Designing a Garden

ALLEN PATERSON   CAMDEN HOUSE

DESIGNING A GARDEN

A GUIDE TO PLANNING AND PLANTING
THROUGH THE SEASONS

CAMDEN
•HOUSE•
PUBLISHING

© Copyright 1992 by Allen Paterson

Canadian Cataloguing in Publication Data

Paterson, Allen
    Designing a garden : a guide to planning and planting
through the seasons

Includes index.
ISBN 0-921820-45-3

1. Gardens – Design.   2. Landscape gardening.
3. Gardening.   I. Title.

SB473.P38 1992   712   C92-094742-5

Design by
Linda J. Menyes

Cover photographs by
Walter Chandoha

Colour separations by
Hadwen Graphics
Ottawa, Ontario

Printed and bound in Canada by
D.W. Friesen & Sons Ltd.
Altona, Manitoba

Printed on acid-free paper

Published by Camden House Publishing
(a division of Telemedia Communications Inc.).

Camden House Publishing
7 Queen Victoria Road
Camden East, Ontario K0K 1J0

Camden House Publishing
Box 766
Buffalo, New York 14240-0766

Trade distribution by
Firefly Books
250 Sparks Avenue
Willowdale, Ontario
Canada M2H 2S4

Box 1325
Ellicott Station
Buffalo, New York 14205

To my colleagues at the Royal Botanical Gardens,
who have borne a stableful of hobbyhorses with
remarkable equanimity.

A beautiful garden is both a work of art and a work in progress: a considered, slowly developing association of trees, shrubs, perennials, annuals and structures such as patios and walls.

CONTENTS

The traditional perennial border shows little colour until June. For earlier colour interest in my garden, tulips planted deeply among the perennials go on happily from year to year.

WHY GARDEN?

oubtless, the old cliché about it being better to travel hopefully than to arrive has much validity in the world of gardens. Why plant trees that take 50 years to reach adolescence let alone adulthood? Why garden at all? This is a question that my invaluable Camden House editor Jennifer Bennett suggests, indeed demands, that I attempt to answer before launching into the body of the book that follows. Putting aside all thought of the effect that a pleasant, planned and planted garden will have upon the value of the house when it is sold, it is, I would suggest, just plain ridiculous to wait until one is sure of having arrived at a final home to start serious garden making. (There is only one final home, and then somebody else does the planting!)

Why garden? The important thing is to obtain all possible enjoyment from a bit of ground while it is "ours," contingent upon our chosen lifestyle. I say this from experience, because my family's garden, which is really the subject of this book, is ours only as long as I continue in my job as director of the Royal Botanical Gardens in Hamilton and Burlington, Ontario. The opening chapter of the book describes in part the acre or so of land that is—for now—the Paterson garden.

I should emphasize at once that it is not a complete garden: it doesn't have everything that we might want—and certainly not what other gardeners would find essential. There is no swimming pool. Wouldn't it be marvellous to have a pool? A formal rectangular pool it would be (not a kidney-shaped irrelevance impossible to relate to any existing line), with a pair of little classical pavilions to house the works and the changing rooms—all enclosed by vine-draped walls; no unclothed chain-link fence here. That would be water for sybaritic pleasure. Think what it would do for ageing backs after a busy afternoon of weed-

10

My garden is mine only as long as I continue to be director of the Royal Botanical Gardens in Hamilton and Burlington, Ontario, yet the temporary quality of this trusteeship does not diminish our pleasure in sights such as this June scene dominated by alliums.

ing. Similarly, there is no purely ornamental water other than the creek in the valley, whose glitter can be seen only before the trees leaf up. A small pond down by the moist spot that permits our June display of Japanese primulas would put them into better context, and other waterside plants, now impossible, could be grown.

Furthermore, certain of my gardening friends consider it a lapse, almost of morality, that this garden includes no serious attempt at a rock garden. Even the inherited rock bank has been allowed to revert to maintenance-free ground cover. No gentians, no saxifrages and not a draba in sight—even with our glasses on. Although many rock-garden plants are extremely beautiful, associating them into the general garden scene is difficult, simulated Alps are seldom successful, and the choicest alpines, it seems to me, are best grown in containers. Sadly, therefore, the following pages offer little to rock-garden aficionados, who should turn at once to the reading list at the back of the book.

These are the most obvious lacunae. Doubtless there are others. This is not one of those texts rashly entitled *All About* . . . or *The Complete Book of* . . . . Such are seldom what they claim. This book tries not to dictate but to encourage. What

you grow, then, is not so important as the spirit in which you grow it.

To garden is to underline one's sense of place, because it commits one to a custodial role—almost a trusteeship—of a bit of ground, a commodity that is becoming ever rarer: they are not making any more of it. A garden offers a sense of belonging that even the grandest apartment cannot give. Yet it does not necessarily offer permanence. Perhaps the acceptance of this truth may encourage those who are keen to garden but know or believe they are likely to move in five years or so. Much of the pleasure and satisfaction is in the study, the preparation, the doing and the anticipation.

Success is no more certain in a garden than on a tourist's journey. Yet sometimes, wonderfully, it does all come together. For instance, you get off the train, and Venice's railway station is as ordinary as any other; you carry your bags out to the vaporetto—a ferry that looks as though it might be setting off to the Toronto Islands—and then suddenly, you are in the world of Canaletto. Vivaldi's *The Four Seasons* seems to sing upon the air.

Our backyards may be less dramatic, but they can provide similarly joyful moments. A lily or a Himalayan blue poppy grown from seed flowers

Although success is no more certain in a garden than on a tourist's journey, there are times when, wonderfully, it all comes together. Here, foxgloves ascend through a lush perennial bed of poppies, dianthus and irises.

for the first time; the peach tree gives a small basket of baby-skinned, summer-blushed fruit; our new potatoes taste like nothing else; and the peas . . . ! Like that first breathtaking view of the Grand Canal, anticlimax is just not possible. And, like travel, it all becomes strangely compulsive. We might do well to remember Hilaire Belloc's lines on quite another subject: "The Doctors, as they took their fees / Murmured, 'There is no cure for this disease.' " Destinations in the garden be-come elusive, simply highlights on a journey of increasing fascination. One lives for the passage of the seasons, that seamless tapestry of the year that I will emphasize throughout this book.

So I invite readers—gardeners-to-be and gardeners now—to travel with me along a number of garden paths. It should be fun, and it could be rewarding. Certainly it would give me pleasure to pass on the contagion for all to catch.

—*Allen Paterson*

A successful
garden does not
just happen; most
beautiful gardens
are ever-develop-
ing amalgams of
desire, design and
commitment.

A LOVELY LOT

Garden making, for me, is less a chore than a pleasant obsession, so I am lucky to live on an acre or so of land just calling out to be gardened. I have a lovely lot, in both senses of that phrase. Our house, a pretty, added-to clapboard cottage, sits at the eastern edge of the property, facing the street on the only flat bit of ground. From this plateau, the ground rises gently to the south and falls almost precipitously to the west and north. A classic southern Ontario ravine-edge lot, it has the wonderful advantage that the ravine is a beautiful valley embracing a considerable creek. It offers us a view of a stretch of the Niagara Escarpment half a dozen miles away, a vista that comes and goes with the weather. Clouds on the horizon sometimes look like the mountain peaks that Ontario has only in dreams. My lot of land is a joy throughout the seasons, but a joy planned and contrived and capitalized upon, as any reasonably successful garden must be.

A successful garden does not just happen: it is an ever-developing amalgam of desire, design and, it must be added, commitment. That may sound daunting, especially to first-time garden owners who have glimpsed a spectacular perennial border down the street and have seen, in the local bookshop, volumes packed with fabulous photographs—most of which depict English gardens that enjoy a very different set of circumstances from their own and merely provoke envy or depression. Glossy magazines add to the beginner's belief that beautiful gardens are only for the prosperous.

They are not. Most beautiful gardens happen slowly and can be created with as much or as little cash as the gardener can spare. But how to start? Actually, the books, the magazines and the gardens seen on the way to work or on a country weekend do help. They begin to inspire an almost subliminal list of what is possible in terms of both design and the plants which furnish that design. The analogy of building a house from scratch and furnishing the rooms is obvious, with one enormous difference: although some of the architectural features in the garden are inanimate – walls, a pool, a fountain perhaps – most of the furniture is alive. Plants make a garden; indeed, they define a garden as such. A garden is a place for growing plants. This furniture, then, only gradually fills its rooms, and it needs care and attention. First, there is the problem – or better, the wonderful potential – of choice. However apparently unpromising a site, it can give a happy home to a huge diversity of plants. But how to choose them, arrange them, succeed with them, enjoy them? How, indeed, to make a garden?

To begin, one basic question has to be asked. What do we want? This question has several facets. How central to our lifestyle is the garden to be? How much time will be spent in its cultivation? Is it to be merely the place where the house sits, or is it to be a significant part of the world we consciously inhabit? At this stage, it is necessary only to accept that these semiphilosophical questions exist, not to answer them in any final way, because with knowledge and practice, one's tastes will be changed and one's horizons broadened. There are endless examples of reluctant Saturday-morning lawn-mowing captives who become wonderfully accomplished garden makers, often to their initial surprise and increasing delight.

For some people, the garden path narrows as they begin to concentrate on a single type of plant, such as dahlias or rhododendrons, or on plant types, such as alpines, tropical orchids or hardy aquatics. These people eventually become experts in their field, join or form specialist societies and discover a lifetime of interest and fulfillment. Their sole focus in the layout of their lots becomes the provision of perfect conditions for their plant pets. The role of people in their gardens is much less important.

Another route, the one I follow and find more sympathetic (though I do love rare and exotic plants), is more concerned with the garden as an extension of the house. In this way, the garden can be seen as a series of interconnected rooms with different uses and pleasures at various times of the day or year. Individual plants or groups of plants, though chosen, I hope, with care, are of rather less significance than the design as a whole. A garden is then like a big, living, three-dimensional walk-through sculpture inhabited by plants and people. It is seen from a multitude of angles, with some sight lines being much more important than others – the one from the kitchen window, for example, since we are apt to stand at the sink for many hours. But even the 3-D analogy is not sufficient, because the furniture of these outdoor rooms is living and growing. The fourth dimension, time, is an inexorable ingredient as the seasons unfold year after year. The observance of the changing of the garden throughout the year is an old-fashioned delight that maintains a link with the past, when weather was more than mere transient pleasure or inconvenience; good or bad, it affected the lives of people who were still a part of nature in its broadest sense. Postindustrial urban humanity, it seems to me, is unlikely to become deeply concerned about environmental issues, however dire, without some personal commitment and even fear. A garden does give a toehold.

So, back to the how and why and where of design; back to the question, What do I want? The sky – or, to be more precise, the extent of the ground – is the limit of what can be done. But even that truism is broadened by the desire to garden. Almost anything is possible. All good gardeners push back the bounds of local myths, written texts and the plant-hardiness zone maps, one of which is nevertheless included in this book as a guideline. I have seen ripe lemons and olives in London gardens, English holly and the mimosa-like pink siris here in Burlington, Ontario. Surprise is a constant.

DECKS, TERRACES, PATIOS

My list of desiderata starts outward from the back door of the house, where I want a deck, a terrace or a patio. The chosen name indicates one's attitude to this most obvious outdoor room. "Terrace" suggests something to look out from and possesses a certain grandeur; "patio" has a southern ring, redolent of summer drowsiness; decks are wooden, and the nautical association implies openness. What I want is something that combines the best of all these, a sitting place from which to enjoy the garden I have made and the countryside whose view I have appropriated. The ideal deck must be out of sight of neighbours, protected from cold winds early and late in the

14

15

I have a lovely lot, an acre or so of southern Ontario land just calling out to be gardened. This is the view from the terrace in September.

season, sunny in winter and shaded in summer, when it offers closeups of my favourite scented flowers. It must be dry underfoot and have immediate access to the house—to the kitchen door, at least—and to the adjacent part of the garden. A city plot might be all patio, a flower-filled room with its own bit of sky.

Usually, a terrace will not take up all of the garden space, but it should be big enough to permit what is wanted of it, to hold the equipment of outdoor summer living: a table with chairs and almost as many reclining chairs. My own inclination here is to relative simplicity—furniture that can be left out and only its cushions brought in, with luck, before a thunderstorm. If complicated or bulky furniture has to be transported in and out, the problem, apart from storage, is a tendency not to use and enjoy it for those short half-hours of sun, especially early and late in the year. Visits to home-and-garden shows will indicate what is available—as well as what one refuses to pay—and what is compatible with one's ideas for outdoor living. Some patio furniture, it must be said, is so pretentious that it would be almost impossible to live up to, let alone lie down on.

The presumption that an outdoor room is at the back of the house is not a rule cast in stone. Indeed, there may be more than one patio. A front-garden one that is also the access to the front door, partly enclosed by vine- or rose-clad walls, gives beauty and function to a piece of property that is apt to be sadly underused. So long as the back-garden-only convention is disposed of, several otherwise neglected spots may be ideal for some use some of the time, such as alfresco meals in sun or shade.

Our front door is in a corner formed by an addition made to the house in the 1950s. A low yew hedge separates the wide front step from the lawn. This wide step faces southeast—ideal for an early-morning cup of coffee or a simple breakfast on a weekend when the low sun shines through the birch leaves. In high summer, the same spot is in shade from before noon and is the coolest corner for an evening drink.

On the other side of the house is the main "living room" of the garden. There, we have a terrace from which the garden slopes away to the west. No part of our garden is more used. When I sit in a lawn chair (and it is vital that, however maniacally one gardens, time is taken to sit back, reflect and enjoy the product of one's exertions), my eyes pass over lawn, borders, woodland edge plantings and on to the distant view. The south-

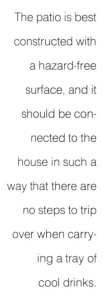

The patio is best constructed with a hazard-free surface, and it should be connected to the house in such a way that there are no steps to trip over when carrying a tray of cool drinks.

west exposure, with eastern shelter provided by the house and northern shelter by an evergreen planting, makes this spot wonderfully warm on windless winter days; we have had Sunday lunches out there even in January. In summer, it is hot, and shade is essential from midday on if the butter is not to turn to liquid in minutes.

Some shade is usually desired. A new terrace can be made pleasant with a big garden umbrella or two. Fortunately, we inherited a fine yellow-wood tree (*Cladrastis lutea*) that was planted some 30 years ago at the terrace edge. Its delicate tracery casts almost no winter shade, and anyway, the October to March sun is low enough to shine in under the main branches. Then in late May, just as we begin to wish we had sensibly invested in an umbrella like everyone else, the delicate young leaves unfold, framing every vista, and long strings of white pea-flowers open, casting their scent upon our world. The fragrant two weeks that follow are among the glories of this garden, and the moving, dappled shade is a joy all summer long. If I had a new garden, choosing as big a tree as I could afford for this position would be an early consideration. I would grow my own patio umbrella.

In situating a backyard or side patio, conve-

nience to kitchen and dining or living room is important. The connection with the house is best if there are no steps to trip over with a tray of cool drinks. The terrace surface, too, needs to be reasonably hazard-free.

Well-constructed wooden decking gives the quality needed for above-grade levels. At grade, some form of paving is necessary. Grass has neither the capacity to endure hard wear, especially under trees, nor the ability to dry quickly after a rain. But how to choose? The depth of one's pocket cannot fail to have some effect, but it must always be remembered when making the choice that there is no part of the garden seen or used more. Here, quality counts.

PATIO PAVING

Concrete poured *in situ* is to be avoided if only because it is so irrevocable. Blacktop shares the same problem, and its colour absorbs all radiant sun heat and breathes it back even after the sun has set. Split stone is always my first choice; its colours are complementary to plants, and the inevitable slight imperfections encourage natural weathering to the soft tones gardeners admire when visiting old, established gardens. One of the most effective ways to use natural stone is as square or rectangular flags of random size. No formal or geometric pattern is built up, but there is a gentle weave of horizontals and verticals – a sort of do-it-yourself Mondrian in stone. Where a source of natural stone occurs locally, it can even be cheaper than synthetic alternatives. Cost of transportation from a distance, on the other hand, can make stone expensive.

In this case, recourse to manufactured alternatives is possible. These become more diverse each year, and the phrase "synthetic stone" need no longer have a pejorative ring. Only their diversity causes difficulty in choice. Beyond price, the uppermost thought should be how the garden can best be joined to the house. The terrace is the connective, so the material of which it is made is significant. Just as local, natural stone suits its surroundings, so should an alternative choice.

One possibility is the material that forms the house exterior, which will help the design flow out from the house. This does not imply that the brick used for walls is suitable for the ground (though it might be) but that rows of the same brick could be used, for instance, to frame panels of inexpensive concrete slabs. Simple geometric patterns can be constructed to repeat the lines of existing features of the house – doors, windows, and so forth.

Now there are companies that offer patterns far beyond the common rectangle. Circles, shells, fans and other motifs almost approach the black and white arabesques of sidewalks in Lisbon. But in the garden, design must not be too frantic. The hard landscape is only a part of the scene, and while vital as the bones of the design, it is also the frame for the luxuriance and brilliance of the plants. Natural stone colours are usually the best. Paving that resembles kaleidoscopelike Neapolitan ice cream is invariably unwise. Desperate hopes that such a selection, made in a moment of euphoria, will tone down in time are always disappointed; it remains a mute but loud – or loudly mute – reproach to carelessness of choice.

Construction of paved terraces is by no means beyond the capabilities of most reasonably handy gardeners. The desire for speed encourages us to employ professionals, but there is a real pleasure in deciding upon position and size, designing the pattern and ordering or gathering up the materials, perhaps incorporating a few *objets trouvés* – cobbles from a seaside holiday, a slab of stone picked up on a country walk – to

make the terrace unique, not bought off a shelf. And there is pleasure, too, in slowly doing the work. It is much like weaving or knitting in permanent materials – though not necessarily in irrevocably permanent positions.

PATHS

Paths, which inevitably direct garden traffic, can be made from the same materials as terraces and steps. Paths should be made of level, nonslip stone, brick or pavers set in sand. There may be an edging band of similar material or perhaps preserved lumber to support adjacent beds or grass – avoid metal or plastic edgings, which may be tidy but seldom look better than dreadful.

A path width of five feet (1.5 m) is the minimum to permit two people to walk abreast. That is the width of the path to our front door, which has grass on one side and a foundation border on the other. This path is one of the bits of the garden where plants are allowed to overlap the edge – but only a little; formality and full width are needed here. At the side of the house, however, the path that links the front with the main back terrace is very different, though the same width. This one, made of natural split limestone (inexpensive if you live near a quarry), has a lavender hedge on one side and mixed planting on the other; the plants tumble over the edges, so by the end of the season, strollers must walk single file. If it were the only way to reach the backyard, this path would be unsatisfactory, but here, it is part of the planned cottage-garden scene. Beyond this, terrace paving and decking act as a wide path along the back of the house. From here, formal paths are not needed; one simply walks on the lawn to reach all other parts of the garden. But care is necessary. While grass is remarkably resilient, it cannot take unlimited wear;

For a patio surface, split stone is my first choice; surface imperfections encourage natural weathering to soft tones sympathetic to plants.

the lawn must be wider than a path with a hard surface. In this garden, one area that receives a lot of traffic has steppingstones sunk into the grass. Mowing is unhindered, and no wear tracks develop–a simple, cheap solution.

Grass in heavy shade never builds up a turf strong enough to take more than minimal foot traffic. Paths in woodland, therefore, are best made of woodchips (which will need annual top-dressing as they decay) or gravel. The latter also makes a good alternative for a formal path if solid materials are too expensive.

Paths are obviously vital to the way a garden works, so it is wise to avoid poured concrete and similar irrevocabilities unless one is certain the design is perfect and unlikely to change. I, for one, no longer have such self-confidence.

Our hard winters play havoc with external masonry, so for walls, one must set the foundation below the level at which the ground freezes. Paving stones have no such requirement. So long as they are set on a few inches of gravel topped with an inch (2.5 cm) of sand, all is well. The gravel ensures good drainage; it is, of course, water moving constantly from its liquid to solid state and back again that causes heaving. If some stones do lift a bit, the unevenness is easy enough to rectify in spring–no concrete, no cement needed–and a little more sand can be swept across the area to fill interstices and gaps.

Some people think there is a major disadvantage to this relatively simple, nonconstructionist approach to terrace, path and patio making: weeds. There is nothing, they will tell us, to prevent seeds from germinating in the cracks. Quite true, but I do not consider this all bad. On the contrary, the growth of vegetation causes the hard structure to soften, to be garden rather than house, to develop a rapid maturity. There is a classic picture in many gardening books showing the main path to the front door of Rosemary Verey's house in Gloucestershire, England, that has become something of an icon. There, the stone path between the double row of sentinel Irish yews has become colonized by a flower garden of rock roses (*Helianthemum* cultivars) in every soft pastel colour. It is a picture that could hardly have been contrived, but once it began to develop naturally, it was encouraged by a sensitive owner. Serendipity wins again.

Rosemary's path also demonstrates the effect of what can be called, rather grandly, micro-

habitat. This same phenomenon of colonization has developed in our Ontario terrace and paths, to which, I should boast, Mrs. Verey has given personal approval. Here, random chunks of Niagara Escarpment limestone, seldom smooth enough to be called paving but blissfully cheap, have developed their own flora, as close to a bit of aromatic Mediterranean terrain as our winters permit–self-sown lavender, catmint, thyme, artemisia, and so on. These plants like the heat coming off the stones, their roots approve of the perfect drainage, and we like the scent that is given off when, inevitably, we walk on them.

A halt to this invasion must be called eventually –or better, continuously and delicately–or there would be no path and no terrace. I permit the surrounding flowerbed to flow onto the hard paving while ensuring that there are still the shapes and spaces I want. Also, not all the volunteer seedlings are desirable by any means. It is extraordinary what comes up in spring in the area around the bird feeders, and of course, the traditional garden weeds are always on the lookout for an empty niche. Dandelions are everywhere endemic and unacceptable in paving, and for us, a little prostrate spurge seems to find the tiniest cracks between front-path pavers perfect for extending its empire. Hand-weeding this takes no more than a couple of hours over the season. Spot drips of weedkiller are my answer to dandelions and other deep-rooted perennials, but I do not spray, or I would lose many of my favourites, including seedlings of blue spiraea, or bluebeard (*Caryopteris x clandonensis*), and even young mountain ash trees. It never ceases to amaze me how many good garden plants seed themselves and can be used elsewhere if the almost overwhelming propensity to tidy a garden to within an inch of its life is resisted.

STAIRS

When the garden lies either above or below the terrace, there is the need for connecting steps or possibly ramps if wheelchairs are to have full access. Effective steps, arranging for changes of level, are almost the most important architectural statements one makes in small gardens. They invite movement and progression of the eyes and the feet as you enter another dimension of that walk-through sculpture which is your garden. They usually need to be wide enough for two people to go abreast–single file makes for an un-

Level paths of nonslip stone, brick or pavers set in sand will guide traffic safely through the garden. Paths narrower than five feet necessitate walking single file.

sociable walk—shallow enough for easy movement, broad enough for the whole foot and utterly steady.

On our often precipitous site, we have a lot of steps, all homemade and of varying success. One set is made of blocks of limestone (not smooth enough), two are made of sawn stone (not wide enough, but it would be bank-account ruinous to buy more), and several are just cut into the ground, with rough log risers and woodchip steps (simple but rather erratic). The best for use, almost equally inexpensive, go from the terrace to the top lawn. They consist of a dozen railway ties—two or three per step—practically a cliché material in Canadian gardens, often despised but,

for us, invaluable. Pressure-treated lumber would be aesthetically preferable constructed in a similar fashion—a 9-foot (2.7 m) width, 5-inch (13 cm) risers, 18-inch (45 cm) treads. The bottom step gives on to a stretch of stone that meets the lawn—stepping down onto lawn creates bad wear marks—while the top step supports and edges the terrace stone. These steps, too, have a foundation of gravel, which permits plant growth at the point where riser meets tread. We have encouraged English ivy on one set of steps and periwinkle on another to grow across the back of each step and provide, as it were, leafy risers. *Cotoneaster dammeri* works equally well, and other evergreens can be found. In all cases, the

Our best set of steps, from the viewpoint of ease of use, consists of a dozen railway ties. Their gravel foundation permits the growth of English ivy where risers meet treads.

plants soften the hard structure and add another dimension to the planting. One further set of steps in our garden, the first one built, is also made of railway ties but mistakenly has only one tie per step and hence is uncomfortable, especially to walk down. But the steps have become colonized by forget-me-nots that reseed each year. That stairway is like a small blue amphitheatre for weeks in spring, almost unusable but too beautiful to change.

Steps up or steps down imply contours. On each side of the steps, the ground may be left as a slope, grassed or cultivated. But its maintenance poses a continual problem, especially if the slope is steep: grass is difficult to mow, and cultivation provokes soil erosion. The alternative is to terrace the ground and build retaining walls to support the soil at each level. The raised beds thus created offer some of the best possible sites for exciting gardening. Drainage is improved, always a factor in our heavy clay. Also, plants can tumble forward, and they are closer to the eye, the nose and the hand.

If I had a flat site in which raised beds were not an inevitable part of the design, I would construct one or two, perhaps surrounding the main sitting area. They offer so much opportunity for special

planting. With my entrenched desire for privacy in this highly domestic part of the garden, it is pretty certain that I would give the raised beds a backing of walls, fencing or simple trellis to support summer vines. I find one of the major mysteries of many even rather grand current housing developments to be their nakedness. Windows overlook windows, deck looms over deck, not a foot can be put outside without it being observed by people next door or across the street. While I have little wish to be watched, I want to watch others even less. Strangely, when the source of noise is invisible, it is much less disturbing. The pattern of most row housing is much more civilized, it seems to me. In Britain, elegant terrace housing is a major architectural genre, where each house has a small, high-fenced yard. Here, row housing is a slightly pejorative term, but call them town houses, site them on vastly expensive city real estate, elegantly walled, pave the yard, call it a patio, and all is well.

TERRACE PLANTINGS

Even without the sociological overtones, this garden feature, the patio or terrace, is where I want the first flowers to appear. Whether the terrace be the entire lot or just a portion of it, whether entirely enclosed for privacy or only sheltered from wind and the windows of others, this is where everything starts. From under a five-foot (1.5 m) boxwood bush on one side of our terrace peep the earliest snowdrops, capitalizing on heat escaping from the house. This is mid-February. And there is something showing colour in the bed almost until Christmas. Without doubt, this is the most important part of the garden, because it is in view from the house and it is where, in summer, most people are for most of the time. So we want long-season interest and colour and scent, from the earliest spring bulbs to the last flourish of fall chrysanthemums.

If this really is the entire garden, there is little difficulty in furnishing it with flowers. It is possible to discard that which is past and continually bring from pots, or in pots, another batch of bulbs or annuals purchased in the garden centre down the road. But while I have no objection to bringing in a bit of emergency colour, this is not quite gardening – or "not quite cricket," as the Brits refer to socially unacceptable behaviour. The area needs its permanent plants, both shrubby and herbaceous, and perhaps a tree, even in a tiny

The area on and around the terrace is the most important part of the garden, because it is in view from the house and it is where, in summer, our family and friends spend much of their time.

courtyard. Permanent plants are what demonstrate the seasons and provide the pleasures of anticipation. Within that setting, the summer annuals have a vital place. These traditionally bloom from late May to September, but protected patios and town courtyards in most of the country can usually steal as much as an extra month at both ends.

Of course, one can fill the beds with perennials, leaving little space for annuals. My 8-by-15-foot (2.4 by 4.6 m) bed to the south of the raised terrace is filled with boxwood and snowdrops and the sort of cottage-garden miscellany that goes through the seasons without much external help. It is warm and west-facing, with late-afternoon shade from the yellowwood. The bulb sequence continues after the snowdrops with a few clumps of early dwarf water-lily tulips (*Tulipa kaufmanniana*), some scillas and dramatic crown imperials (*Fritillaria imperialis*). As these decline, the spears of June-flowering alliums appear. A big clump of *Helleborus atrorubens* flowers in April, the colour of dusky plums, and its hand-shaped, near-evergreen leaves provide furnishing throughout the year, staying green even under our erratic snow. Also in April, self-sown seedling forget-me-nots and honesty (*Lunaria annua*) begin to show colour here

and there, and they will be good throughout May. Behind are a couple of early roses, the utterly hardy eight-foot-tall (2.4 m) white rose of York (*Rosa x alba*) and the dwarf, deep pink apothecary's rose (*R. gallica officinalis*). June is their month, which they share with clumps of blue catmint tumbling forward to seed itself in the paving. The ferny grey foliage of artemisia fills out over the declining bulb foliage, English ivy trails about, and should there be a gap, which is unlikely, a few gentle annuals can go in. *Salvia farinacea*, good till October, is a favourite here.

Such planting never gives a blaze of glory, but it does provide continual interest and requires very little work. But it cannot be entirely neglected: the artemisia may need reducing, the catmint is clipped over after flowering to encourage regrowth and a later display, the roses are dead-headed, and only one dead forget-me-not is left to spread its seed (otherwise, there will soon be a forget-me-not lawn). But this is part of the simple pleasure that such a cottagey collection gives.

It is extraordinary how different a habitat only a few feet away can be, and how necessary it is when choosing plants to take this into account. Below the big yellowwood tree that makes our summer sitting out so pleasant, the raised bed

Beds edging the terrace should have some permanent plants, both shrubby and herbaceous, because they demonstrate the seasons and provide the pleasure of anticipation.

is inordinately dry, and continual watering would be necessary to maintain summer annuals, most of which would resent the shade anyway. But until the tree's leaves unfold in late May, it is a very desirable spot, ideal for spring bulbs. Here, we wanted a strong statement, so 50 peacock tulips were planted a foot (30 cm) apart. In eight years, they have increased so much that from many original bulbs, there now come five or six flowers, rather smaller than the first year's Dutch-grown blooms but, I think, preferable. It took a couple of years to find the right permanent ground-cover plant for the tulips to grow through, but now lamb's ears (*Stachys byzantina*) demonstrates its worth. By the end of winter, its mat of downy fo-

liage has declined to almost nothing, and one pulls it away just as the coral-pink tulip leaf shoots pierce the soil. Regrowth begins as the tulip leaves yellow, and for the rest of the year, lamb's ears provides a soft grey carpet with hardly a gap for annual weeds—which anyway hate drought and semishade. No work needed here at all.

CONTAINERS

A bit of open soil seems to be the desire of all humans who do not follow a nomadic life. This implies ownership of land, yet one may venture down narrow alleys between tenement blocks in any part of the world and, looking up, see plants hanging from windowsills and parapet walls. In the lands of the Mediterranean, every flat surface that can hold a pot seems to do so. Few village houses have much in the way of a garden, yet clustered around a doorway or a wellhead are geraniums, four-o'clocks, aloes, spider plants, asparagus ferns and pots of basil—anything to add green to the surrounding aridity—in every possible receptacle that will hold a little soil and a plant or two. Often an old chipped terra-cotta urn or oil jar, highly covetable by more sophisticated garden makers, jostles for space with tins, superannuated saucepans and handleless jugs.

These are peasant versions of the elegant 2,000-year-old Roman courtyards excavated at Pompeii and Herculaneum, where the pots are still in place, like their grand equivalents on the Spanish Steps in Rome. Plants in pots have a proud history, and their use is just as valid for gardeners now. Containers raise plants significantly above their fellows and enable gardeners to have greenery and flowers on decks and terraces where there is no soil. Chosen with care, containers add an air of distinction to any focal point.

But the mélange of tins and old kitchen utensils admired through the rose-tinted spectacles of a tourist in Europe does not travel well. Our North American version is apt to be recycled tires—not easy to recommend but not to be sneered at. The intention is a good one: to give a few plants a presence they would otherwise lack. If one cannot find or afford the perfect urn, then lesser things will have to do, and the plants must be so luxuriant as to hide the "mechanics." Conversely, a particularly beautiful pot can be a focal point in its own right. It becomes a piece of sculpture, invariably more satisfactory than many of those mass-produced statuettes, too saccharine by half.

In general, though, containers are meant not so much to attract the eye as to contain, to grow plants in. That being the case, their ability to hold sufficient growing medium is obviously vital. A few years ago, there was a vogue for "contemporary" shapes in concrete, including elegantly shallow saucers a yard (1 m) or so across. They are still about. Incapable of holding more than a few inches of soil, which dries out disastrously in hot periods, these containers seldom support the desired luxuriance. But placed in front of a couple of big but taller pots, such a container might be filled with water (its drainage hole plugged) to hold a single pot of one of the wonderful water

cannas or *Cyperus alternifolius*. Such contrasts of pot shapes and plant silhouettes are striking.

In our climate, gardeners worry about whether to leave a pot outdoors for the winter even if the plants do not survive. Concrete and stoneware can overwinter successfully here; terra cotta, the staple of warmer areas, cannot. Wood, in the form of half-barrels, is safe enough. So, too, are those grand cube-shaped boxes with finials at the corners known as Versailles tubs. Soil can be left in all of these, and the containers can remain *in situ*.

It is a chore to empty and store big containers, but the work can be helped if, instead of filling the biggest with planting compost, you pour in bark chips into which smaller pots are plunged up to their rims. Then, at the end of the season, only the finished plants are removed and the containers are trundled off to the garden shed or the back of the garage. For protection on the site, it is enough to wrap containers with burlap and plastic, but as by their very nature they are placed in commanding positions, I could not, in all conscience, recommend that anyone live with such an eyesore for almost half the year—though I note that many people seem able to avert their gaze. By April, the squint must seem almost congenital.

All of the above presumes that even permanent containers hold impermanent plants. To be realistic in our climate, it is wise to accept this, just as Louis XIV's gardener André le Notre had to accept that if His Majesty wanted 2,000 orange trees at Versailles, then every one would have to be carted in and out of the orangery every year.

Within the setting of the terrace, container-grown summer annuals like alyssum, marigolds, begonias and impatiens can play a vital role, providing colour, texture and height.

But we are often equally demanding. In a new garden, the immediate value of a pair of shrubs raised to greater effect in containers and flanking a doorway or path entrance may be irresistible. Choice is restricted to the most winter-hardy, drought-resistant species that also have an interesting shape. Thus while boxwood or clipped yews appear in every grand garden in the south, here, we can use cedar, the only really safe evergreen, although it is apt to look dark and rather sullen in winter. Better to accept a less formal shape and choose quick-growing deciduous shrubs with attractive form and a long season of interest, such as golden ninebark (*Physocarpus opulifolius* 'Luteus') or variegated Cornelian cherry (*Cornus mas* 'Variegata'). These are helped if the container is lined, sides and bottom, with half-inch polystyrene to insulate the roots from frost. You might also want to add to the potting compost one of the almost magic new materials such as Viterra or Supersorb, which hold vast quantities of water. In our garden, however, containers are used for less permanent plants, so the soil mix can be ordinary compost.

While we want brilliant summer annuals on the terrace, it is obvious that there is not a spare bit of ground, so we concentrate them in a few huge blue Chinese pots. Since the pots are stoneware, they do not need winter protection, and even when empty, they earn their keep visually. In mid-May, those in full shade get impatiens and begonias. Those in sun we fill with a mixture of things to give colour as well as scent and height and tumbling exuberance. Of course, these annuals need regular watering and feeding, but the roots are not competing with permanent plants and growth is prodigious. Even simple annuals such as petunias planted in raised containers can develop a luxuriance that those in conventional beds seldom attain. And when they grow close to the nose, one realizes how fragrant some of them are.

Summer is a season one would wish to prolong, but it moves inexorably into fall and toward the first real frost. It will turn the impatiens to a sad and soggy heap overnight, and nothing can bring the flowers back to life. Many of the other annuals will take three or four Fahrenheit degrees of frost (−2°C) without undue damage and live to flower another day. Just when the moment of truth comes depends upon one's area, the year and, to some extent, oneself. Certainly, killing by frost is something I wish to put off as long as possible,

because so often, that first icy night is followed by two weeks of Indian summer. With us, early to mid-October is apt to be the end of the annuals in the open garden, but we usually get another couple of weeks out of the pots by the simple expedient of keeping a few old towels on hand to throw over the flowers on suspiciously clear and chilly evenings. It is the work of a moment that gives a gardener the wonderful feeling of being able to push back winter.

If, on the other hand, an unexpected cold snap does away with the annuals, it is well worth buying a few pots of outdoor chrysanthemums to plunge, pot and all, into the bigger terrace containers to celebrate the season. Some chrysanthemums can take as much as 10 Fahrenheit degrees of frost (−5°C) and still maintain colour through November. All this, it will be realized, is in defiance of the common Canadian myth that colour in the garden cannot begin until mid-June and has to stop on Labour Day. What nonsense!

FOUNDATION PLANTING

In discussing plants that grow close to the house, one must make mention of so-called foundation planting. Certainly buildings, especially new houses, need visual anchoring into their site; a house rising from a sea of blacktop or even lawn can be a depressing sight. The frequent antidote is a random collection of junipers and other conifers against the house. While they ease the baldness, they do little to make a garden, especially where grass spreads uninterrupted to the road.

As has already been emphasized, the walls of the house can provide protection, sun or shade, a measure of privacy for ourselves and similar virtues for plants that might not succeed in the open garden. There is, however, one obvious disadvantage. We have a border facing east and south that stretches from the front door the length of the original cottage, but inevitably, because it is under the windows, almost all of its good things are entirely invisible from indoors. And although I am very fond of our neighbours and have no inherent objection to casual passersby, my gardening activities are not altruistic.

The way to remedy the situation is to use the border not just as the edging to the front path but as part of a fuller garden scene that can be enjoyed even from indoors. If the flower border under the windows is left in place but the conventional foundation planting is pushed out to the

24

A building needs visual anchoring to its site, best provided by flower borders used not just as path edgings but as part of a fuller garden scene that can be enjoyed even from inside the house.

property or street line—it is all pretty resilient stuff, after all—then immediately, there is the beginning of a sense of enclosure to the front yard. The planting does not have to be tall if you feel it would be antisocial to bar all eyes or if, as I do, you enjoy sharing some, but not all, of passing activity. Then, on the inside of that basic planting, facing the house and in view of the windows, one can add a sequence of seasonal colour.

This takes one out into that part of the lot, and once outside, one looks back to that border under the windows full, let us hope, of good things. I play this game to the utmost, growing plants against the house that enjoy its protection. We have three hardy hollies bred in North America—

two 'Blue Princess' for splendid winter berries and one 'Blue Prince,' the vital pollinator without whom nothing much, beyond leaves, would happen to the princesses. Below them are spring bulbs, some pulmonarias with early-spring drooping bells of pink and blue and some of the same dusky purple hellebore that is on the other side of the house. Its Mediterranean cousin *Helleborus corsicus* is also here but, without protection, is apt not to flower; in spite of this, its fingered, pale green leaves earn its place in summer and fall.

Between the windows, a magnolia has reached the cottage eaves in five years. This is 'Jane,' one of the hybrids, all with girls' names, produced by the U.S. National Arboretum. It is not attached to

the wall but grows close to it, because forward-jutting branches are removed, usually at flowering time, to bring into the house. Its narrow, wine-dark goblets the shape of champagne flutes appear in a heavy flush in May and then intermittently throughout summer. This long-flowering habit is inherited from one of 'Jane's' parents, *Magnolia liliiflora* 'Nigra' (*M. quinquepeta*).

At the southeast corner of the house is one of the best plants we inherited: a fine clump of Oregon grape (*Mahonia aquifolium*). It is also one of the best of all broad-leafed evergreens we can grow. Shiny, divided leaves, slightly prickly and thus evocative of holly, turn bronze in winter. Tufts of bright yellow flowers in spring—where we see our first hummingbirds—are followed by purple fruits that are marginally edible. It is truly a plant for all seasons. In winter, the leaves can become sun-scorched, so before that happens, I prune out the most exposed branches and use them for indoor decoration. Those not needed at once stand in water in the earth cellar, where they keep for months until required upstairs.

On the wall behind are a couple of clematises, both similar to their original species. The little blue-purple bells of *Clematis viticella* make a good show in June, but that cannot be said of 'Duchess of Albany,' a *C. texensis* hybrid. After three years, the promised cascades of red flowers have not materialized, although it grows like a weed. It needs either serious talking-to or moving—probably both. Established plants do not take kindly to root disturbance, but I do not take kindly to costive clematis and it will have to take its chances. The moral is obvious: not that this is a bad plant but that I have been a bad gardener, giving a hybrid of *C. texensis* too shady a spot. More summer sun should do the trick. If it lives.

I have been at pains to describe some, just

some, of the plants that grow in the small borders on a couple of sides of our house and help to knit it to its site. Throughout, the emphasis is upon interest in all seasons: flower colour, flower scent, fruits and foliage with attractive year-round texture, all adding up to effective furnishing. The analogy with the interior rooms of the house remains underlined by the fact that patios, decks, terraces, steps and paths are the most contrived parts of the garden.

CHANGING THE LOT

What of the rest? What is the rest to be? We are back to the basic question: What do I want? Beyond the artificiality of the garden next to the house, there is a limit to the amount of contrivance that is possible and desirable. Of course, we know that Louis XIV turned a wasteland of bog and heathland at Versailles into one of the greatest gardens the world has ever known. But he had great artists and designers and a bottomless purse and could even turn the army out to dig the canals. Few of us are in such a situation, and even if we were, human attitudes, sensibilities and tastes have turned away from such gratuitous manipulation of the land. We wish to work with, not against, natural forms and local conditions. And we are wise to do so.

Plants have five major requirements for healthy growth: light, air, warmth, water and nutrients. In fully environmentally controlled greenhouses, almost any plant from any place can be grown. But in the open garden, gardeners must match every individual plant's needs to the conditions the site can offer. There is no point, for instance, in planting out the range of conventional annuals in an area that is heavily overhung with trees; petunias, marigolds, salvias, and so on, are sun-loving tropicals. Plants originally adapted to boggy or marsh conditions are bound to be a disaster in a dry, sunbaked border. It is all pretty obvious, one might say, but to find out what wants what where, one must first turn to the texts and catalogues with lists of shade lovers, sun lovers and moisture lovers (I prefer to work in the affirmative, rather than offer lists of shade haters, et cetera). Always, however, expert advice must be taken with the traditional pinch of salt. Texts (except this one) are apt to err on the side of pessimism, and often a bit of TLC works wonders.

Nevertheless, in designing one's lot and designing with and for plants, the existing environmen-

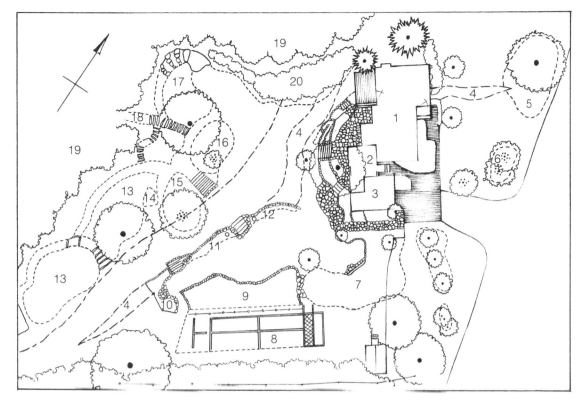

My garden:
1. Main house
2. Garden room
3. Garage
4. Embankment
5. Spring bulbs and hostas
6. Snowdrops, daffodils and day lilies
7. Shrubs, perennials and herbs
8. Vegetable garden
9. Perennial border
10. Perennials
11. Perennials
12. Perennials
13. Shade and woodland plantings
14. Seat
15. Snowdrops and English ivy
16. Shade and woodland plantings
17. Shade and woodland plantings
18. Steps to valley
19. Woodland
20. Forsythia (mixed)

tal factors can never be disregarded. To completely change them is often impossible and seldom desirable. An exception might be the construction of a garden pool. It would be difficult to grow water lilies any other way (though I have seen small varieties in tubs). But amelioration is always a possibility, because it is the basis of gardening. A heavy clay soil can be drained and its texture improved over time by deep cultivation and the addition of compost and other organic materials. The same additions, miraculously, help sandy soils retain moisture and grow a wider range of plants – which is why no garden should be without a composting system, however basic.

While gardeners must work within the limitations of shade from buildings or fences, tree shade is often more in our control. In the most extreme cases, whole trees can be cut down or lower branches removed to open up the site, but – and this is a big but – much thought must be given to such a course of action. That tree may be the product of a century of growth, it is probably the dominant visual factor in the garden, it may well screen a lot of things best left unseen, and it may frame views and vistas in a way that nothing else can. Woodman, Spare That Tree is an old song best kept in mind. Much amelioration of the garden's conditions, however apparently unpromising they may be, happens by the very act of planting and the ongoing care of those plants.

Recently, there has been much publicity about how tree and shrub growth around houses can help economize on the use of fuel. In winter, reduced wind lessens heat loss, while in summer, tree shade on the house puts fewer demands upon air conditioners. It is surprising that when such economic reasons for lush planting exist, so many houses sit in a wasteland of lawn, gobbling up further energy in the form of fuel as they suffer the weekly haircut.

How satisfactory, therefore, to find such hard-nosed justifications to add to the real reason for planting one's lot, the aesthetic one. It is the desire for beauty that motivates most gardeners: the gradual building up of considered scenes, large or small; the arrangement or rearrangement of plants; the consideration of foliage texture and flower colour; the conscious celebrations of the seasons that are for most of us as close as we shall get to artistic expression. Even if we cannot paint like Poussin, play the piano like Paderewski, sing like Sutherland or sculpt like Sansovino, we can take and give pleasure in our immersion in the natural world.

There is no clear
beginning or end-
ing to the garden
year. Hardy bulbs,
such as tulips, daf-
fodils and scillas,
and spring-bloom-
ing perennials,
such as trilliums,
flower early in the
year. They spend
the rest of the
season building
their strength.

YEAR-ROUND IN
THE GARDEN

During my first years in Canada, I used to rise like a hungry trout to a juicy fly when I heard the inevitable remarks every October (sometimes even earlier) on the theme of "I suppose now you can sit in your office till May with your feet up?" My equally inevitable response was to indicate impolitely up where I would willingly put my feet, one at a time. Attempting to cultivate a sense of ineffable superiority, I now keep quiet, more or less, but still find it difficult to understand why normally intelligent people are willing to write off half the garden year. Even when temperatures are around 4 below zero F (−20°C) and frost is two feet (60 cm) into the ground, the garden is still there—still visible from the windows, still able to be walked around.

Just as one has to work with one's soil, helping it here and there as necessary, so one has to work with the seasons. Every year is different and cannot be dismissed as a formula, or we start to ally ourselves with those sweetly naïve visitors from the south who arrive in Canada in July wrapped in furs with skis on top of their cars. (I don't think they are a myth; it is amazing how many Niagara Falls and Fort Erie residents of the frozen north swear they have witnessed the phenomenon.)

The important thing is not how cold or how hot things become or even how wet or dry a year is—although those things matter too—but that there is no clear beginning or ending to the gardening year. Each year starts the year before; each year prepares for the next and the next. There is, of course, a rightness, a sequence of activities and festivals almost like that of the church, with its hymns such as *We Plow the Fields and Scatter* and *As the Green Blade Rises*, and so on. Indeed, the cultural connections are closely interwoven because the festivals of the religious year celebrate humanity's dependence upon the land. In an urban society, the activity of growing plants links us to our most distant roots.

DECEMBER, JANUARY

It is convenient that the turn of the year, which no doubt all major religions celebrate, is a suitable time to begin, conceptually, the garden year. Christmas presents are opened (and gardeners are easy to buy gifts for—the number of trowels and waterproof label markers lost indicates that another never comes amiss, so that we need not find, in John Betjeman's words, "that hideous tie, so kindly meant"), the cards come and with them, often, the seed catalogues, their rivals in colour, happiness and hope. There are brilliant annuals on the front cover, vegetables of incredible perfection on the back, and somewhere in the middle is a picture of a very pretty girl crouched over a cornucopia of produce in a floral background that makes *Les très riches heures du Duc de Berry* seem positively mean by comparison. Clearly, 'tis the season to turn from the turkey and start thinking about the future.

It really does make sense to plan some of the summer scene now. There was, you remember, that dreadful gap in the front border, that enormous row of lettuce in which every plant matured at the same moment and that wonderful show of gladioli when you were on holiday—or so your neighbour said. Planning or no planning, these sorts of things, I find, happen again and again, but at least it's fun to try to repair last year's disappointments in a flurry of fine New Year's resolutions. Some might even be followed up.

The catalogues, too, act as a wonderful *aide-mémoire*, reminding us of things seen, read about and desired. Now is the time to tick them off; however good the local garden centre, it is inevitable that, as with all retail stores, what you particularly want at a given moment will not have come in yet or will have just sold out. When this means missing a whole year, it's pretty serious.

But of course, one must try to be sensible about what can reasonably be grown from seed and what has to be brought in as plants. This decision depends entirely upon one's facilities and patience. I never cease to be amazed at the way in which basement rooms are rigged up as environmentally controlled plant chambers with banks of lights and rows of boxes and pots of plants in every stage of development. But you don't have to be a do-it-yourself whiz kid—though it helps—to take advantage of the now easily available compact units of one to several lit shelves that allow propagation by seed or cuttings. Personally, though, I must confess to remaining in the spare-bedroom-windowsill age—just as I write this book with a pencil and my kind wife types it up.

FEBRUARY, MARCH

To make the most of the northern seasons, it seems sensible to start some of this year's garden furnishing indoors and bring it to a stage at which, when put outside, it can move forward, hardly noticing the change of site. But the ability to provide winter warmth and light and even impeccable watering and feeding is not enough. Sown in ideal indoor conditions when the snow is still deep outside, summer annuals will germinate in a week or two, whether they are vegetables or ornamentals. They will probably grow more quickly than they would if sown outside, even in high summer. So what happens if they are ready to transplant weeks before the last expected frost and when it is even longer before the soil is sufficiently warm to encourage the roots of these young coddled creatures?

It is necessary to curb the natural, even atavistic, impulse to rush into a seed-sowing mode as soon as one notices the evenings getting just a breath longer day by day. The starting time is something we long for and, I fear, often delude ourselves about. First, one must carefully separate frost-tolerant plants from the really tender tropicals such as petunias and marigolds. Mid-May is usually the best time to plant the tender plants; mid-April or even mid-March is fine for the hardier ones. Parsley and sweet peas, for instance, can survive a couple of degrees of frost and can move directly into the garden, leaving the cold frame ready for the first lettuce plants.

The second point to remember is that it takes different lengths of time for different species to germinate and develop sufficiently to plant out. Indoors, lettuce comes up in five or six days, broccoli a day or two later. In little more than a week, the seedlings are ready for pricking out into separate containers. Parsley and celery need more than twice as much time. Eustoma (also called lisianthus) germinates well in a couple of weeks, but the seedlings seem most unwilling to move beyond the two-leaf stage, so some gardeners start this charming new "prairie gentian" in January or February. Basil moves along quickly

It is convenient that the turn of the year, which no doubt all major religions celebrate, is also the time to begin, conceptually, the garden year.

enough under glass but deeply resents any cool weather and is generally best not put outside until June. The plants gardeners raise from seed each spring range from the fully frost-hardy, such as honesty and love-in-a-mist, which can germinate outside in the autumn and overwinter outside as small seedlings, to the truly tropical begonias and impatiens. In short, every plant has its own agenda that reflects its geographical origin, which is a good reason for discovering the background of even the most common garden plants. The amount of heat we can provide puts limits on what we can start ourselves at home and when.

So what to do? As mentioned already, the committed gardener with, it must be admitted, time to attend to them, will start quantities of plants under lights in optimum temperatures. My own pre-spring system is much simpler: I concentrate on things I know I shall not be able to buy either in time or at all at the local garden centre – I grow almost exclusively the earliest vegetables, as described in the chapter "Designer Vegetables."

I also start a few flowers indoors. Sweet peas are among the most deliciously scented of flowers, perfect for cutting from June onward. After seed germination, they need to grow slowly in cool conditions, hence the February activity. Ger-

mination, which is often erratic can be helped by chipping a tiny sliver off each seed coat to allow moisture to penetrate and activate the sleeping embryo. Three seeds are sown to each plug in a six-pack on a warm windowsill. As soon as the seedlings emerge, they are brought down to the garden room. Initial stem growth is thin and wispy, and only later do leaves and tendrils begin to unfold. This is the natural behaviour of annuals that, in the wild, start their lives down among the grasses and other perennials which they must push through quickly to reach the light. This is unnecessary for our seedlings growing in plugs with no competition, but we cannot fight evolutionary behaviour. However, after three or four leaves unfold, if the short tip above is carefully pinched off, the plants are provoked into developing much stronger shoots from the leaf axils. I grow just a dozen and a half sweet peas, and when it's time for them to go outdoors, I plant six around each of three wigwams of twiggy branches. If flowers are continually picked for indoor enjoyment, production will continue well into August. Once the plants set seed, it is the end of flowers for that season, but seeds should be collected for next year's February sowing.

The indoor seedlings mentioned so far are

grown without special conditions (apart from a bag of bought potting soil) and without much effort beyond the basic care of watering. I grow them because they are not available from the garden centre at the time I want them and because I enjoy the activity and deep pleasure that comes from preparing plants almost surreptitiously, while all is still ice-hard outside, to be ready to take advantage of the earliest stirrings of spring. Some gardeners will turn their basements and houses into production lines and continue to sow, prick out and pot up vast numbers of tender annuals that must wait until frosts are definitely past in May or even June, depending on area and site. This is not for me; the couple of flats of impatiens needed for late gaps in the woodland garden and a few petunias or geraniums for containers by the house are easily bought.

MARCH, APRIL

By late March, certain outdoor activities are a more profitable use of whatever time I wish to put into the garden, and with the golden stars of winter aconites now shining amongst drifts of demure snowdrops, the floral season has begun. I want to miss none of it.

The major task for me is the big perennial border. Already, the monkshoods are showing new leaves indicative of root growth beneath. Over the next month, I will lift, divide and replant the more overcrowded clumps of phlox, day lilies, Shasta daisies and all the marvellous perennials that will give such a beautiful display from late May until October and beyond. This can be an enormous job and utterly daunting to many aspiring gardeners, but as with any physical activity, the need to do it must be balanced with the time available and one's idea of work. When one's garden becomes nothing but a chore, it is time to move into an apartment. Long before that dreaded step is taken, however, sensible planning can reduce the most tedious tasks.

The wise gardener – a member of a smug breed I make an annual resolution to join – will have kept a careful garden diary of the previous season to note that the Shasta daisies really are too tall for the front and the shocking pink bee balm and golden day lily are not ideal companions. More simply, it is wise to remember one or two colour infelicities; to realize that this clump of phlox has become too big, is starting to lose vigour and needs dividing; and to work on the

precept that only about one-third of the border will receive serious attention in any one year. The rest is merely cut down (now, not in the fall – see page 91 for the rationale for this) and the soil gently pricked over (take care not to tread on the emerging tulips) and given a two-inch (5 cm) dressing of compost, the heap having thawed out in the nick of time.

From now on, my 25-yard (23 m) border needs almost no attention except a little weeding in the early stages – compost always brings in seeds all ready to germinate. By late June, perennial growth is so dense that nothing can seriously compete. Some deadheading is desirable to prolong the display, while some plants are best left because the seed heads are the extension of the display. Delphiniums are the only plants to be staked. The rest hold each other up, more or less, and there certainly is not time to fuss about it.

APRIL, MAY

Early April is also the time when the shade-tolerant plants in the woodland beds are starting to move, and they do so with incredible speed. One week, everything seems to be asleep; the next, the first bloodroot is in flower. There is not much serious work here but a lot of gentle and pleasurable facilitating. A great mat of soggy dead hosta foliage is pulled away to permit the emerging daffodil spears to get to the light; unrotted tree leaves are taken off that patch of scillas and *Anemone blanda*. Old leaves of epimedium are clipped off to let the new foliage develop in parallel with the delicate sprays of flowers. April and early May is a time of finding forgotten woodland plants as they push up to flower before the tree canopy above shuts off their light.

But here, plant growth is not strong enough to crowd out weeds, and these areas become invaded from the wild world beyond the garden. Jewelweed, annual spurge and garlic mustard, our garden's worst curse, would take over entirely without some serious intervention in May and June. Again, however, it is sensible to play the weeds' own game by introducing desirable plants that match them in vigour. The later bulbs emerge from a blue sea of self-sown forget-me-nots that are pulled out as soon as they have flowered. Only a few need stay to set seed for next year's display. Then, as the bulbs start to go to rest, naturalized black-eyed Susans take over. Along with day lilies, hostas and lily-of-the-valley, they can keep the invaders at bay for the rest of the year. The aim is to keep the soil covered by the growth of desirable or temporarily acceptable plants in a continuous, but not flat, carpet. Open ground is an invitation to weeds, and they will invariably accept with pleasure—their pleasure.

May is a month of preparation and promise. However much one has tried to stagger work in the vegetable garden, there is probably still a bit of ground to dig over. Almost everything can be sown or planted now. So, too, can the bright summer annuals go in as soon as frosts finish—the marigolds, impatiens, petunias, begonias and such. Indeed, there is so much activity preparing for high summer and polishing the barbecue that spring is apt not to be appreciated. Certainly in most of Canada, we do not have the extraordinarily extended spring of England that can last from February to June (after which, the canard goes, it becomes autumn), but neither is our spring a fleeting moment between winter and summer. The weather is typically erratic, blowing hot and cold, affecting early tulips or late daffodils. Only if a gardener is foolishly dependent on a display from just one variety is the season other than exciting and productive.

May is the time of the flowering trees (magno-lias, cherries, crab apples) and the most spectacular of flowering shrubs (forsythia followed by lilacs, viburnums and the first of the roses). A hot spell does indeed reduce the display of a single shrub to a few frustrating days. (But we do well to remember the year it seemed to go on for weeks. Why does the negative seem to stay in the mind longer?) This is why the planting of a magnolia or a lilac needs to be part of a considered association of complementary plants such as crocuses and colchicums at the base to give, respectively, March and September flowers. A clump of day lilies for foliage texture and July flower, a clematis clambering up for a sudden early-summer surprise and a fuzz of silver seed heads in fall: garden design means choosing plants and using each site to its greatest potential.

May is also the month when most gardeners feel they should start to worry about their lawns. It is not a worry that I often share, as people would recognize if they saw what goes under that title here during a summer drought. Certainly, one cannot fail to admire the classic billiard table lawns of Oxford and Cambridge colleges, but that climate is very different from ours—as is the traditional head groundsman's recipe: "You rolls it and you mows it twice a week for 300 years." Equally unacceptable today are the frantic feeding and soaking with chemical sprays in parallel with prodigious use of water. Hand cultivation is possible for emerald postage-stamp-sized lawns, while for large areas, consideration can be given to variations, such as different height cuts for different uses or wildflower meadows with mown paths. Few things are more beautiful. But such variations, like so much of my own garden ethos and activity, are greatly at odds with the common obsession for garden tidiness.

Here is a hobbyhorse I had better ride for a moment because it affects so much possible garden pleasure and activity. There are entrenched myths that need personal evaluation rather than blind acceptance. I met a neighbour one day sweeping up the fallen green flowers from a fine ailanthus (tree of heaven). "It's a dirty tree," she complained. "We probably ought to cut it down." I protested that in fact, common though it be, it was a very beautiful plant that framed her charming house delightfully. "I've never thought about that," she replied. "I thought it was a dirty tree." That dire phrase occurs again and again as if it were not entirely natural for leaves and flowers

34

In May and June in southern Ontario, the growth of the first non-bulbous plants such as irises and peonies—the one tall and elegant, the other heavy and lush—soon hides the declining foliage of spring bulbs.

and fruits to fall, as if gravity were not a fact of life. Admittedly, there are times of legitimate complaint—the gust of wind that sends the heap of fall leaves back from where you've just raked them or (my own problem) the activities of a pack of squirrels in my huge black walnut chewing on the nuts and spitting out the bits. I can deal with the mess—perhaps that is the rent one pays for the tree's year-round beauty—but I do resent the squirrels' looking so smug while I'm doing so.

And again, much of the admiration lavished upon the endless images of English gardens in coffee-table books is in fact based upon the luxuriance of their tumbling plants. There seems to be an almost contrived untidiness—an untidiness that is not only acceptable but admirable. Why, then, if it is desirable in books, should it not be desirable in fact? What is this fear of growth, of plants doing well? The questions I am often asked about this shrub or that are: "How do you prune it? When do you cut it back?" As if control were more important than cultivation. Effective garden making, I believe, comes from combining the architectural, the imposed and the human-made with the natural—the plants and the effect the seasons have upon them.

But back to lawns. One needs to ask the same questions already posed about the garden as a whole: What do I want? What is the lawn for? Is it to be frame or foil? Is it for access to ensure the garden's flow? Is it for children's games? Or is it the apparently easiest way to "control" the land surrounding the house, keeping it flat with a ride-

on mower that also conveniently avoids giving exercise to the owner?

Leaving out the last defeatist rationale, the answer is probably in the affirmative for all the other roles. And while we would, no doubt, all choose perfectly smooth turf—with those alternating two-toned bands of green that are only possible with a low-cutting cylinder mower, preferably operated by someone else—the final question must be: Is it worth it? Is it worth the chemical insecticides and fungicides and herbicides and even wormicides as well as the thousands of gallons of water? Is it worth the time and effort and money, especially if a "lawn-care" contractor is brought in? Obviously, many people will say yes, but the environmental movement will gradually insist upon less draconian systems and, it must be accepted, less immaculate lawns.

I am willing to live without a grass monoculture and am happy when white clover, self-heal and other carpeters appear. Less acceptable are plantains and dandelions, and it must be confessed, crabgrass is a most insidious brute. Against the latter I am happy to accept a single spray in April to inhibit germination of its seeds; for the rest, "live and let live" is my usual motto.

What about fertilizers? In one sense, a lawn is as much a crop as a field of corn. Continually "harvesting" its leaves is bound to deplete the soil in which it grows. Leaving what is cut where it falls to return its nutrients to the soil is a help, but cuts must be frequent and light, for a thick layer of mowings will rot on the surface and kill the living grass beneath. In addition, while I have no desire for the commercially exploitive feed, weed and water regimes, I consider each year the need for an autumn dressing of slow-release nutrients and a spring spot attention to broad-leafed weeds. Effective, satisfactory garden making is based on a continual series of considered decisions, not on a rule book.

MAY, JUNE

Lawns aside, as we come to the end of May, we are at the busiest, most exciting and often most beautiful time in the garden. The shade-loving plants under the north wall or in the woodland beds—trilliums, Solomon's seal, foamflower and lily-of-the-valley—are in flower, and their foliage is still young and fresh. In the perennial border, the late tulips meet the first of the nonbulbous plants, such as peonies and Oriental poppies.

Effective garden
making comes
from combining
the architectural
with the natural:
the plants and the
effect the seasons
have upon them.
Within this mar-
riage, there may
be little need
for a lawn.

Leaf growth is prodigious and soon joins up to hide the declining foliage of the spring bulbs.

Only in the most formal bedding schemes is it necessary to lift the tulips and daffodils planted last October. People who do not count the cost (who are seldom home gardeners) can treat the spring display as an annual expense, throw away the bulbs and start again next fall, a prodigal and almost sinful waste. If it seems necessary to mask the natural transition from spring's decline to summer's ascendency, bulbs can be lifted with all their foliage left on and replanted in a trench in the vegetable garden—or in the few yards of cultivated ground one might keep as nursery—watered in and left until the leaves have done their job by feeding the bulbs that will produce next year's flowers. By early July, the dry bulbs can be taken up and stored in a cool place until planting time comes around again—only three months ahead. In informal areas, there is no need for this: day lily foliage, for example, entirely hides that of daffodils going to rest behind it, a perfect seasonal sequence that has innumerable variations. Even in my small formal bed by the front door, I prefer to plant my young summer annuals between the declining tulips at the beginning of June. Perhaps the annuals even enjoy

the early protection. In three weeks, the bulbs' leaves have yellowed and are pulled off whole, and the summer stuff has the space to itself. Come autumn frosts, the annuals are removed, a little rotted compost is forked in and all we have to do is wait for the tulips again—squirrels permitting. It really is very simple.

Summer is a time when we seem to have written off bulbous plants as a visual force in the garden until next spring. But it need not be so. There is a wonderful range of summer-flowering bulb and corm plants that add a lightness and variation in foliage and form not easily found in other groups of plants. Some are permanent—as permanent as most perennials are—needing only occasional lifting and replanting. In this category are the true lilies (*Lilium* spp). There are lilies for almost every garden position and soil condition, flowering from June to September. Hybrid garden lilies require good drainage, yet the wild L. *michiganense*, six feet (2 m) tall, luxuriates in the wet river valley below this house and the West Coast L. *pardalinum* is happy with its feet in running water.

Rich feeding and regular care are given by lily aficionados with the show bench in mind, but fine garden effects come from lilies treated as fully permanent residents. In my garden, the white,

In June, the press of garden activities can get a bit out of hand, with weeding, staking, pruning and the last of the planting to do.

pink-flushed *Lilium regale*, with wonderfully scented trumpets, pushes through an evergreen ground cover of English ivy at the base of *Magnolia sieboldii* and shares its spot with snowdrops (long out of sight before it appears). The plan was for the lily and magnolia to flower together, but in most years, the lily is a little late. Nevertheless, it was a nice idea in my mind's eye. In a woodland area, the dusky Turk's cap (*L. martagon*) has settled in. Brilliant tiger lilies survive for years in old, abandoned cottage gardens. Many others can be tried; they can be expensive at the outset, but they are truly perennial if well looked after.

The classic planting time for most lilies is early autumn, when bulbs are plump and fleshy roots are still attached, although even the tired-seeming bulbs still lurking on garden-centre shelves will often do surprisingly well, and a job lot on sale is worth snapping up. A strange exception to early-autumn planting is the Madonna lily, *Lilium candidum*, which should be moved soon after flowering, when it takes a short summer rest before leafing up in the fall.

Other fine summer bulbs are not winter-hardy, but I would not want to be without them: South African gladioli (especially the small types); Mexican tigridias, like clusters of brilliantly marked butterflies; galtonia, the so-called summer hyacinth, with tall spikes of white bells; eucomis, the green pineapple flower that floral arrangers die for; cannas, with their dramatic leaves but muddly flowers that are rather a disappointment; and at the very end of the season, *Acidanthera bicolor* (*Gladiolus callianthus*), with heavily scented white-and-purple flowers. And there are others. All need planting in mid-May in groups between lower-growing perennials. They will need to be lifted five months later and the bulbs or corms kept in barely moist peat in a frost-free but cool place till next year. My prejudice against the treadmill of dependence upon annuals weakens with these lovely plants, not least because each fall as they are lifted, one finds that most have increased in number and size like the best gilt-edged stock.

One expects most herbaceous perennials to flower over a long period and, if religiously dead-headed, to repeat off and on during the season. But May turning to June sees two favourite plants appear so splendidly for a short time that we cannot legitimately expect anything more. Irises and peonies, the one tall and elegant, the other heavy and lush, combine to make a show that is like no other. Peonies, I find, are almost too permanent for a mixed perennial border. They like to be left alone. While I admire a long border devoted to these beauties, my limited space has only two or three clumps beneath an old moss rose (they just manage to flower together) underplanted with daffodils and colchicums to give early and late interest to the same spot. This seems a better way to use a small number.

Similarly, the rough-and-tumble of my big perennial border does not give bearded irises the air they need to build up their rhizomes after flowering. Also, the need to lift and replant them after flowering every three years or so is a bore in a season when one doesn't want the inevitable gaps so caused. This is a combination of unacceptability that makes me increasingly admire the irises down the road at the Royal Botanical Gardens, where I can get an annual visual "fix" from a couple of acres of them without having to do the work myself.

In small gardens, it is difficult to justify plants that demand year-round space for a short season of glory. So if my garden holds fewer bearded irises than it once did, the genus is represented at other seasons. Indeed, the little bulbous irises share the earliest spring with crocuses and scillas. *Iris danfordiae* is yellow, I. *histrioides* clearest blue, while I. *reticulata* blooms in shades of purple and blue and smells of violets. Other permanent species follow: I. *sibirica* in early June and the four-to-five-foot (1.2-1.5 m) forms of I. *spuria* for a further month. Unlike the bearded irises, these maintain a good leaf presence throughout the summer; also, they need dividing only when the clumps grow too big for their spots.

I have similar reservations about another favourite flower—perhaps *the* favourite flower. This same time, late May, brings us to the start of rose season. The yellow 'Canary Bird' is soon followed by other shrub roses and species and near-species roses. They have a short and delicious season, and like most other flowering shrubs, they are virtually pest- and disease-free. Only as gardeners become determined to grow modern everblooming roses do the inevitable problems of black spot and rose mildew well up. There is an associated difficulty with most modern hybrid tea or floribunda roses. For at least half the year, the bushes not only do not earn their keep but look positively ugly; traditionally, too, they demonstrate their difficulties in isolation, without associative planting. This is a subject that will be discussed in its own chapter.

For this reason, I have restricted my own rose growing to a very few old-fashioned varieties and a couple of modern varieties ('Nearly Wild' and 'Sea-Foam') that seem almost immune to the rose scourges. Then, once again, I go down the road to the Royal Botanical Gardens to enjoy that incredible rose garden vicariously, knowing the effort that goes into such a display.

If there is a time at which the press of gardening activities really does get a little out of hand, it is June. Keeping up with the weeding, a bit of staking, the last of the planting and the pruning of early-flowering shrubs is all very well. Most of it will get done, and unless one becomes positively paranoiac, it must be accepted that it really doesn't matter terribly, even if in a weak moment last winter you agreed to host a meeting of the local garden club. ("What a pity you weren't here in April—the daffodils were superb," you can loudly cry, and "Of course, in July . . . !")

JUNE, JULY

But what does become difficult to live with is success. Suddenly, even in a small vegetable plot, the broad beans, the first peas, the lettuces, radishes, spinach and early strawberries start to come to maturity, and it is unthinkable that they should not be gathered, eaten and enjoyed at their peak of perfection. Picking and preparing them is surprisingly time-demanding, and this, of all times, is the moment of the year when other members of the family (even reluctant children) may need to be asked to help. A word of warning here may not be out of place: if children are not to be put off gardening, it is vital that they be asked to do only the more agreeable jobs, such as pea picking, which have ongoing rewards as well as the ultimate treat at the end.

The "Designer Vegetables" chapter demonstrates how every yard of the vegetable plot is kept used and moving with catch crops and successional crops throughout the growing season. Thus, as the early crops in June and July are harvested, the spent plants are immediately pulled up and taken to the compost heap. The ground is forked over with a little well-rotted compost, and while it is still moist—soil that has been protected by plant growth maintains a moisture level that the sun and wind pull out of exposed areas—the next seeds are sown: more carrots and lettuces, main-crop chicory and radicchio, et cetera. If each crop is replaced in its season—I try to get an hour in early in the day—the kitchen garden maintains its productivity and a wonderful visual fullness, like the type of living cornucopia invariably carried by the goddess Flora in old prints.

June is traditionally the month of roses. Indeed, before the introduction of the China rose (*Rosa semperflorens*—"always flowering," as it was first called), June was almost the only month of roses. Rose species and the heritage roses derived from them were, and are, just another group of late-spring-flowering shrubs. They flower wonderfully, but they flower just once. Their annual *raison d'être* gone, pollination, fruit set and seed development become the parade leading, they hope, to the propagation of their species. Aesthetic considerations are only in the eye of the human beholder—or perhaps of the bee, but even its appreciation is ultimately utilitarian.

June also is the month of a number of other fine flowering shrubs on which this garden depends for much of its spring-turning-to-summer effect. They are described more fully in the chapter on trees and shrubs. Every one we enjoy is representative of many more that could have been chosen. On the edge of the woodland, highbush cranberry (*Viburnum trilobum*) grows wild. Its simple flat plates of white flowers are hardly dramatic (its real value is a six-month show that begins as the berries colour up in August); much more striking are its Oriental relations, and we grow several. Nearby, and also happy in a lot of shade—even the black walnut shade that is traditionally death to everything else—we have V. *tomentosum mariesii*, whose tiers of horizontal branches look as if covered in white confetti; a short-lived display (quickly taken by birds) of pale cherry-red berries follows.

Across the lawn, a 12-foot (3.7 m) V*iburnum x carlcephalum* flaunts its tennis-ball-sized flower heads. Its flowers pink in bud, opening creamy white and wonderfully scented, this shrub epitomizes the first warm, balmy nights of early summer, when it glows in the dark and throws out its perfume on the drifting air; mixed with the scent of late lilac and early mock orange, it's an intoxicating blend.

With all shrubs, growth follows flowering, and if any pruning is to be done, this is the time. Remove whole branches that have flowered rather than clipping the bushes over as if they were rather poor topiary. Forsythia, especially, must be dealt with so that the long wands that will carry next year's flowers will grow. Here, I am concerned that the forward growth of the long forsythia bank does not overwhelm the band of day lilies in front that gives July and early-August colour on that side of the garden.

Topiary, of course, usually refers to plants pruned into fantastic shapes—balls, pyramids, giant peacocks or whatever—but one form of topiary is common to most gardens: hedges. We have only a few yards of low boxwood and a little yew, whereas neighbours have long stretches of cedar. At the Royal Botanical Gardens is an extensive hedge garden demonstrating the use of more than 100 different trees and shrubs. All of us are out with the shears in early July, maintaining the formal effect that our hedges give to the garden—enclosing, framing and enhancing. Their value is enormous.

Obviously, shrubs that give a subsequent berry display are only pruned to keep the desired shape until that display is over. Pruning may be done a few weeks later or not for several months: pruning is a very movable feast. In this category come the edible soft fruits too. Gooseberries and red currants can wait until winter for pruning, but the canes of raspberries that have borne fruit are cut off at the base the moment the crop is complete. This enables the new canes for next year to develop and ripen properly and provokes a much greater second crop on the autumn-fruiting varieties. These begin to fruit again in about six weeks and continue into late October.

Early July sees the floral balance between shrubs and herbaceous perennials finally tilting in favour of the latter. The Chinese flowering dogwood (*Cornus kousa chinensis*) and our native pagoda dogwood (C. *alternifolia*) continue to dominate their spots, and the great clump of bottlebrush buckeye is showing its potential, but almost suddenly, it seems, the spotlight is on the perennial border. Its most important effect occurs when all the foliage meets and no soil shows. Then the planned (and unplanned—often the best) floral combinations take the eye. Delphiniums and catmint, goatsbeard and Shasta daisies create a blue and white scene. At the other end of the border, a day lily, a true lily, cimicifuga and macleaya combine creams and buffs. A little later, bright pink phloxes and bee balm are cooled by clouds of grey artemisia.

This all sounds terribly grand *House & Garden*, with shades of British garden designer Gertrude Jekyll—and indeed it *does* look good from May to No-

The July border looks best if it is full of plants, everything supporting everything else. Almost the only requirement is a bit of deadheading to keep them all blooming.

vember, writes he smugly. It looks good because it is so full. Because everything supports everything else—except the delphiniums, which are programmed to lie horizontal unless prevented from doing so—there really is very little to do but enjoy it throughout the whole summer. All that is required is a bit of deadheading, Sussex trug basket over the arm, sharp secateurs and no bending down. One only wants a floppy hat and wash-leather gloves to be positively Sissinghurst!

JULY, AUGUST

An Ontario July garden is not, however, able to drift endlessly in an Anglo-Saxon idyll. Temperatures are high, humidity is hell, mildew on the phloxes is doing wonderfully, and no rain is forecast for the foreseeable future—none of which worries the crabgrass in the lawn in the slightest. All these things—and a lot of others—are facts of life that one must come to terms with. They can be helped but not avoided. The garden will lose all pleasure if everything has to be fought. All of us must make choices. Some are forced upon us. Here, water pressure is so poor that only one sprinkler is possible—and that is best turned off if someone wants a shower. Thus lawns are never watered. What water there is must be kept for the vegetables, now maturing at a great rate, and for the borders that are most likely to suffer permanent damage.

Plants that require little watering—and so fare best during the hot days of summer—include lamb's ears, foreground, yellow coreopsis and, in the background, 'Gold Plate' achillea.

The woodland edge stuff has had its season, and while some impatiens were put there a few weeks ago to extend the interest, this may well be an area that has to be sacrificed. A pity, but it doesn't really matter. On the other hand, it is wonderful how things do come back (generally plants prefer to grow rather than to die) even after they have apparently reached the point of no return. Our swaths of black-eyed Susans in arid half-shade can go limp for days but recover unharmed after a thunderstorm. Similarly, even after a couple of weeks of drought, two hours from the sprinkler can be enough.

What must have help are the newly planted shrubs whose roots have not had time to develop and annuals whose roots never do. Plants in containers—where the majority of our relatively few annuals grow anyway—cannot be neglected. Hand-watering, with a balanced fertilizer added weekly, is an inevitable but not necessarily disagreeable task. Standing with a hand-held hose certainly is time-wasting and foolish-looking, so this garden has water sources for dipping watering cans into, a far quicker method. A giant Chinese pot doubles as a focal point at the end of the bean arbour; barrels catch rainwater from the garage and garden room roofs. When the rain fails, they are kept topped up by the hose. Thus the distance water has to be carried is short. Such activity has another virtue. It keeps one in touch with one's plants to note their needs and to observe their progress, their beauty in development, their success.

Mid- to late July is about as late as one can sow any vegetables and expect them to reach harvest before the season really does close in. One needs to choose quick-maturing varieties, the "early" ones used at the beginning of the season. Because soil is warm and temperatures are high, their speed of development is doubled. Each seed packet gives the time in days necessary to give a crop—anything below 60 or so is a good bet. The simple salad greens are obvious choices. So, too, are peas, dwarf beans (though, in this garden, the bean arbour continues to produce like Rupert's Magic Basket and will until the frosts) and even a second group of summer squash—zucchini, courgettes or whatever one wishes to call them—if the first has given up or looks as if it is about to.

Keeping up with high-summer harvesting of maturing crops continues to be vital throughout

Ornamental kale, foreground, is an annual that will survive the first frosts, providing colour beside fall-tinted shrubs like Japanese maples.

August. Zucchini become zeppelins within a week, and even the politest of neighbours hides when you appear with yet another unsolicited gift. Beans soon go stringy if not picked every other day; when this happens, which it is bound to if holidays have intervened, it is necessary to be ruthless and take them to the compost heap. Otherwise, one never catches up and is sentenced to eat old, substandard beans for the rest of the season. To continue to pick means to continue the harvest; once the plants are able to develop ripened fruit (and beans and zucchini *are* fruit), they have fulfilled their reproductive destiny and are content to die. So if an absence is unavoidable, it is wise to find a neighbour—preferably without his or her own vegetable patch—to keep up the good work and be as ruthless a harvester as oneself.

AUGUST, SEPTEMBER

There are mornings in the garden in August when a heavy dew and a surprising coolness make us think of autumn. By early September, this refreshing air becomes the norm and, combined with the Labour Day weekend and imminent back-to-school, is apt to lead to conventional thoughts that all is over in the garden. Nothing could be

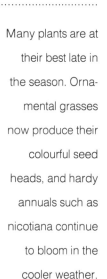

Many plants are at their best late in the season. Ornamental grasses now produce their colourful seed heads, and hardy annuals such as nicotiana continue to bloom in the cooler weather.

further from the truth. Certainly it is a time when, walking around, one realizes that it is too late to do anything that will have much effect this year. The depredations of what we call the lace doily beetle on the hosta and ligularia leaves show only too clearly that slug and snail traps should have been more liberally set down earlier in the season. But the knowledge that "it's too late now" does have its own gentle charm: early autumn brings pleasures of reflection in addition to the new satisfactions of the moment.

Lots of lovely plants are only now at their best. Morning glories are tumbling over the cedar rails on one side of the vegetable plot; against the trellis on the garage, they are scrambling up the old rose 'Zephirine Drouhin,' whose mainly early-season display can be accepted in this way. The ipomoea trumpets send one off to work with a picture of incredible perfection that is renewed daily until the first hard frost, which is still, one hopes, weeks away.

In the Mediterranean, this is the time when the summer drought is broken by the first rains for months. Immediately, weed seeds germinate and a brown world takes on a tinge of green. Suddenly, too, dormant bulbs are triggered into growth. Most of the hardy bulbs we grow are from the Mediterranean area, and they behave the same way here. The pink goblets of colchicums, like huge crocuses, push through the parched earth. Here, a row enlivens the declining day lily foliage in front of the forsythia bank and gives beauty to a spot that would otherwise have nothing. There are a number of true crocus species, such as *Crocus zonatus* and *C. speciosus*, that also flower in September and October, with their leaves following later. At this time, too, we look for the little pink shuttlecock flowers of the hardy *Cyclamen hederifolium,* one of the joys of the season. Though these

few bulbs flower now, most of the others are in rapid growth at the root, as a clump of daffodils shows if accidentally dug up. This should remind all gardeners to get on with new bulb planting as soon as possible. The real wise virgins will have ordered just the ones they want from mail-order catalogues back in June and will be anxiously awaiting delivery; the less prepared will find plant-centre shelves groaning with Holland's best, each box irresistibly illustrated. In the mind, winter passes like a flash; suddenly it's spring.

But in the real world, time is not quite so fleeting, and there are other garden activities that help to prepare for even greater success next year, especially for organic growers. As blocks of vegetables are cleared, mostly the frost-sensitive tropicals—tomatoes, peppers and eggplants— a two-inch (5 cm) layer of well-rotted compost is spread and rye seed raked in. This germinates in a few days, overwinters as a grassy covering and is dug in during April as green manure. It is a wonderful soil improver and soil conditioner at virtually no cost.

SEPTEMBER, OCTOBER

By late September, the days are noticeably shortening. The crickets and cicadas start to creak without the necessary lubrication of high humidity and heat. We look at the late-evening sky and listen to the weather forecast. Surely the first frost cannot be long delayed. However, many plants, even those in flower—roses, late perennials (hardy chrysanthemums and monkshood have yet to start their show), sky-blue caryopteris, and so on—pay no attention. They are good for another month at least. But impatiens and dahlias and basil will blacken overnight. After this, there is often a delicious Indian summer for a further few weeks before a second frost and the subsequent slow slide into real fall. Therefore, there is no rush at all to "tuck the garden up for the winter," so often recommended as if a new ice age were imminent. The season provides so much enjoyment that it is foolish to switch into the fully winterized mode until a couple of months later.

Tubers of dahlias, rhizomes of cannas, corms of gladioli and montbretias, bulbs of pineapple flower (eucomis) and summer hyacinths are lifted sometime during October and their tops cut off (and composted—*everything* is composted). I spread the bulbs for a few days on the floor of a dry shed to reduce moisture content a little and

After the leaves fall, the bones of the garden become more evident. These include buildings and other structures, evergreens and the bare branches of deciduous shrubs and trees.

then store them in boxes, right way up, in barely damp bark chips. They'll spend the next six months in the cool but frost-free earth cellar.

Other tender perennials don't have such convenient resting organs that they can fully hibernate, but I cannot bear to throw away the couple of dozen geraniums that have worked so hard to give colour to the terrace pots and the little dry bed by the kitchen door. So they get similar treatment. Lifted, their tops reduced by half and all dead leaves removed, they are replanted at once, packed closely together in moist bark chips. Even with little light, most are able to survive in a state of suspended animation in the earth cellar until brought up in March, when they are potted separately and reinvigorated for next year. This procedure gives a comforting continuity to the gardening seasons—and with geraniums costing a couple of dollars each, it is worth the small effort entailed.

NOVEMBER, DECEMBER

When winter really does set in, a number of permanent pot plants whose summer home was on the terrace will give interest to our unheated-till-December garden room. These plants are left out as long as possible, because they are attractive on the terrace and anyway the garden room is our dining room while it is warm enough. There are a couple of camellias and shrubby marguerites, a big oleander, a clivia and a few fuchsias; a hanging basket of ivy-leafed geraniums will, even if not worth keeping over the whole winter, continue to give colour until Christmas. All of these are cleaned of dead flowers and foliage before they take up their winter quarters; plants do furnish a room. Any with pests such as whitefly are consigned to the compost.

Outside, the leaves colour, often providing some of the most brilliant displays of the whole year. When they fall, the value of evergreens as vital "bones" of the garden becomes really apparent. So, too, do the lines of walks and walls and the beds themselves even when they are almost empty. Plants that hold their seed heads—sea hollies and sedums in the perennial border (none of which, in my garden, is cut down until spring, as it is far too valuable a sight from our windows) and hydrangeas and honesty on the woodland edge—take on a new dimension. Areas of evergreen ground cover—English ivy, ajuga, and so on—all help to link *this* autumn to *next* spring and to maintain visual and aesthetic interest over the dull but not dead months ahead.

44

Trees and shrubs
form the per-
manent structure
of the garden,
framing views
while providing
shade from the
sun and protection
from the wind.

LANDSCAPING WITH TREES AND SHRUBS

A plot that aspires to the title of garden cannot succeed without suitably chosen trees and shrubs. They make up most of the skeleton, the bones of the design without which the place is little but an amoebic jelly, however bright it is with marigolds and petunias in the high-summer months.

Woody plants provide perspective and a sense of permanence. They frame many views and are the objects of others. They help to moderate all the excesses of the elements, providing shade from the sun, protection from the wind—which can have a significant effect upon costs of home air conditioning and heating—and developing a microclimate that makes possible the cultivation of lovely plants that are quite impossible in the treeless, shrubless site next door. They give privacy while enhancing the architecture, whether they are informal screens or rigorously pruned hedges. In their own right, they can be dramatically beautiful in fragrant flower, fruit or foliage. Most of them are virtually trouble-free, with few significant pests or diseases. And the eulogy could go on.

All of these benefits keep me in a state of continual surprise at the unfurnished, unfinished and uncivilized subdivisions that make up so much of current suburbia. Even the dreary euonymus and juniper "foundation planting" (the ultimate cliché) with a desultory blue spruce in the corner of the front yard is better than nothing, a base to build upon. But why, one wonders, the paucity of plants and ideas?

Excuses are not difficult to find and are apt to be repeated ad nauseam: The "average" North American household moves every five years; why, then, plant for permanence? (What about adding value to the real estate?) Nothing will grow in my area/soil/climate. (Was it a desert before your house was built?) The garden centre has so little choice. (Look farther.) I don't know where to start. No problem, let's do so now. But first the usual question: What do you want? It was posed in the first chapter of this book, and by now – if you are still with me – it might be answered, at least in concept. What are the woody plants that will provide the desiderata you have identified?

What one needs to do first is make a list of favourite shrubs or small trees. It is bound to be too big a list for the space available. No matter at this stage. Persevere. Next, note when each is at its best, in flower or fruit. Now, do you want a blaze of spring glory or a sequence of more restrained effects? The answer is probably, if rather unrealistically, both. But with the right combination of trees, shrubs and herbaceous plants, including bulbs (which are themselves herbaceous perennials), it is possible to approach the ideal.

Generally, one wants trees to sit under in the summer and to cool the sun room or perhaps the living room with its big south-facing picture window. One wants some defence against the neighbours' busiest windows. One wants it now. But the ideal garden tree that combines the virtues of beauty with incredible speed of growth until it stops at 25 feet (7.6 m) hasn't been invented. And if it had, it would be so common that we probably wouldn't plant it. The problem is that most small garden trees remain small because they are slow-growing; rapid growth is apt to lead to considerable size.

CHOOSING A TREE

However, even really small plots can accept – indeed, need – a taller tree than is usually imagined. Consider those tiny backyards, usually in an older part of town, that are veritable oases because of an old inherited black locust, pear tree or even the much maligned tree of heaven. Of course, the tree drastically restricts what else will grow, but all gardening is a balance between the possible and the desirable. Another fact is that the closer the tree is planted to the house or to the place where the shade is required, the quicker the results. The same plant on the boundary will take years longer to do the same job.

Beyond speed of growth, one must consider the desired form and "weight" of the growth and leaf canopy. Close to the house, many gardeners want foliage that is light and delicate, late to unfold and early to fall. The locusts fill this bill wonderfully, as do birches if you are in an area not too plagued by borers. Evergreens, on the other hand, are not suitable; the classic English Victorian image of summer-afternoon tea on the lawn under a great cedar of Lebanon is possible only if the lawn is so vast that heavy coniferous shade will not overwhelm the garden and half the house as well.

Farther from the house, the diversity of desirable trees is positively daunting. Choice will depend upon personal likes and dislikes, upon soil type and local conditions. There are useful guidelines, but within the ability of a given plant to succeed, nothing is inherently wrong with any preference. There is, incidentally (as I mentioned in the previous chapter), no such thing as a "dirty tree." All trees drop something sometime unless they are made entirely of plastic.

If the scale of the landscape is large and includes the good fortune of a frame of existing native trees, it is wise to keep a balance between what is natural or nearly so and what is obviously contrived, organized garden. For instance, if one wishes to grow magnolias – who doesn't? – the delicate, small-flowered but ultimately tree-sized species such as *Magnolia kobus* or M. *salicifolia* associate most happily at the woodland edge, whereas the grand, extravagant, sophisticated saucer magnolias of the M. *x soulangiana* type are better in the garden proper.

Similarly, trees that have been selected for their variation from the basic type, such as those with variegated or golden or purple foliage, are best kept within the garden scene and not taken far into the country. The same sort of choice can be made with flowering crab apples and flowering cherries: the delicate, near-wild *Prunus subhirtella* types versus big-flowered Japanese cultivars such as P. 'Kwansan.' These two groups of invaluable spring-flowering trees also exemplify different cultural needs. The cherries hate heavy clay soils, while the crab apples prefer them to the cherries' choice of drier sandy loams. Fortunately, gardening on a small scale generally means that soil amelioration and contrived drainage are possible.

CITY TREES

A phrase that has become popular in recent years to emphasize the importance of trees in town is "urban forestry." I have no question whatever about the concept's importance. In addition to the virtues of providing shade and wind protection, trees have been proved capable of reduc-

The grand, extravagant saucer magnolias are best kept out of wild gardens and planted, instead, as part of more organized areas closer to the house.

ing air pollution. But their major significance is visual—the civilizing, enhancing effect of tree tracery seen against the works of humanity. And it is here that the phrase "urban forestry" fails. Forestry has one overriding concern: to produce the largest possible quantity of wood pulp or timber. Optimum planting distances for each species are known and followed, side branches are taken off or shaded out to a considerable height to obtain the single straight trunks that are the economically required norm. People's requirements of trees in towns and gardens are very different. Multiple trunks are often vastly more attractive than bean-pole straightness, and distances vary according to visual and amenity needs.

A small walled courtyard—a perfect outdoor room—that I know in Brantford, Ontario, is about 20 by 30 feet (6 by 9 m). It was wonderfully designed by a well-known landscape architect and contains three large trees: a pin oak (*Quercus palustris*), a honey locust (*Gleditsia triacanthos*) and a katsura (*Cercidiphyllum japonicum*). Just outside the wall is a tall old white oak (*Q. alba*). Together, the trees offer variation in form and colour, time of leafing up and fall tints. If left to become mature, each could grow big enough to overwhelm both courtyard and house. But this is gardening, not forestry, and it will be possible over the next 10 years or so to take out whole branches to maintain a balance between the leaf canopy and the

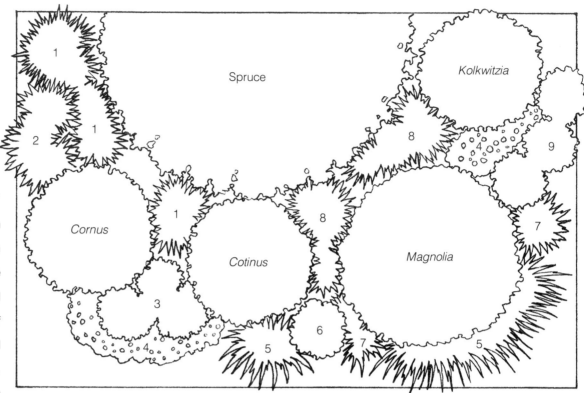

Spruce

Kolkwitzia

Cornus

Cotinus

Magnolia

The area under an existing tree such as a blue spruce could be planted with a selection of shrubs, bulbs and day lilies.

1. Yellow daffodils
2. *Hosta*
3. *Hydrangea*
4. Snowdrops and crocuses
5. Day lilies
6. *Buddleia*
7. White daffodils
8. Tulips
9. *Caryopteris*

sky. Then perhaps one or even two of the trees will have to be felled entirely if all balance and control is not to be lost, and the garden will move into another phase. Naturally, such sequential progress will be considered and planned for when the garden is first designed. There are alternatives that makers of such small gardens can consider. The courtyard could ultimately accept just one mature tree. One carefully chosen specimen, the honey locust for instance, sited to give shade where it is most required, will eventually provide the combined effects of the existing three trees. But it will take some years to reach the stage of effective furnishing. Can one wait? Or can one afford to buy a really large specimen and hire the crane and the necessary labour to swing it over the house and plant it?

In really restricted spaces, even a single tree may be thought too overpowering. Yet summer shade, dappled and moving the way a table umbrella's can never be, is still desirable, and there are a few plants that will fill this bill, quick to grow but never too tall. A couple of them are North American natives. If it were rare, our own common sumach (*Rhus typhina*) would cause lineups at garden centres. Though we pass acres of it along the highway, we seldom see the form and

grace of a single specimen with just three or four stems. In a town courtyard, it has an extraordinary elegance, from the fresh unfolding foliage of May to October's fall brilliance. The female plant then holds its Venetian-red fruit candles through winter. In Europe, where staghorn sumach is truly exotic—that is to say, not native—it is well appreciated. Here, there is the usual difficulty that prophets have in their own country.

Even more dramatic in leaf is angelica tree, or devil's walking stick, a species of *Aralia*. Which common name is used is apt to reflect the user's opinion, but in fact, the names are needed in sequence. First, there is the summer canopy of spreading, lacy, angelicalike leaves. In August comes a froth of tiny cream flowers, then pink-tinged fruit, which ripens black in September and attracts flocks of cedar waxwings. As the nights cool, the weight of all this finery suddenly seems too much and it abruptly falls. Bare, thorny 10-foot (3 m) stems are left—the walking sticks.

Both sumach and aralia are suckering plants that will try to colonize the whole yard. It is no problem to pull up the shoots that appear, but planting in a big, bottomless container saves the bother. A concrete sewer pipe ring is ideal because it both restricts and frames the plant.

But what of evergreens? In this climate, we are restricted to coniferous species—no evergreen oaks, no *Magnolia grandiflora* (just possible in New York), no tree-sized hollies like the *Ilex pedunculosa* that grows in Philadelphia, no eucalyptus as in California. Here, big evergreens mean conifers, either natives such as the lovely white pine or species that come from high altitudes with severe winters similar to ours, such as blue spruce (*Picea pungens*) or Austrian pine (*Pinus nigra*), from the Rockies and the European Alps respectively.

A SAMPLE GARDEN

Realizing that their winter shade may be unacceptable in very small gardens—and that a very long shadow is cast by a 30-foot (9 m) tree in low winter sun—the gardener should also note the strength of form and texture these plants give to the planned garden. I have already made fun of the desultory blue spruce as the only plant in a front lawn, but a superb association of plants could be based upon that lone tree. Conventional though it be when standing alone, it both gains and gives when used constructively. However ordinary or initially unappealing a tree may be, deep thought must be given before the chainsaw is brought in to irrevocably demolish the growth of many years. Far better to build upon it as one of the "bones" of the new garden. Here follows one of the many possibilities, indicating the way a gardener can build upon existing plants of importance and, over two or three years, develop an association of ongoing attractiveness.

In April, a couple of yards (2 m) away from the branch spread of the spruce, one might plant a saucer magnolia. Even at three feet (1 m) high—a good, affordable size to start with—it will have a few of the silky, furry buds that on a big plant are almost as ornamental as pussy willow catkins. They are effective from November leaf fall till spring, through snow and frost. In May, the fur will fall away and one will get the first hint of how a mass of these pink chalices will someday look against the grey-blue of the spruce. Three yards (2.7 m) to one side, one might take out another circle of grass for a beauty bush (a foolish name, really, because there are dozens of potential contenders for the title; the one to which it is usually given is another Oriental, *Kolkwitzia amabilis*). As the magnolia bloom ends, the beauty bush opens its little buff-pink foxglove flowers. In five years, at 6 to 10 feet (2-3 m) high, its arching branches

will look like a floral fountain, remaining elegant when the flowers give way to rusty seed heads. All this against the once lonely spruce.

The magnolia's neighbour on the other side might be a purple-leafed smoke bush (*Cotinus coggygria* 'Royal Purple'), whose dark, lustrous leaves are crowned with a froth of pink "smoke" in midsummer. Beyond, in more shade, one might plant the white variegated dogwood, *Cornus alba* 'Elegantissima,' which will light up its spot throughout the growing season and then catch the low winter sun that tinges its twigs deep cherry-red.

Just three or four plants added, and the whole front yard begins to take a new lease on life. But one cannot stop now. It has become only too apparent that having a number of shrubs, each in its own little bed, is an awful bore when it comes to cutting the lawn—and how maddening that the mower broke a major branch off the magnolia.

So in September, the decision is made to do what might have been planned from the beginning if one were starting from scratch: incorporate all the new planting into one bed. The turf is skimmed off and placed grass side down in the bottom of the trench as the ground is dug. Now there is the opportunity for a Proper Garden. Elizabeth Sheldon's book of that name is obligatory reading for those whose plant horizons are lifting. And how very fortuitous: the local garden centre has just received its consignment of spring bulbs. It is now possible to plan for colour from early March: a couple of dozen snowdrops planted in groups of six just a few inches out from the shrubs' stems, ditto for crocuses and scillas. These are just for starters, floral hors d'oeuvres. This small investment will grow year by year until the ground around the deciduous shrubs is carpeted.

The real need is to choose things to complement the main actors in the spring pageant. Early yellow daffodils would be fine, but personally, I would prefer white 'Ice Follies' or 'Beersheba' when the magnolia comes out, then late pink tulips to fill the gap until the beauty bush takes over. Numbers do not have to be great at first. More can be added in later years, and the bulbs may increase naturally if conditions are good.

Paradoxically, if all goes well, that won't be the case for some of the bigger bulbs. As the main shrubs grow and their branches meet, it must be accepted that tulips, especially on the edge of the spruce leaf canopy, will become shaded out and begin to decline. However, after five years of good service, they will have fully earned their keep. Moved to another more open spot, they may still build up good bulbs again.

But in the early years, there is a lot of empty space in the new bed. Soil, I believe, is for growing plants in. It is not an aesthetic experience in its own right, so it makes sense to add more plants at once even though, ultimately, they will be crowded out. We have so far arranged for floral interest from March through June and good foliage into the fall. But high summer and early autumn need help from some fairly low shrubs. *Hydrangea arborescens* will give interest throughout all that period as its flower heads change from green through creamy white to buff. A few day lilies add colour in July, a dwarf buddleia in August and blue caryopteris in September.

SEASONAL SEQUENCE

This sort of planting pattern can be easily copied, sometimes by building upon existing plants, sometimes by starting from scratch. In either case, it is wonderful how quickly the garden becomes furnished and starts to develop the vital vertical dimension. There is no lack of fine woody plants to choose for any climatic zone. In the following paragraphs, I will explore a seasonal sequence that will give flowers, foliage or fruit for 12 months of the year. They are plants that grow in my garden, some inherited, many added. In most cases, I expect my plants to earn their keep by giving more than a single-season display.

Amelanchier (serviceberry, Saskatoon berry, Juneberry, shadblow or snowy mespilus) is a typical example. For just 10 days in early May it is the epitome of spring, its wandlike branches wreathed in white blossoms. Less than two months later, its pink-purple fruits are ripe, ornamental and delicious if you can beat the robins to them. Then in October, the leaves fall in a blaze of orange and red. A plant for three seasons at least – or to be more exact, a range of plants, for *Amelanchier* is a genus with at least a dozen species to choose from, small, medium and large.

However, the flowering year begins with the witch hazels. One could say that the year *ends* with witch hazels if one chooses our native *Hamamelis virginiana*, which flowers in November. But its yellow petals appear as the foliage turns the same colour, and so they give little show. The spring-

flowering species make more sense for gardens. Close to one of the doors at the Royal Botanical Gardens Centre is a huge 'Arnold Promise.' As I pass it daily on the way to my office, I am able to appreciate its sequential virtues. The pale green, downy summer leaves put on an unrivalled autumn show as they develop concentric rings of gold, orange and scarlet. When they drop in early November, one gets a sudden mind's-eye signal of spring, for the flower buds are exposed, looking like clusters of suede *petits pois*. In milder climates than ours, they will open for Christmas. Here, a few will start to show colour in late February in some years. Usually, however, it is a month later when the twisted, inch-long (2.5 cm) petals unfurl to cover the bush in clear yellow. The flowers are amazingly frost-resistant and can take whatever the season brings. What a start to the year, underlined with perhaps a clump or two of purple *Helleborus atrorubens* and golden winter aconites at its feet. At home, we have a close cousin of the Arnold Arboretum's selection called 'Jelena,' whose typical spidery flowers are coppery red, more remarkable than the yellow in closeup but less effective in the garden scene.

SPRING-FLOWERING SHRUBS

Yellow is the predominant colour of early-spring shrubs. Witch hazel is followed by *Cornus mas*, the Cornelian cherry, with little puffballs of pale yellow and sometimes a good autumn show of red fruits. An easy, utterly hardy shrub – or eventually a small tree with interesting flaky bark – it shows up well against a coniferous backdrop.

Of course *the* spring shrub is forsythia. (May I appeal here for pronunciation which shows that it is named after a Mr. William For*syth*? I followed him as curator of the historic Chelsea Physic Garden in London – almost 200 years later – and feel I owe it to him to try.) A problem in zone 5 and colder has been that some forsythias, although able to survive perfectly well, have been reluctant to bloom because their flower buds were killed above the snow line in winter, making the whole exercise pretty pointless. New selections such as 'Northern Gold' and 'Sunrise,' bred in Ottawa and elsewhere, are virtually guaranteed to perform.

Forsythia is common, but that in no way detracts from its value if used properly. Unfortunately, it takes almost any treatment without complaint and therefore often receives it. The fre-

There is no lack of fine woody plants for any climatic zone, but only in warmer areas does the term "evergreen" include trees that are broad-leafed, not coniferous.

quent short-back and sides haircut after flowering entirely ruins its typical open habit. Each plant should be considered both as an individual and as a component of the border that is allowed to touch and interrelate with its neighbours without getting out of hand. This is the essence of all pruning; it should not develop into guerrilla warfare. Thus, unless bulk is desired to build up the plant, the classic way to deal with spring-flowering shrubs is to cut out a portion of branches that have flowered to encourage development of new shoots to carry next year's display. Yet forsythia is so prodigal that it can take more than this. I cut huge branches soon after Christmas, stand them in water in the earth cellar and sequentially bring them into the warmth upstairs. The flowers soon open – essence of spring. (You can do the same with *Cornus mas*, but it smells rather of old fish boxes.) Then more forsythia is cut close to Easter, when one finds the flower-arranging ladies at the church are suddenly even more than usually friendly. The brilliance of most forsythias in the garden needs toning down with white honesty or white daffodils in front and some help – day lilies perhaps – for summer, when it is merely another green-leafed shrub. But then, too, it is valuable because forsythia maintains its greenness much

longer than most shrubs, dropping its leaves only after they turn purple in late November.

Well before forsythia is finished blooming in mid-May, other fine plants are coming into their own. The magnolia season begins with *Magnolia stellata*, its brilliant white flowers opening wide like sea anemones. 'Royal Star' and 'Centennial' or the gentle lilac-pink 'Leonard Messel' are the forms to search for. They are not difficult to grow, but because of their early flowering – sometimes starting in late April – a bit of protection provided by buildings or other shrubs is appreciated. Soon afterward come the saucer magnolias with their great pink-and-white goblets that smell of exotic fruit salad. *Magnolia x soulangiana* and its forms eventually make small trees. If well sited, one becomes the dominant plant in a small garden, around which the design will develop.

As these finish, another favourite magnolia species opens its first flowers. These are like little parachutes, deliciously fragrant, and only when you turn one up do you see the purple interior. They will appear intermittently until late July. Throughout the summer, the leaves' milky-white undersides flash in the wind, and in autumn, there are spectacular scarlet seed clusters. This Oriental paragon is *Magnolia sieboldii*. Do plant it.

52

The closely related rhododendrons and azaleas are fairly particular about habitat, requiring well-drained, acidic soil and some shelter from wind and sun. The cool white of the flowering dogwood in the background balances the intense pinks and reds of these site-specific plants.

But now we are ahead of ourselves. Late May and June can provide more marvellous shrubs than even the biggest garden can accept. If one is interested in a lilac, better come to the Royal Botanical Gardens in late May to pick out a favourite from the 800-plus growing there in the Lilac Dell. All of them are named and, to a critical and informed eye, all are different. The scent of just one bush is an intoxicating proclamation that summer is around the corner. But although a selection, from typical lilacs to the Canadian Preston hybrids and the Japanese tree lilacs, extends over two months, any single bush is good for only two weeks, and the foliage is not much to write home about for the rest of the year. Here

is the sort of choice one needs to make consciously: is that couple of weeks of flower and evocative perfume worth it? If so, it is sensible to plant snowdrops and crocuses and daffodils around the lilac's base, as we do here, in order to get a bit more value from the space; 2 weeks out of 52 is not enough.

As the lilacs bloom, so do the viburnums, often just as highly scented. Everyone knows our native highbush cranberry (*Viburnum trilobum*), a loose, shade-tolerant shrub of woodland edges with simple flat heads of white flowers. These make a gentle, unspectacular show, but in fact, few spring plants have a longer season, because by July they ripen cherry-red bunches of fruit that hang on the branches until the following spring. The closely related European V. *opulus* has a yellow-fruited form that is happy here right under the big black walnut—a valuable attribute.

Viburnum carlesii, known as Korean spice, eventually becomes a compact six-footer (2 m) with round heads of intensely fragrant flowers, pink in bud and opening glistening white. Still more spectacular and twice the size is V. *x carlcephalum*, a hybrid whose wonderfully scented flower heads are as big as croquet balls, though their season is short. Here, *Euonymus fortunei* scrambles up it and pushes out nearly evergreen branches covered with winter fruit, so again, a single space is doubly used. For small gardens, another Korean spice hybrid, V. *x burkwoodii*, is a more sensible choice. With the same desirable attributes of flower and scent, it has a six-week season. The lustrous leaves with suede backs hang on till December, giving the garden a furnished look. By the time they do drop, next year's flower buds are already developed and distinctive.

But if I could have only one viburnum, I think it would have to be one of the Japanese *Viburnum plicatum* forms whose wide-spreading branches, carried horizontally, become overlaid with a spread of white flowers like tablecloths of finest Nottingham lace. This is an architectural plant to build a border around. In some years, a good, if fleeting, display of red berries follows, but the birds soon gobble them up, and in autumn, the leaves turn deep purple before falling.

RHODODENDRONS

Then, of course, it's rhododendron time—at least it would be if I put my mind and a lot more effort into it. As it is, we have a couple of bushes of the small-leafed 'P.J.M.,' which is common, easy and to be depended upon to appear healthy throughout the year and to flower well. The clear purple looks lovely with pale primulas or doronicums at its feet. Sadly, so many rhododendrons in northeastern North American gardens look hideously ratty; their fine flower clusters, for the short period they are there, seem to emphasize the lacklustre leaves and miserable habit.

I love rhododendrons. I've admired the tiny *Rhododendron lapponicum* on the shores of Baffin Bay and seen R. *campanulatum* flower against a backdrop of Himalayan snowfields at 10,000 feet (3,000 m). I have drooled over the wonderful collections in West Coast and British gardens, where flowers bloom from January to July and the foliage is fabulous beyond that. Occasional lakeshore gardens in balmy Oakville, just west of Toronto, could almost be confused with Surrey, England. But in your garden? Much is possible. Equally fine is a new rhododendron garden I admire in Terra Cotta, Ontario, a zone or two colder than here, demonstrating that almost anything is possible if trouble, time and money are effectively combined. First, a white pine wood was created, then attention was given to the medium —soil is too simple a word—in which the rhododendrons were to grow. The naturally limy soil there is absolutely useless by itself and mere amelioration just a temporary expedient. To provide a low pH was essential. PH is the scale by which soil acidity is measured; pH 7 is neutral, while pH 4 to 5 is ideal for acid-loving plants like these. Quantities of pine needles were put through a shredder and mixed with an equal quantity of peat moss. A foot or so (30 cm) of this was spread beneath the trees and the young rhododendrons planted with a sprinkling of flowers of sulphur. A spring dressing of ammonium sulphate is given both to maintain the low pH and to provide nitrogen naturally lost as the organic matter decays. Occasional chelated iron deals with any lime-induced chlorosis caused by alkaline irrigation water. Drainage is perfect. Further medium is added as necessary.

Thus in an entirely unsuitable spot yet with ideal soil conditions artificially provided and with carefully contrived shelter from wind and, especially, from winter sun, a wide range of climatic-zone-3 rhododendrons flourish. This is why evergreen shade was chosen rather than the conventionally recommended oak trees. Of course, the shade must not be allowed to become too dense. The *Rhododendron yakusimanum* hybrids like the shadiest spots, and small-leafed 'P.J.M.' types, such as 'Olga,' a lovely early pink, grow with abandon. But this is garden making at a level few of us can attain. It needs real dedication.

Herein is the real secret of success. First, the choice of species or cultivars must be suitable. This means not restricting one's choice to the very few locally available but searching beyond and researching the possible. Second, the association of plants must be effective to build up a garden picture that causes the viewer to exclaim not only, "How lovely," but, "Of course, why didn't I think of that?" Such an effect does not depend

Leaf colour can vary from pale through dark green to variegated, greyish or purple. Here, a variegated dogwood and a lime-green robinia oversee a contrasting bed of spiky sea holly.

ered forms: 'Buckley's Quill' resembles nothing so much as torn-up paper. Their season is as short as lilacs', but for a half-shaded spot where it does not get bleached by midday sun, the golden-leafed form of P. *coronarius* is worthwhile, as is the uncommon variegated type. Both flower well for their moment.

Variegation is caused by a reduction of green chlorophyll in some or all of the leaf. Most such plants occurred originally as mutants or branch sports, which were noted and subsequently propagated vegetatively. Back in the 17th century, Oxford University Botanic Garden had a collection of what they called "striped plants," whose oddness was observed without the reason being known. Since that time, the number of plants whose leaves are striped, marbled or blotched with white or gold has increased dramatically. Without variegation, the range of desirable hostas would certainly be vastly smaller and our houseplant palette greatly reduced. Everyone would agree that an all-green spider plant is not worth growing.

SUMMER COLOUR

With shrubs, lack of chlorophyll is apt to reduce vigour, as one might expect, taming rather coarse plants for garden use. The green-leafed ninebark (*Physocarpus opulifolius*) is hardly worth planting, but its golden-leafed form 'Luteus,' which unfolds as brightly as forsythia flowers, is a splendid thing. So, too, are the variegated dogwoods. *Cornus alba* 'Elegantissima' has fine, white-splashed leaves decking dark red stems which show up especially well in winter after the leaves drop. Such foliage dogwoods offer little in the way of flower, but the garden effect is seven months long.

Our barely native flowering dogwood (*Cornus florida*), a Carolinian forest species found only as far north as southernmost Ontario, is a wonderful plant, but it produces its flower buds in autumn and holds them throughout winter, so it is very vulnerable to hard frosts. Many springs are flowerless or see only mean, frost-pinched bracts —the four petal-like growths that surround the central "button" of little flowers. A better choice, certainly possible into zone 5, is C. *kousa chinensis*; our now 20-foot (6 m) bush is one of the best things we inherited. This is another of those ideal plants with a seasonal sequence of delights. In early June, the flower bracts unfold the palest green. Gradually, they turn cream, then pure

upon a large amount of land and a deep pocket (though both help—the Wildean aphorism that nothing succeeds like excess has a certain awful truth) but could be confined to a small, half-shaded border against the house where the necessary amelioration can be effectively concentrated. What is important is that keen gardeners capitalize upon soil (light and naturally acid) and situation (agreeably mild) beneath high natural oak woodland (for dappled shade) and use their rhododendrons as just one layer in a natural-seeming stratification of trees, shrubs, herbaceous plants and ground covers.

Rhododendrons, incidentally, do not have to be evergreen. Deciduous species such as the exquisite Korean *Rhododendron schlippenbachii* and a host of species and hybrids from cold regions of the world are better adapted to our winters than the big-leafed evergreens. For garden effect, remember that individual plants do not make a garden—always it is their effective combination with others.

Rhododendrons see out June with help from a range of white-flowered deutzias and related mock oranges (*Philadelphus* spp). The latter have a delicious perfume and exquisitely modelled flowers as long as one avoids the double-flow-

Ivy on my chimney is one of several climbers, some flowering, some predominantly leafy, that provide visual and thematic linking of house and garden.

white. The display continues for weeks. There are still a few dotting the branches in August. From September till the end of October, their succeeding orange-pink fruits hang on long stalks like glass Christmas tree decorations. And then comes the fall leaf effect, purple and bronze. What a plant!

With us, the bottlebrush buckeye (*Aesculus parviflora*) is *the* plant for late July. On the edge of the lawn is a 15-foot (4.6 m) clump of this fine suckering shrub, which is dramatic when holding its foot-high (30 cm) "candles" of white flowers. Rooted suckers taken off in years past also grow in quite heavy shade and still flower well. Their unfolding leaves are flushed pink, and they drop clear yellow. Here is another easy but strangely neglected plant. It is ideal as a front-yard shrub, informal yet able to be contained to any size. If it is underplanted with snowdrops and English ivy, its position gives continual interest.

Clear-blue-flowered shrubs are unusual in northern gardens. California has its wonderful range of ceanothus. Bluebeard, or blue spiraea (*Caryopteris* spp), is a small alternative for us. This grey-leafed, aromatic plant becomes a cloud of blue, and as the flowers drop from their calyces, the latter take on a metallic sheen like oxidized

bronze. Only three feet (1 m) high and wide, it is a front-row shrublet, or it can be used as a low, loose hedge. In spring, it is pruned back to about half its size. With full sun and good drainage, it may even produce self-sown seedlings that can be moved to other spots or given to deserving friends. In our garden, these seedlings appear in cracks in the stone-paved paths.

FALL AND WINTER

By September, the season for flowering shrubs is almost over. Depending on the previous winter, the mop-head hydrangeas will or will not be earning their keep. *Hydrangea paniculata*, however, can be relied upon to carry its pink-flushed heads. Visual emphasis moves toward the products of earlier flowering—the fruits of crab apples, viburnums, hollies, and so on, which are at first combined with fall leaf tints and then blaze alone. Only the size of one's garden restricts what can be a superb show at this time.

If I could have only one plant to celebrate fall, it would be *Euonymus alatus*, one of several plants known as burning bush. Bright it certainly is, but it is not a fiery colour. Around the end of September, the small leaves turn a vivid cherry-pink, and the show lasts a month. At the same time, the

Clematises have twisting leaf stalks that must be trained as they grow. Like other climbers, they provide a valuable sense of height, enclosure and privacy in the landscape.

covers of the fruits fall off, revealing little orange seeds that hang on after the leaves have dropped, entirely changing the pattern. The true species from China and Japan eventually grows quite big, 15 feet (4.6 m) high or so, and is rather the shape and size of a really happy Japanese maple. With its lower branches pruned off, it would make the ideal small tree for a town courtyard, but unfortunately, it would take 20 years to do so. A naturally smaller form, 'Compactus,' is half the size but has all the advantages of the wild plant. Its compactness is not the tight, inelegant shape that is the curse of so many dwarf mutants mistakenly recommended for small gardens.

If one is lucky, an occasional seed germinates naturally in the sort of serendipitous position that one would never have thought of (or dared to try) oneself. At the very base of our big yellowwood outside the garden room is a four-foot (1.2 m) burning bush. The soil is so dry there that the shrub manages only five or six inches (13-15 cm) of growth a year, but we bless the indolence that prevented its being moved when we first noticed it. Now, the combination of gold and cherry-red in October winds up the season with a fine fanfare flourish.

November comes, and most of the leaves are down. It is going to be four months before the first witch hazel flowers stir a spidery petal – a third of the year. But the garden remains. As snow comes and goes and as extreme cold waxes and wanes, our wish to get out into the garden varies, but always we see it from indoors. It is still there. The shapes of the shrubs, the lines of the paths, the silhouettes of the trees, the long blue shadows of winter, all these combine to provide the invaluable bones of the garden. Now they can be observed from inside. Every room has a view, and we can observe calmly and critically, unencumbered with the confusion of colour or, because it is so cold out, the compulsion to immediately rush out and do something. *Such* a relief.

Questions abound. Does the front line of the big back border sweep suitably, or are the curves too mean? What closes that vista before it ends at next door's clothesline? Would we get a glimpse of the creek or the elegant church tower if that tree were pruned or even removed? What can I plant or build to take the eye from that dreadful electrical substation across the road? Would a pergola (in my mind's eye, elegantly draped in morning glories and ripening grapes) be the ideal addition to link this with that? Let's not give each other Christmas presents this year; we'll commission a gazebo on the edge of the ravine instead. Winter is the time to plan, to plot. Even if the more expensive flights of fancy never get beyond the drawing board or the back of an envelope, it will not be time entirely wasted, and it does help to hurry spring along.

There is, I think, a necessary comment that the reference to a pergola provokes. Especially in new gardens, in new subdivisions where the builders have just left (and have also left some nasty detritus that you will not find until later because it is hidden under the imported cosmetic layer of topsoil), even the short three or four years it takes to build a basic framework of trees and shrubs seems interminable. One wants immediate height, enclosure, privacy (at least I do), a feeling of ownership – this is ours; after all, the mortgage is killing us – and a sense that we are putting our stamp, our style, on the property.

CLIMBERS

Fortunately, there is one invaluable group of plants that seems perfectly programmed to help. All plants need light and will go to almost any lengths to reach it at the expense of competitors.

Old-fashioned roses combine with clematis—this is 'Lasustern'—to give a cottage-garden effect on a house wall.

Trees have evolved extraordinarily complicated methods of producing a permanent skeleton (we call it wood) and highly sophisticated methods of plumbing. How *do* the water and the plant nutrients it carries reach the top foliage of a 300-foot (90 m) giant redwood? No wonder it takes time to build the body to support all this stuff. In the race to succeed and survive, some plants have replaced the ability to develop heavy supporting woody tissue with extreme speed of growth. But this means that after a few fighting feet, gravity wins and such a plant falls flat on its face, unless, of course, it can hold onto something else. These are the wonderful shrubby climbers that are invaluable in all gardens to clothe walls, drape pergolas, clamber up steep banks and hide ugly sheds by putting on 10 or 12 feet (3-3.7 m) of growth in a single season. Climbing mechanisms are yet another wonder within the world of plants. Grapevines have sensitive tendrils that wind round anything they touch like the slenderest simian fingers. Boston ivy goes one step farther, with tiny sucker pads at each tendril tip to deal with flat surfaces. Clematises have twisting leafstalks that, once firmly in place, can be dislodged by nothing short of secateurs, which is why clematises must be trained as they grow. Like geese, they can be led but not driven. Honeysuckles twine, while roses have hooked, downward-pointing thorns that double

A pergola—two parallel fences joined by overhead bars—supports a wisteria, one of the traditional climbers that quickly give a furnished look to a new garden and further visual dimensions to an old one.

as defence. Once its new shoots have pushed up through a host shrub, only the collapse of that support will bring the rose down.

These climbers are the sort of plants which naturally colonize the treetops in tropical jungles or which, carelessly introduced into a climate softer than that from which they came, overrun untold acres of land. In the southeastern United States, Japanese kudzu vine is so rampant it looks like something out of science fiction. Climbers grow fast. Fortunately, an advantage in our climate is that in spite of impressive speed of growth, no climbers need grow impossibly out of control.

Species by species, climbers for our gardens exhibit all the virtues of normal shrubs: splendid scented flowers, fine foliage and beautiful berries. At the Royal Botanical Gardens are two extensive collections designed especially to help gardeners choose. On the huge pergola whose arms enclose the rose garden, there are traditional twiners such as wisterias, trumpet vine (*Campsis radicans*) and honeysuckles (*Lonicera* spp), tendril climbers such as porcelain vine (*Ampelopsis brevipedunculata*) and examples of traditional shrubs, such as crab apples and even magnolias, that can be trained on a framework as espaliers. The dozens of clematises have their own collection,

including large- and small-flowered hybrids and species that flower from May till October; the range is positively daunting.

All of these climbers and many others are ideal for quickly giving that furnished look to a new garden and adding further dimensions to an old one. A pergola—which is, after all, just made up of two parallel fences joined by overhead bars, the sides filled with cedar trellis or tightly strained fence wire—can carry the line of an important path out into the garden. Its sight line could be closed with an urn or a planted pot on a stand. A backyard terrace might carry a pergola roof on just a row of uprights, the upper members joined to the house. The terrace ends might have single-sided pergola "wings" to give privacy or protection from cold winds. These and other trellis structures, combined with good planting, help to give early vertical emphasis.

The walls of the house can be used as support for climbers. Nothing gives a cottage-garden effect more quickly than self-clinging Boston ivy (*Parthenocissus tricuspidata*)—the effect extends indoors, too, if you leave the windows open long enough. More control comes from attaching a trellis or panels of fence wire to walls that require furnishing as part of the consciously designed scene. At the base, plant one or two climbers such as the *kordesii* rose 'William Baffin' with clematis 'Frances Rivis,' which will give early interest. Then, in June, add just one morning glory, 'Heavenly Blue,' to throw out a few sky-blue trumpets with the fall flush of roses. Such associative planting inevitably results in blossoms that are less perfect than those a single cherished plant would give, but it extends seasonal and foliage interest so that the black spot and the mildew matter much less — to the point at which a spray of baking soda in water can take the place of proprietary chemical fungicides. If some mildew persists, so what? It has its own life to lead.

PLANTING TREES AND SHRUBS

When to plant our trees and shrubs deserves the most careful consideration. After all, they are expensive. Perfect plans and impeccable choice add up to very little if the plants do not grow. As is so often the case, although there are rules of planting, they need to be accepted for what they are — guidelines that should be adapted to our own conditions and convenience so that we can help our plants adjust to new life in a new place, an adjustment bound to cause them stress.

Spring and autumn are the usual planting times, although as the garden centres demonstrate with their rows of trees and shrubs in pots, anytime from April through October is possible. The plants used will also affect the season chosen. Obviously, any plant of doubtful winter hardiness in one's area needs to have as long a period as possible to establish itself before facing winter. For these, the cool weather of early spring is best. To wait will bring sudden hot days with desiccating winds that can play havoc with young shoots and unfolding leaves unsupported by a well-developed root system.

As summer approaches, that danger is ever more present, so it is best to wait until early fall for most planting. Then, days are again cooler, rains more likely and irrigation not immediately lost to evaporation. Soil, too, is warm, so roots quickly take hold. Left too late, however, the plants are forced into immediate hibernation and are ill suited to survive the winter months ahead.

These concerns affect even plants that have been well established in pots. They need feel little planting shock unless the roots are stunted and matted from too long a pot life. Those that have been lifted from the nursery rows and are sold bare-root or balled-and-burlapped (that is, wrapped in sacking to keep some soil around the roots) clearly need even greater care; the bare-root plants must be fully dormant in early spring to survive transportation and planting.

Soil preparation is equally vital. Holes need to be about twice the size of the rootball, and the subsoil should be loosened and improved with rotted compost. Too deep a planting must be avoided. With small plants from pots, it is easy to keep the top of the rootball at the new surface level. The former soil level of bare-root plants is also pretty obvious. The uppermost roots coming from the trunk should be only just covered, as can be observed in wild-growing or otherwise established trees. In wet soil, if it is suitable for planting at all, trees are best planted on a shallow mound. When planting large specimens, it is wise to ask for family assistance to ensure that they are upright and do not sink as the soil is returned and firmed around the rootball.

Staking is something of a vexed question. Recent research suggests that the branches waving in the wind provoke stronger root growth. But with standard trees, especially in exposed positions, some initial help is certainly necessary to keep the base of the young trunk supported.

It is very desirable to be able to ensure follow-up care once the plants are in. Planting "up at the cottage" or wherever, with a month's subsequent absence, is apt to be a recipe for disappointment. It is necessary to water the new trees and shrubs at planting time and subsequently until they are established. An antidesiccant spray to reduce transpiration may be desirable for evergreens. A similar effect of protecting new plants is obtained by wrapping them in open-weave burlap (*not* plastic). For spring-planted stock, a temporary screen on the sunny or windy side is sufficient, but after a fall planting, the overcoat may need to be worn from November through March. In Japan, winter wrapping has become a positive art form, involving elegant canopies of reed and thatch, bandages and guy ropes to prevent branches breaking under the weight of snow. It is unlikely that home gardeners would be tempted to go to such lengths. In any case, it must be emphasized that beyond the first winter, as with roses, if the method needed to enable plants to survive for almost half the year is visually intrusive and ugly, either the system or the plant must be changed.

There are hundreds of different roses, hardy and tender, shrubby, climbing and miniature. Something of the ancestry of modern roses can be ascertained by looking at their thorns. Climbing roses have thorns that hook downward to hold up the canes.

ROSES FOR ALL

An image of the perfect rose is easily brought to mind: the scrolled petals organized so that each encloses the next, slightly furled; the colour soft as velvet, yet glowing with a silklike sheen; the scent warm, sweet yet spicy. This imaginary picture is less easy to bring to perfection in the garden—though it is by no means impossible. I am always surprised that reluctant gardeners who complain about the difficulty of growing this and the problems of succeeding with that are willing to persevere with a few languishing hybrid tea roses that, though excessively laboursome, earn neither their keep nor their space. Many other roses are preferable. To find them, it helps to know something of the origins of roses, because as with any group of plants, their background tells the gardener something of their likes and dislikes, which can be taken into consideration in cultivation and in breeding.

Although authors vary in their estimates, it seems there are about 120 distinct wild roses. A few are so closely related that some botanists insist they do not deserve to be considered separate species. But then, one must remember that just as plants can be classified, so can botanists—into two major groups, the lumpers and the splitters. (If all the lumpers had their way, gardeners would have fewer plant names to learn.) In any case, the wild roses—more than a hundred, as all will agree—are spread around the northern hemisphere. While there are species native to the mountains of southern India and the hillsides of Mexico, none of them cross or even approach the equator except by way of human hands.

Almost all roses, therefore, are plants of temperate climates, which gives one the immediate hope that they will succeed in our gardens. Unfortunately, the situation is not quite that simple. Certainly there are roses from the prairies and the climatically equivalent steppes of Central Asia that can take anything our winters are likely to throw at them, as can the little burnet rose (*Rosa pimpinellifolia*, R. *spinosissima*) and the ramanas rose (R. *rugosa*) from Scottish and Japanese seashores respectively. But there are also roses from the Mediterranean, from mild and moist western Europe—think of photographs of those swags of pink and white wild roses hanging from Devon's deep hedgerows—and from the even damper and warmer sub-Himalayan hillsides.

So from a simple geographical survey, one can guess with reasonable certainty whether this or that *Rosa* species is likely to succeed in one's garden. Depending upon its native habitat, one can also gather whether it is a low bush or a rambling climber and therefore where and how to grow it.

One can understand something of the ancestry of even the modern hybrids by examining their thorns. Almost all wild roses are aggressively armed, but bush roses have straight spines, whereas climbers have thorns which are hooked downward, so that once they have pushed new shoots up into a shrub for support, nothing short of the death of the host will bring them down. We can even choose to grow them that way.

SPECIES ROSES

Among the so-called species roses are some wonderful garden plants, and indeed, these relatively unimproved types play the first clear notes in the garden's annual symphony of roses. Here in Burlington, Ontario, several yellow-flowered species open from early to mid-May. All are elegant, six-foot-tall (2 m) vase-shaped bushes with fernlike foliage that becomes entirely hidden at flowering time. Father Hugo's rose (*Rosa hugonis*) is pale yellow; the incense rose (R. *primula*) is primrose-yellow. Better still, perhaps, is R. 'Canary Bird,' which is from China, like the others, and is probably a true species despite its name.

It must be emphasized that these roses are shrubs, and like most shrubs, from lilac to lavender, they flower once and once only. The ability of most modern hybrid roses to flower off and on throughout the summer leads to an unfair expectation of wild roses and their immediate offspring. They have other and entirely distinct virtues, so any comparison with the hybrids is pointless. Each group has its attributes that, as garden makers, we choose to use to our advantage or not.

Very soon afterward, perhaps the last week of May, the double yellow 'Harison's Yellow'(*Rosa x harisonii*) blooms. Again, it flowers but once, and if blooming coincides with a sudden hot spell, it is sadly fleeting. Nevertheless, it is an important plant in North America, having appeared in the garden of a New York lawyer, George Harison, in 1830, when there was no other double yellow rose on the continent. Its ease of propagation soon spread it around. Today, it is an essential plant in the restoration of heritage gardens.

At the Royal Botanical Gardens (RBG), it flowers with two forms of *Rosa foetida*, an unkind name that one's nose does not fully validate, although certainly, for a rose, the scent is a disappointment. These are 'Austrian Yellow' (of which 'Harison's Yellow' may possess a few genes) and 'Austrian Copper,' known in French as 'Rose Capucine.' *Capucine* is the French word for nasturtium, and if one pictures orange-red nasturtiums tumbling across the paths of Monet's Giverny garden, one can imagine that the sudden blaze of colour, like a Turner sunset—to use another painterly image—is both strangely unseasonal and unroselike. The petals are yellow on the outside and a nasturtium vermilion on the inside, producing a brilliant bicolour effect that breeders laboured long to bring into the spectrum of modern roses. Unfortunately, their success at the turn of this century included another of the 'Austrian Copper's' genetic traits, a dire susceptibility to black-spot disease.

The grace and simplicity of single roses—which, of course, all true wild species are—have been consciously retained in the work of a number of breeders. In the 1930s, the German Wilhelm Kordes, whose concern for winter hardiness in that continental climate was as great as ours, worked with extremely hardy Siberian forms of the burnet rose, crossing them with selected garden roses. The results, such as 'Frühlingsgold' and 'Frühlingsmorgen,' are six-foot (2 m) bushes with a wonderful June display. The former has four-inch (10 cm) flowers with two layers of creamy yellow petals. Its cousin has huge single flowers, pink flushed with yellow. Both are sweetly scented. Again, one has to choose between a one-time prodigious display, as these give, or a flowering period that is meted out gradually throughout the season. One that has the latter is Ohio-bred 'Golden Wings' (again with the burnet rose in its parentage), a fine four-footer (1.2 m) whose exquisite flowers are made up of five waved petals set off with a boss of darker stamens. Vastly

63

Father Hugo's rose is one of the first to bloom in May, but like most of the other species, its lovely flowers appear once and only once each year.

bigger, and a favourite of mine at the RBG, is 'Flamingo,' whose slender buds open into wide, soft pink roses from June to October. All of these give the lie to the belief that hybrid roses invariably need winter protection. It depends upon their origin. The 'Flamingo' at the RBG has some stems that are six inches (15 cm) around.

Rosa multiflora, the hardy Asian species frequently used as an understock for our garden roses, makes a fine froth of white in June, followed by crowds of tiny red hips, and while only the wildest gardens would wish to use it—for there are better things—its sequence of early-summer flower display and subsequent fruiting is worth pursuing in more desirable species and hybrids.

In the northeastern United States much more than in Canada, R. *multiflora* has gone wild and even weedy, forming big, domed, freestanding shrubs or clambering up hedgerows.

One of the very best species roses is *Rosa moyesii* from the China-Tibet border. Its glowing crimson flowers of perfect heraldic form are followed by an August-to-October display of shining, sealing-wax-red hips. On a glowing fall day, these strangely elongated hips, exactly the shape of upside-down wine carafes, can elicit a sense of euphoria almost equal to that given by the contents of a carafe—and with no aftereffects. "But," you might say as you look at the catalogue description, "where on earth can I put a 10-foot-high

One of the best species roses is *moyesii*, whose perfect crimson flowers are followed by a fall crop of elongated hips the colour of red sealing wax. This is a compact selection, 'Geranium.'

(3 m) rose? And anyway, I'd need to go upstairs to enjoy it!" Fortunately, rather more compact is a *moyesii* seedling introduced from the Royal Horticultural Society's garden at Wisley, England, in 1938. This is called, rather confusingly, 'Geranium.' Its hips are a bit plumper, but otherwise, every virtue is there. It does well at the RBG, where it should be seen both in flower and in fruit.

Even simpler are the rugosas (*Rosa rugosa*) from northern China, Korea and Japan. Generally, I deeply disapprove of using a species name as the common name of a plant: it's too often done by gardening name-droppers showing off their botanical facility. In North America, however, the "common" names ramanas rose and Japanese rose mean nothing to most gardeners. Calling them "rugosas" is a good way out. Rugosas are as hardy as old boots and virtually disease-free. They thrive on the rocky sea cliffs of Maine, where the typically lilac-pink species has colonized acres. In the garden, they are beautiful and even economically useful. The hips, the size of 'Sweet 100' tomatoes, make the best of all rose-hip conserves, not least because of their size.

Rosa rugosa has been used as a parent of a number of garden roses, but invariably, these hybrids leave most of the wild virtues behind, so we are wise to stay with the true species and what are probably seedlings or branch sports from it. All have the typical lustrous, wrinkled foliage that clothes the bushes to the ground (so all make marvellous hedges) and turns clear yellow before falling in November; all have a fabulous fragrance; all have a good June display and then erratic bursts of flower till the end of the season. Beyond this, one has a choice: to fruit or not to fruit. Only the less full and less long-lasting single flowers are gradually replaced by a crop of developing fruit that remains after all flowering

is done. There are four fine fruiting singles: white, yellow-eyed R. *rugosa alba*; claret-coloured R.*r. rubra*; the robust 'Scabrosa,' whose flowers are a sort of violet-crimson; and 'Frau Dagmar Hastrop,' pale pink, half as tall as the others at about three feet (1 m), the perfect small-garden rose.

If bigger double flowers are the choice, then one has the violet-red 'Hansa' or the more purple 'Roseraie de l'Hay' and the well-known papery white 'Blanc Double de Coubert.' Good flowers on the latter are a triumph, but its petals do brown easily in rain and hot sun.

The old rugosas are all proven garden plants of about a century's standing, and though it would be agreeable to be patriotic, the recently named Canadian rugosas such as 'Jens Monk,' 'Henry Hudson' and other Explorers do not seem to me to be any particular improvement, pleasant though they be.

Such are the traditional and restricted expectations from roses in the garden that the above reference to good autumn colour in rugosas may have come as a surprise. In fact, there are other shrub roses that have this attribute—as we fully expect from a number of flowering shrubs in other genera—and sometimes even the virtue of distinctive foliage earlier in the season. Perhaps the most striking is that of *Rosa glauca*, also known as R. *rubrifolia*. Either name is descriptive, but added together, they are perfect, because the reddish (*rubra*) leaves are overlaid with a glaucous bloom like that on purple plums and grapes. The leaves are carried on purplish, thornless stems. The little pink flowers are very fleeting but are quickly replaced by sprays of red hips that add to the quality of the effect. This is a wonderful rose to associate with herbaceous plants: the blues and purples of delphiniums early in the season and New England asters at the end. Flower arrangers find it irresistible, though their cutting is not always to the benefit of the plant. R. *glauca* is one of the few roses to accept quite a lot of shade. The foliage then takes on a greyish cast, which is just as attractive.

It is a pity—but doubtless inevitable—that our wild North American roses are considered of little garden account. But the shiny-leafed, compact little *Rosa nitida*, medium-sized R. *carolina* and the tall—about five feet (1.5 m)—R. *virginiana* are all splendid plants, admirable for shrub borders or informal hedges. Their attributes include ease of cultivation, pink flowers of various shades, fine

'Henry Hudson,' which has rugosa parentage, is one of the Canadian Explorer series of roses hardy enough to over-winter without protection in most northern gardens.

red hips and brilliant red and gold autumn colour. The two latter species have been grown and cherished in England since the 18th century, in both their original single- and subsequent double-flowered forms. Perhaps, like the Constitution, they should be repatriated.

There is, of course, one essence of roseness that has been mentioned only in passing: scent. A rose without a perfume is hardly worthy of the name. There is no doubt that 20th-century breeders' pursuit of bigger and brighter roses tended to relegate scent to a subsidiary role—in general, older roses have good perfume while many visually dramatic modern varieties have little—but it is not fair to praise all old roses and damn all

new ones. Many modern roses have superb perfume. Each must be judged on its individual merit by each gardener. The sense of smell differs greatly from person to person, and although recommendations from friends or textbooks are valuable, ultimately the choice is one's own, best tested by visiting major rose gardens or rose nurseries that have open days during the summer.

In his splendid book called simply *Roses* (Dent, 1978), rose breeder Jack Harkness lists particularly worthwhile selections under a number of headings and grades them on a point system. In the perfume category, four, all modern, rate 9 out of 10: three are hybrid teas and one, 'Margaret Merrill,' a floribunda of Harkness' own raising. It is noted that 'Margaret Merrill,' whose flowers are white with just a hint of blush, has sweetbrier, or eglantine, in its ancestry. This is *Rosa eglanteria*, described by Shakespeare: "I know a bank whereon the wild thyme blows, / Where oxlips and the nodding violet grows / Quite overcanopied with luscious woodbine / With sweet muskroses and with eglantine."

The scent is not only for "a midsummer night's dream" but for any moist evening, when sweetbrier throws out perfume upon the air from both its rather fleeting flowers and its foliage. Harkness gives a full 10 points to a *Rosa eglanteria* hybrid – 'Austrian Copper' is the other parent – called 'Lady Penzance.' It is not, however, a plant for small gardens; its formidably armed canes grow 10 feet (3 m) long in a single summer.

Again, I should emphasize that when choosing roses – or any other plants for that matter – one should always consider the effect of the whole plant as a part of the garden's furnishing. Keen iris buffs, rosarians or rhododendron enthusiasts may be more concerned about the show bench and the subsequent joys of polishing silver trophies, but that is an entirely different subject on which I shall resist further comment. I entered the brief discussion on sweetbrier and its Penzance hybrids because of their attribute of scented leaves. Some modern roses grown for their flowers also have valuable foliage – even in a bad black-spot year. They may not be scented, but glossy, robust leaves help the general effect immeasurably. The orange-yellow flowers of the hybrid tea 'Glenfiddich' are superbly complemented by its young purple shoots.

HERITAGE ROSES

The discussion of rose foliage moves us legitimately into the wonderful world of old-fashioned, or heritage, roses. Any book on roses will document what we all seem to know almost instinctively: that roses have been cherished by successive cultures in the Far East, Asia Minor and Europe for several thousand years, that roses have been used as demonstrations of riches and conspicuous excess – a Roman emperor is said to have literally drowned guests at a banquet by having vast quantities of roses cast down from the ceiling – and that the rose is such an icon of purity and beauty that the Christian church appropriated it as the symbol of the Virgin Mary herself. We all know, if distantly, of the Wars of the Roses (in spite of the name, as nasty and brutish as any other civil wars), when the rival factions of 15th-century England took white and red roses as their respective emblems, and we learn the myth that a rose with pale pink-and-white striped flowers, the 'York and Lancaster,' miraculously appeared as a sign of peace. The lore is fascinating to anyone interested in the interweaving of culture and horticulture from earliest times, although it seems not very relevant to the day-to-day activity in our home backyards. (A local library may have a copy of my own *History of the Rose* – published by Collins but now out of print – that follows the story further.)

Where history becomes significant, however, is in the realization that the dawn of the 19th century was as important a time in the history and development of garden roses as it was in European history. One beam of civilized light in the darkness of the Napoleonic Wars was an order from the British Admiralty that any ship's captain who captured an enemy ship and found himself in possession of plants destined for the Empress Josephine's garden should dispatch the plants to her at once. From 1804 until her untimely death in 1814, Josephine brought together at Malmaison, just south of Paris, the most extensive collection of roses the world had ever known. Though doubtless wonderful in early summer, however, the collection would disappoint us today. Nothing much bloomed after June, and the colours were almost entirely confined to white, pinks and reds. Nonetheless, within the Malmaison collection were some splendid roses that are as gardenworthy today as they were then, when the choice was so much more restricted.

ALBAS AND GALLICAS

Rosa x alba, for instance, is distinctive for its bluish green foliage, which is seemingly resistant, if not immune, to black spot and mildew. This rose makes a fine backdrop to a white garden association, which it will enhance wonderfully when in flower. Pickering Nurseries, in Ontario, one of North America's major sources of old roses, lists 16 albas. They vary in height, size, fullness of flower and the amount of pink suffusing the basic white expected of R. x alba. All have a superlatively sweet perfume of varying strength. 'Great Maiden's Blush,' with origins before the 15th century, is certainly to be chosen if one has room for only a couple of shrub roses. It has good, grey-

kitchen herb bed, nothing could be more delightful or more suitable than a row of the apothecary's rose, R. *gallica officinalis*, once grown by the acre in France for the making of conserves and the flavouring of medicines. A single plant today is equally to be cherished for its dramatic show of wide, semidouble flowers, cherry-red with a boss of golden stamens.

Sometime in the early to mid-1600s, a bush of the apothecary's rose produced a branch sport that amazed all who saw it. Dubbed 'Rosa Mundi,' this still amazes with its brilliant white-and-red-striped flowers. Grow it and enjoy the remarkable flowers and lovely scent. Quite possibly, a bud or two will open clear cerise, a sport back to the original—two plants for the price of one.

Other fine striped gallicas still available include 'Tricolore de Flandre' and 'Camaieux,' while extraordinarily unroselike mauves and purples occur with 'Cardinal de Richelieu' and 'Belle de Crécy.' Most of these roses are from 19th-century France, but they are entirely winter-hardy here, and though they appreciate appropriate doses of TLC, they can actually put on a good show in poor, stony soil. The fact that they survived in old gardens through a century of neglect and changing fashion is proof of this.

DAMASKS AND CABBAGES

There are two other groups of ancestral types that include roses worth consideration even though they flower just once for four or five weeks of glorious display from the beginning of June. There are the cabbage roses and the damasks (*Rosa damascena*). The latter have downy, rather greyish foliage and often nodding flowers. The pale, striped 'York and Lancaster' already mentioned is one of these, historically interesting but not a first choice. Nor is the kazanlik rose, R. *damascena trigintipetala*, unless one plans to build a still and produce one's own attar of roses. That sounds like a good idea until one learns that in Bulgaria, where this rose is grown commercially in huge quantities, it takes some 200 pounds (90 kg) of morning-gathered rose flowers to make one precious ounce (28 g) of rose oil.

Better to choose just one or two particularly beautiful cultivars: 'Celsiana,' perhaps, with clusters of wide open, semidouble flowers, clear pink turning to palest blush, or the little three-foot (1 m) 'Leda,' whose dark red buds open to white with a fringe of red all around. This is also known

green foliage and will make a freestanding bush of six feet (2 m) or so, or its back branches can be trained against a wall or a fence—even a shaded one—allowing the others to cascade forward. This is just how it behaves on the west wall of our garage, shaded after lunch in summer by the big yellowwood. The flowers have the delicate blush of pink that the name implies. Rather more richly coloured forms have suitably suggestive names such as 'La Séduisante' and, ultimately, 'Cuisse de Nymphe Émue.' 'Queen of Denmark' (strictly, 'Koenigin von Dänemark') is an early-19th-century version with intensely doubled flowers in the strange quartered form which many old roses display and which 20th-century breeding of high-centred hybrid teas did its best to leave behind. Any historical survey of roses is a survey of fashion as well.

If the albas are tall and lax, the gallicas (*Rosa gallica*) are correspondingly short and compact and thus ideal for small gardens. Because they sucker from the base—provided plants are indeed on their own roots and not budded onto rootstocks as are all modern garden roses—they make excellent, self-renewing low hedges three or four feet (1-1.2 m) high. For enclosing a herb garden or, more simply, for demarcating a utilitarian

68

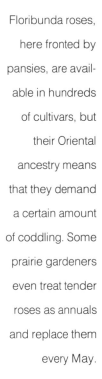

Floribunda roses, here fronted by pansies, are available in hundreds of cultivars, but their Oriental ancestry means that they demand a certain amount of coddling. Some prairie gardeners even treat tender roses as annuals and replace them every May.

as the 'Painted Damask.' But the best of all is 'Madame Hardy,' dating from 1832, one of the most beautiful white roses in existence. The intensely double flat flowers are quartered and have a little button eye of green carpels. Damask roses need a good garden life to show off their best. Prune out weak, twiggy branches as soon as flowering is over, and reduce the new long summer shoots by a third in March.

This treatment is also necessary for the cabbage roses, such as the species itself, the rose of Provence (*Rosa centifolia*). They are cabbagelike only in that the overlapping petals, layer upon layer — the hundred leaves suggested by the species name — hide the centre of the flower, as a good cabbage does its heart. These roses probably date from the 16th century, but their origins are difficult to be sure about; damask and alba roses are possibly in their background. More to the point is that they include some of the most fascinating old roses available anywhere. 'Robert le Diable' and 'Tour de Malakoff' are either loved or loathed, their flowers passing from shades of pink through lilac-purple, ending up a sort of dove-grey. These and other biggish centifolias, potentially four to five feet high (1.2-1.5 m), are apt to flop with the weight of their flowers, so they

should be given some support — three stakes joined by a circular iron band is ideal — or they can be allowed to fall over a low wall. Smaller types such as the charming three-foot (1 m) 'Petite de Hollande,' which has small, intensely double pink flowers, need no such help.

These cabbage roses are splendidly winter-hardy and need no cosseting. Neither, therefore, do their extraordinary sports, the moss roses. There are, or were, dozens of these, many of them intentional products of 19th-century breeding programs, but unless one wishes to build a collection or is especially enamoured of unusual colours, no choice could be better than the original of the race, 'Common Moss,' or 'Old Pink Moss,' dating from the 17th century. A fully opened flower seen alone would appear to be a typical, exquisite cabbage rose, clear pink and wonderfully perfumed. But turn it over, and one will see that the sepals and the flower stalk are all grown over with sticky glandular projections that look for all the world like green moss. When the flower is in bud, this covering is, of course, entirely apparent. This "moss" has an intensely aromatic scent different from, though no doubt a part of, the fragrance of the open rose. Its pure white variant 'White Moss,' or 'White Bath,' is just as lovely. Both the pink and the white moss roses grow about four feet (1.2 m) tall. They are the very epitome of the heritage old-fashioned rose.

MODERN ROSES

The Empress Josephine's Malmaison rose garden, though one of sensational early-summer display, was created at the very threshold of the era of modern roses, which bloom far longer. What changed everything—though it took a century for the full effect to be apparent—was the introduction to Europe of garden roses from Canton, one of the Chinese treaty ports. A couple of these Chinese species arrived in the mid-1700s, but hybridization was in its infancy, and nothing much was done with them. But in 1792, a Mr. Slater brought in what was first called Slater's Crimson China, then the Chinese Monthly rose. Soon formalized as *Rosa semperflorens*, the ever-blossoming rose, it was as exciting as if today someone suddenly introduced a delphinium-blue rose, the seemingly impossible. This delicate tea-scented species made it possible at last to have roses in flower even in northern European gardens from May till Christmas—or beyond in a mild year. Breeding programs developed the Bourbons—I grow the lovely thornless climber 'Zephirine Drouhin' against the garage wall—as well as Portlands, tea roses, hybrid perpetuals and, later in the 19th century, the hybrid teas.

These, at last, are what everyone expects in a modern rose—that epitome of "roseness" I described in the first sentence of this chapter. However, everything comes with a "but." Genes from China roses contributed scent, colour and remontancy (recurrent flowering) but also susceptibility to damage from low winter temperatures. China roses are plants of the warm temperate world, whereas many of us live and garden in a continental climate of extremes in which a bad winter can carry off entire bedfuls of fine plants. Not that this stops keen rosarians in any way; on the prairies, some actually lift their roses every fall and overwinter them in their basements as I do dahlias.

Before reviewing a few of the myriad modern roses—hybrid teas, floribundas and grandifloras—it is worth discussing their use in the garden and their value in the full garden scene. What do we want of them, and what do they do for us—and is it enough? For many people, the ability to grow a few fine modern rosebushes and see their perfect blooms is fulfilling and sufficient. It is their greatest joy to go out on a fine summer morning to find the dew still bejewelling those silky petals. Two or three cut for the house surpass the grandest floral arrangements.

But a major theme of this book (and only too obviously a major hobbyhorse of its author) is the year-round furnishing of our gardens. This is something the traditional modern roses—a bit of an oxymoron there—are unable to do by themselves. Their tender *Rosa chinensis* ancestry sees to that. Even in climatic zone 6 at the RBG, we protect our hundreds of bushes from late November until mid- to late March. Some years, it may be unnecessary, but it is not a risk we dare take. So we have domes of shining white plastic over polyfoam insulator, giving the impression of a space station more than a garden, an effect I would find entirely unacceptable in my own backyard. (If we could be sure of snow, the white plastic would be much less intrusive.) It is worthwhile seeing the RBG rose garden in winter, however, to compare this glaring protection of the modern roses with the uncovered roses beyond. These are the shrub roses, the species and the heritage roses, happily accepting whatever winter might bring. The RBG's modern rose beds were not much more attractive in winter when the traditional, vastly more laborious method of earthing up each bush to the height of a foot (30 cm) was adhered to. Of course, this is the system that most backyard rose gardeners are bound to employ. In late fall, after the first hard frost, the bushes are pruned to about half their height and soil is drawn up around the stems. It is usually necessary to bring more soil in so as not to expose the roots. An additional covering of straw, leaves or—provided Epiphany is not too late—Christmas tree branches may be used. All are gradually removed in spring. What a business. What a sight.

It is acceptable, I suggest, only beyond the view from the house windows. A row of favourite tender cultivars might grow, for instance, in the kitchen garden. Converting much of the vegetable plot to a cutting garden may be a more sensible use of that space, perhaps, when the children are grown and there are fewer mouths to feed. There, any method of protecting the bushes that is known to work in one's area is satisfactory regardless of what it looks like. The alternative is to treat tender roses as annuals and replace them every May with pot-grown plants from the garden centre. This I reject out of hand as a way of life, because it is neither gardening nor a method of effectively furnishing the garden space, although, naturally, it is both convenient and sensible for filling a gap or two. There is no lack of choice in modern hybrid tea roses. Hortico Nurseries of Waterdown, Ontario, lists about 200 cultivars in the extraordinary range of colours that hybrid teas now possess, as well as a further hundred floribundas.

The third way to have roses in the garden is, of course, to concentrate upon plants known to be winter-hardy in one's area and to build up planned garden pictures with other plants that happily associate with roses. As has been indicated, this is not a problem in relatively informal shrub borders, where rose species and the bigger heritage roses can take their rightful place. Their dramatic if often short floral display will need to be considered in relation to the colour theme chosen. *Rosa moyesii* 'Geranium' is brilliant scarlet, but other R. *moyesii* hybrids include the lovely cream 'Nevada' and its warm pink sport 'Margaret Hilling.' (Neither of these offers the fruiting display of the parent, but instead, they produce a few flowers throughout the summer in partial recompense.) These are superb combined with a foreground of peonies. Some late day lilies would give further interest and foliage contrast.

Old-fashioned roses, such as the moss roses 'Lanei' and 'William Lobb,' which bloom in the purple and lilac range, encourage the use of a foreground of lavenders and hardy geraniums, with stately foxgloves and delphiniums behind. The alba roses suggest a white border association with regal lilies, deutzias and a grey edging of lamb's ears (*Stachys byzantina*). The main display from these roses is over by mid-July, so they are good with later-flowering shrubs such as buddleia, sweet pepper bush (*Clethra alnifolia*) and hydrangeas, which take the spotlight for the next few weeks before *Euonymus alatus* and the bigger grasses join the fall display of rose hips. Then, autumn crocuses (*Colchicum* spp) open their lilac bowls, while out-of-sight daffodils and other spring bulbs are starting their root growth, ready to do their job at the roses' feet from April onward.

A FORMAL DESIGN

The process is very different if one wants an ongoing summer display of roses of modern form as well as extended year-long garden furnishing. This may change the garden from the informal to the formal mode. In a lawn area 20 feet (6 m) square, one might cut out four L-shaped beds enclosing a central square or circular bed. As a focal point, this could hold a sundial, a piece of statuary or a big container—a Chinese pot or half a whisky barrel—with a tumble of annuals in colours complementary to the roses.

In the outside corner of each bed is a clipped evergreen, obelisk-shaped—a juniper or cedar eventually six to eight feet (2-2.4 m) high. The L-shaped beds will hold 10 bush roses planted on 18-inch (45 cm) centres. In so small an area, it is a mistake to have too much of a mixture of roses. Each bed is best kept to one or possibly two compatible cultivars, and the pattern is repeated in the mirror-image bed across the way. I know this is difficult when there are so many wonderful plants to choose from. Possibly you prefer a kaleidoscope (after all, it's *your* garden), in which case, however, it is still wise to balance plants according to size and vigour, or the design of this formal area will be completely lost. Depending on the colour of the roses chosen, the beds are edged with lamb's ears—these beds are small, so the flowerless form 'Silver Carpet' would be best—or purple *Ajuga reptans* or golden feverfew (*Chrysanthemum parthenium aureum*). There are many possibilities. If paths in this little formal rose garden are to be lawn, then the edging neatly meets it. If paving is brought in, then stachys or self-heal (*Prunella* spp) can be allowed to colonize the bed under the roses, whose shade will reduce its vigour. Beneath the ground cover are planted snowdrops, species tulips or *Scilla sibirica* for the pre-rose show. Their declining foliage soon disappears. Alternatively, for real formality, the beds can be enclosed by low boxwood hedging kept to a foot (30 cm) tall and half as wide, which maintains the pattern of the garden wonderfully even when the beds' contents are in eclipse. Further, one might fence the outer lines of the beds to emphasize enclosure. Simple split-cedar rails would be fine in all but the most sophisticated spots.

Here, then, is a place, with its simple topiary, that makes its point for 12 months of the year. Its central path could lead to the front door, or this little formal rose garden could be in a front yard on its own, though its lines and axes must relate to features of the house—windows, a gable end, and so on. Alternatively, such a formal lay-

The centre of this formal rose garden is devoted to a half-barrel overflowing with annuals of complementary hues.

1. Cedars

2. Boxwood hedge

3. Rosebushes

out could lie below a deck or terrace whose steps would meet the central path that leads out to lawn or another planned garden "room." With its ground cover and spring bulbs, the rose bed gives interest as early as the climate permits. Its roses provide pleasure from late May until late fall brings down the floral curtain for the year.

There is, of course, nothing wrong with interplanting roses with summer annuals either, and so long as one is not obsessed with individual bloom quality, therefore avoiding a rigorous spray program, the rather gawky twigginess of modern roses can be greatly helped in this way. Even hybrid teas, whose beds have to submit to the annual earthing up and de-earthing, can grow

out of a frame of annual plants, which should have complementary colours and rather simple, loose forms. Pansies and violas are good, as are pale impatiens and *Verbena venosa* (V. *rigida*). One year, I pushed a few spare pelargoniums in amongst my 'Nearly Wild' roses, which, serendipitously, were exactly the same pink, so we were rewarded with a two-level display of different flowers that were almost indistinguishable from a distance. I must repeat this intentionally and take the credit.

SUITABLE ROSES

This is the basic pattern and these the basic materials, but what now are the roses? Where

Introduced 60 years ago, 'The Fairy,' a continuous-blooming hybrid still considered ideal for landscaping, is capable of surviving severe winter cold.

does one find these winter-tolerant paragons? They must be able to do well with the minimum of winter protection—just straw or evergreen branches to reduce desiccation from cold winds. Conventional mounding would make life impossible for the other plants. Only if the bed is larger could you include (if you insist) some favourite, un-live-without-able hybrid teas. In the centre of the bed where there is neither ground cover nor spring bulbs, some earthing up would be possible without entirely ruining the year-round effect. I would resist the temptation to grow roses known to be tender, however. I would put my row of hybrid teas for cutting in the vegetable garden and choose, for the full garden effect, plants known to be hardy in my area.

The nursery lists are the obvious source, and one searches through them noting cultivars definitely marked hardy. A certain correlation will be immediately observed. Breeders' names turn up again and again: Kordes of Germany, Buck of Ohio, Poulsen of Denmark, Felicitas Svejda of Ottawa, Dr. and Mrs. Brownell of Rhode Island and, more anonymously, Morden, site of an Agriculture Canada research station in Manitoba, now working with another such station at L'Assomption, northeast of Montreal. These are people and places that have worked on the problem of "sub-zero" roses (as the Brownells called some of theirs), and northerners are wise, for our gardens' sakes, to use the fruits of decades of breeders' devoted work instead of lusting after the near impossible. Of course, we all try to grow plants on the borderline of hardiness wherever we live (gardeners in California and Florida continually pretend they live in the tropics and complain bitterly when the occasional killing frost comes along to prove them wrong), but borderline plants should not be important components—not the bones—of the full garden scene. Protect the borderline plants with walls and fences. Those that are part of the framework must be completely safe and secure.

Thus, for that little formal rose garden, you might choose 'Nearly Wild,' one of the Brownells' best and one of my favourite bedding roses. Only two feet (60 cm) high, it carries sprays of single, clear pink flowers over an amazingly long period. One year, I recorded the first flowers opening on May 15. 'Nearly Wild' will also accept half shade without much loss of quality. It is usually described as a floribunda rose, one of the group that has large quantities of relatively small flowers.

Their predecessors, dating mainly from the early part of this century, still have valuable cultivars to offer us. It is significant to note that Hortico recently chose 'Kirsten Poulsen' (1924) as one of their "Roses of the Year" and that Pickering illustrated 'The Fairy' (1932) in the 1989-1990 catalogue, describing it as: "Care-free, continuous blooming, disease-resistant. An ideal landscape rose, also as a ground cover. We have plants which have so far lived for 22 years (and are still thriving!) without winter protection; the past two winters, they survived without snow cover down to minus 25 degrees C (–13°F) without dieback. The blooms are a deeper pink in autumn, enhanced after some frost, when the glossy foliage turns a maroon colour." 'The Fairy's' sprays of double, soft pink flowers look particularly attractive near the grey foliage of dusty millers such as *Artemisia stelleriana* or *Anaphalis triplinervis*.

An even earlier bedding rose is 'Little White Pet,' dating from 1879, vastly better than many later introductions that were claimed to supersede it. As an edging, this might have the low, purple-leafed pansy *Viola labradorica* or clumps of chives (*Allium schoenoprasum*), stolen from the herb garden and easily divided to provide enough for planting a foot (30 cm) apart.

So far, we have concentrated on small bedding roses. Bigger beds can take bigger roses. The smaller cultivars of Dr. Svejda's Explorer series such as the red 'Champlain' and apple-blossom-coloured 'Henry Hudson,' both less than four feet (1.2 m) tall, would be suitable for a formal bed. So, too, would the smaller *Rosa rugosa* hybrids. The old but invaluable 'Frau Dagmar Hastrop' has already been mentioned, and it is now joined by two additional low-growing cultivars, 'White Pavement' and 'Purple Pavement,' to extend the colour range. These are all wonderfully fragrant and offer a good fall display of hips, which, associated with *Sedum spectabile* or *Chrysanthemum arcticum*, finish the year with a flourish.

Another group of roses to look at—and a very mixed group it is too—appears in the catalogues under the general heading of "shrub roses." Of course, all roses are shrubs, but the title is used as a catchall to include garden roses that are not meant to be heavily pruned as are hybrid teas, floribundas, and so on. Thus most are large plants for mixed shrub borders. Some so-called shrub roses happily accept hard pruning and thus flower well at half their potential height. Especially fine are 'Carefree Beauty' and 'Country Dancer,' which are mid- and deep pink, respectively. The flowers, which cover the bushes with wide heads of blossom, have a perfect, small hybrid tea rose shape and are good for cutting. Introduced by Buck of Ohio in the 1970s, both make wonderful bedding roses where space is not too limited.

Meanwhile, gardeners in really cold areas will be grateful for the work of Agriculture Canada at Morden, Manitoba, and L'Assomption, Quebec, where the Explorer rose series, started by Dr. Felicitas Svejda, continues to develop. These are *Rosa x kordesii* cultivars, including 'John Cabot,' 'John Davis' and 'William Baffin,' which is blissfully free of black spot. We await others, not only for more forms and colours but also because these roses succeed on their own roots. If an extremely wicked winter cuts them to the ground, any shoot that arises from the rootstock will be the rose you bought, not some useless sucker.

ENGLISH ROSES

In reviewing the amazing diversity of roses for our gardens, it is easy to see how selection, breeding and fashion have gradually extended the range. The speed of change has generally been rather slow, so it comes as something of a shock to discover an utterly new range of roses that has become available to us only since the mid-1980s. They are the creation of David Austin, a rose breeder from the English Midlands. His aim has been to combine the repeat-flowering habit of modern roses with the fragrance, charm and disease resistance of the old gallicas, centifolias and damasks. Already, more than 50 of these "English roses," as they are now generally called, are listed by Pickering Nurseries under that heading. Other suppliers include them with modern shrub roses. It may be that not all will last—it is also certain that more will appear—and it is as yet too soon to know how definitely winter-hardy they will be. Pickering suggests protecting all of them as one would hybrid teas, except for 'Constance Spry' and 'Shropshire Lass.' These big climbers, which are wonderful but flower just once, came out in the 1960s before Austin's English rose pattern became fully established.

At the RBG, we have most of the newer introductions on trial, and we protect them in the conventional way. But some extra plants have only the protection that comes from their posi-

tion on the north side of a yew hedge. Otherwise, they have full exposure to the elements, yet despite very little snow cover, they have been able to take anything the last three winters have sent. Because they did not need to be pruned to hide under a cover, they show the potential of their considerable size.

So it seems that some of Austin's English roses will give northerners new plants for the full garden scene that I am continually suggesting, and I would recommend to all who love roses to try them. There are near singles and loose semidoubles, but for my choice, I turn to those whose flowers have the flat old-fashioned form yet appear for months and months. The dark red 'Prospero' (one of the Shakespeare series) is a classic with a perfume to knock you over. Next to this at the RBG—as a part of the rose trials, not for harmonious association of colours—we have 'Tamora' and 'Bredon,' both of exquisite form in a pale peachy apricot shade. 'Tamora' smells to me of green apples; 'Bredon,' the pinker of the two, distinctly evokes the aroma of the old-fashioned hard candies known as winter mixture. All three are compact bushes ideal for small gardens. Bigger and very different is 'Graham Thomas' (celebrating the man who, more than any other, brought about the renaissance of old roses in our time). This has a rich yellow rounded flower like a tennis ball with the top cut off, wonderfully tea-scented. Nineteenth-century rose growers, starved for yellow, would have killed for this. Different again are 'Dove,' with palest blush tea-rose flowers above elegant light green foliage, and 'Yellow Button,' a dwarf plant whose rosette-like flowers fully deserve the name.

Descriptions of these English roses could go on for pages; better to visit gardens and nurseries that grow them to pick out favourites and then consider how they can best be used in one's own garden scene. If, as seems likely, some are as winter-hardy as they are disease-resistant, they offer an opportunity to move hardy-rose growing into a dimension much more compatible with the other plants in the ornamental garden. There, all of us can develop our own plant associations of colour and shape and texture in ways that have not already become old hat.

MINIATURES

I have indicated that for small gardens, there are low English roses, small floribundas and

Miniature roses, which look like normal hybrid teas or floribundas viewed through the wrong end of a telescope, are difficult to place effectively in the garden. Here, they are used to frame beds of larger varieties. The climbing miniature 'Mabelyn Lang,' at right, adds height to the garden. The metal edging, on the other hand, adds nothing at all.

even compact rugosas, but all these are giants compared with the real miniatures, roses that may never grow taller or wider than a foot (30 cm) yet are capable of producing perfectly formed flowers exactly like normal hybrid teas or floribundas seen through the wrong end of a telescope. Every colour that modern roses have attained is here as well, but their Lilliputian size makes them appear ill at ease in the normal hurly-burly of garden borders. It must not be entirely pleasant, after all, to be looked down upon by a petunia. Nor is it suitable, as is sometimes done, to put these intensely contrived plants into a rock garden; the scale is right, certainly, but they look like Parisian fashion models attending a Greenpeace meeting. Miniature roses need each other and their own garden space. In containers or raised beds where they are divorced from the rest of the garden and are nearer to one's nose and eyes, they can be stunning. It is possible to find equally minuscule annuals to act as edgings—white or pink sweet alyssum, blue lobelia, and so on—to frame the little rosebushes. Miniatures are the obvious answer for balcony and roof-gardening rosarians. There are mail-order companies that specialize in miniature roses. Some miniatures can endure zone 5 winters, but in general, protection is wise.

CLIMBERS

From the tiny, this review of garden roses moves to the other extreme: to climbing roses that have the potential to be the giants of the rose world. They can be magnificent, taking the luxuriance that only roses can provide up, as it were, into the air. Local nurseries list *Rosa filipes* 'Kiftsgate,' but only for clients in warmer climes. Perhaps this is little cause for regret: the original plant at Kiftsgate Court in Gloucestershire, England, planted in about 1938, spreads 90 by 80 feet (27 by 24 m) around a great copper beech and scrambles higher than 50 feet (15 m) into its branches. Dramatic but daunting. As with miniatures, most rose types are repeated in climbing forms; many hybrid teas have sported to produce climbing variants, but even in zone 6, the shoots have to be taken from their supports every November, bundled together, laid down to be covered with soil or polyfoam or whatever and exhaustingly exhumed each spring. Some people are happy with this as a labour of love, but it's a prickly procedure I prefer to avoid.

So for pergolas, trellis screens, freestanding pil-

Climbers such as 'Pink Cameo' have the potential to be the giants of the rose world. A drawback is that even in zone 6, the tender types must be removed from their supports in fall and mulched—a prickly procedure.

lars and walls, I look for hardy roses. Most of the older rambler roses, though hardy, are not recurrent. They give one magnificent show for a month or so, and that is that. This is not necessarily to be deplored: any plant can only do so much, and that great display may produce as many flowers as a repeat flowerer does over an extended period. Thus, for garden effect, it is possible to add another climber to the same support to precede, succeed or—if excess is your thing—complement the rose show. If the plants are trained against a garden structure, the colour of the roses themselves can, of course, determine their best companions. If they grow against the house, however, the exterior materials must be considered. Scarlet roses against bright red brick lose much of their point—or worse.

For that midsummer display, the famous old fragrant coppery pink rambler 'Albertine' remains unsurpassed after 70 years. 'Seagull,' dating from 1907, is like a huge-flowered *Rosa multiflora* and similarly scented. 'New Dawn' is a particular favourite of mine, with its clusters of silvery pink flowers like small hybrid teas. We turn to breeder Wilhelm Kordes for brighter colours in hardy climbers. The single 'Dortmund' is red with a white eye, 'Hamburger Phoenix' is dark crimson,

'Leverkusen' has big double yellow flowers and good glossy foliage. A couple of Dr. Svejdas' very hardy Explorer series are big enough to be used as climbers. 'Henry Kelsey' and 'William Baffin' are red and deep pink, respectively, and are happily resistant to mildew and even somewhat to black spot. One of Buck's Ohio roses is especially successful as a pillar rose in full exposure at the RBG. This is 'Prairie Princess,' whose deep pink fragrant flowers are almost of hybrid tea quality. In colder areas, it doubtless makes a fine wall plant.

We read, particularly in the English gardening books, of ramblers and climbing roses reaching to the eaves of houses and beyond—a famous Sissinghurst view shows 'Albertine' doing just that. Here, however, some degree of frost damage—and thus loss of length—is inevitable in most winters. When it becomes apparent, shoots must be cut back to a really healthy bud. Sudden intense cold after a mild, wet autumn seems especially troublesome. In the spring, we may see that whole canes have been killed.

PRUNING AND PLANTING

Effective pruning is an essential part of good rose growing. Its role is not to keep plants small—

except with some modern shrub roses, as discussed above – but to encourage the most productive balance of flower and foliage. Pruning begins at planting time. Bare-root roses have to be able to support the aerial part of the plant, which therefore needs to be reduced. Plants delivered for fall planting – by far the best time – will already have been cut down to 18 inches (45 cm) or so and will need only tidying – the odd weak shoot taken out at the base perhaps. Then in early April, all but three or four of the strongest stems are removed entirely, and the remaining stems are cut back to a dormant bud four or five inches (10-13 cm) above the ground. Spring-planted roses get this treatment as soon as they are put in, which, it must be emphasized, should be as soon as the frost is out of the ground. A hot spell in May can otherwise wreak havoc.

With mature plants, the same general pruning pattern is adopted, but it varies in relation to the type of rose. The early-blooming species roses flower on stems that have overwintered. Therefore, any pruning necessary is best done directly after flowering, as one would do with any other spring or early-summer shrub. Just two or three old stems taken out at the base will keep the bush open. The intention, always, is to promote the growth of elegant shoots that lean out with the weight of the flowers. Shrubs and old-fashioned roses and climbers will need only weak wood taken out and strong canes tipped back below frost damage. Modern hybrid teas and floribundas must be reduced to about half their height in late November in order to facilitate winter protection. In spring, after gentle removal of the winter covering, they are pruned almost as hard as when newly planted, leaving just five or six branches, six or eight inches (15-20 cm) high. Subsequently, continual deadheading is itself a form of summer pruning. It is important not to remove too much foliage if the plants are not to be weakened.

Roses are not difficult to grow, but obviously, good preparation at planting time and subsequent care contribute to success. Most soil types are acceptable as long as drainage is decent. The soil is dug deeply with plenty of well-rotted compost or farm manure – peat moss is considered environmentally less acceptable for use in large garden plantings – and each rose receives a couple of handfuls of bonemeal. When planting, it is important to be able to identify a healed wound

where roots meet stem. This is the union where the cultivar has been grafted to the rootstock. (Most commercially grown roses are "budded" thus because it is a quick method of propagation, although it is perfectly possible to root most roses from cuttings and to grow the species from seed.) This union needs to be an inch (2.5 cm) below the level of the surrounding soil surface, the roots having been carefully spread out in the hole and the soil trodden down firmly layer by layer as the hole is filled. If the weather or soil is dry, it is wise to pour in a bucket of water. It also becomes essential, if planting is unusually late in spring, to stand the plants in water for a day (no more) to plump up the buds. Planting later still, using those potted and often almost-in-flower roses from the garden centre down the road, is always possible but is not to be recommended. As mute reproach for this lack of foresight in garden planning, the roses often do poorly.

Restrained feeding – nothing nitrogenous after August, when potassium is needed to help ripen growth – will encourage a continual production of flowers. Irrigation may be necessary, but good soil preparation will reduce the need, just as it helps to produce good healthy plants that resist disease. (We all know how we catch colds when we are run-down and tired.) Yet with many roses, mildew and black spot and various bugs are facts of life. Each of us must decide whether to wage continuous war, spot treat on occasion or live with these plagues. Some combinations of the latter two approaches seem to be the best. Why get out a battery of armaments for Japanese beetles when a daily walk round one's roses, a pleasure in itself, is enhanced by the satisfying crunch as the creatures are dealt with by the best insecticide yet invented: the human finger and thumb in opposition?

In choosing a climber to grow against the house, consider the colour of both. If the roses are not recurrent, more than one type can be grown to prolong the show.

Classic herba-
ceous borders are
dedicated mainly
to perennials,
plants that with-
draw to below-
ground resting
organs during
the inclement
season of their
homelands.

A PERENNIAL PANORAMA

uring the 1880s, a rather opinionated English gardener, William Robinson, brought out *The English Flower Garden*, a book whose aim was to encourage people to change from the overuse of tropical and subtropical annual bedding plants to flowering shrubs and, especially, herbaceous perennials. The change, he asserted, would produce more beautiful but less costly gardens.

The word perennial suggests something that continues from year to year, so an oak tree or a forsythia bush is as much a perennial as a peony. But in this chapter, I am concerned with herbaceous perennials: plants that live from year to year but, during the inclement season of their homelands, have opted to get out of the way. They withdraw to below-ground resting organs of one sort or another—bulbs, corms, rhizomes, tubers or rootstocks—where enough food is stored to stoke the growth of an entirely new aboveground body when conditions are suitable. These are the plants of the classic herbaceous border. They are also central to any garden that does not depend entirely upon tender annuals for floral interest.

Like all successful crusades, Robinson's was a manifestation of its time. His was not a lone voice in the wilderness. The arts and crafts movement had gathered strength, and many fashionable adherents campaigned for a return to a simpler (they imagined) preindustrial lifestyle in which the artist-craftsperson would produce traditional buildings and artifacts by traditional methods. A short English summer season of brilliantly coloured exotics made possible by glasshouses heated by coal boilers needing constant attention was clearly antipathetic to the movement.

But, one wonders, would the movement have become the art form it did without the contributions of a wealthy, well-connected woman whose artistic talents, it is said, were turned from painting to garden making because of failing eyesight? A chance encounter in 1889 brought together the 45-year-old Gertrude Jekyll and an aspiring young architect, Edwin Lutyens. Over the next 30 years, a Lutyens house with a Jekyll garden, whose major component was herbaceous perennials, was the ideal for prosperous people building what we would consider enormous country houses.

EDWARDIAN LESSONS

In terms of the development of taste and garden history, the story of this business relationship is a fascinating and significant one. But what do these "gardens of a golden afternoon," to use the title of Jane Brown's book about the Jekyll-Lutyens partnership, have to say to us? They were made nearly a century ago in another country with another climate. Their scale was often enormous, and they took a small army of devoted and underpaid gardeners to develop and maintain. Not my backyard scene at all.

The apparent extravagance of these gardens led to a belief, especially in Britain's austerity years after World War II, that those golden Edwardian afternoons had indeed gone forever and their gardens with them. Yet careful rereading of *The English Flower Garden* and Gertrude Jekyll's many books brought about a reevaluation that is behind the renaissance of much garden making in recent years. Jekyll worked on a large scale because she and friends who later became clients could afford to and because labour and materials were ridiculously cheap by today's terms, but her real message had nothing to do with size.

The effectiveness of her gardens depended upon consciously chosen plants and their arrangement within a garden whose lines and bones had been carefully planned to relate to the house that it complemented and of which it was an organic part. The message presumed knowledge as well as commitment on the part of the owner either to make the garden personally or to pay professionals to do so. And, the message continued, even given the best professional advice available and with the necessary help, a good garden results only when the real interest and involvement of the owner are factors. It need not be immensely large or laboursome. I believe that much good gardening is done by contemplation, especially on hot, golden afternoons, from the vantage point of a lounge chair settled

in a shady spot. But good gardening does presume some knowledge of plants and an insatiable desire for more. It is this we get from returning again and again to Gertrude Jekyll and those we consider her kindred and, whenever possible, from contemplating the gardens they have made.

Of course, no one can grow plants if they do not know what to call them, and so we come to the vexing question of plant names. Why North Americans should protest more than Europeans about Latin names is not easily explained. There is a fear of elitism, of appearing better than we are (an unfortunate hang-up, it seems to me; few of us are as good as we should be, and a little dissembling might encourage the others). There is also a fear of making gaffes in pronunciation — you say tomayto, I say tomahto; you say clamaytis, I say clemahtis — but so long as one can order the plant one wants and can use the name by which it can be unmistakably identified, it really couldn't matter less. If you are not willing to use the Latin names, be prepared for disappointments; there are at least a dozen different flowers called bluebell. Botanical Latin is certainly a language we need to be able to use, and how wonderful it is to have a language that only needs nouns and adjectives, no verbs or tenses that might slow the flood of invaluable plants into our gardens. The range of perennial plants available is so great, it is vital to be able to read a catalogue with understanding. Speak the scientific names with conviction, and watch the doubters fall back.

No gardener knows everything; indeed, those who have been at it the longest often say they realize they still have much to learn. Every season is new, and one learns and relearns as the years progress. One must be daunted by neither Latin names nor others' successes nor the apparent complexities of some of the tools of the trade. Most "rules" — when to plant this, prune that, harvest the other — are merely long-realized facts that thinking persons can work out for themselves. Cultivation is a word with many meanings. Garden making is a combination of aesthetic sense and an understanding that plants are living organisms which respond to a range of stimuli and carry genetic programs to succeed in certain conditions. There are perennials for every garden and every garden position: for shade or sun, for wet or dry soils, for the front or the back of borders. Some are heavy and solid in effect, others as thin as gossamer. Flower colours can be as bla-

The season-long foliage of plants such as lamb's ears and lady's mantle can be just as important as floral effect in the landscape.

tant as a brass band or as quiet as a clavichord. And as with shrubs, season-long foliage can be just as important as floral effect.

Where possible, it makes sense to match a plant's position in the garden with its natural adaptations to habitat. For instance, early-flowering trilliums and bloodroot from the northeastern woodlands of North America are given shady spots, while the New England asters and coneflowers of open meadows and prairies take full sun without wilting. But habitat predilections are more complicated than that. For example, trilliums grow under trees not necessarily because they prefer shade but because they can accept it and still flower and fruit and reproduce. Many

other species cannot survive in shade, and therefore competition for space, nutrients, moisture and light is less intense in the trillium wood than in the open field beyond. Success in the wild has to balance the possible with the available.

This is not quite the situation in the garden. We remove weeds to enable our chosen plants to grow freely. We water and feed. Thus, we can produce fine trilliums in full sun if they do not have to fight it out with all the other natives that would naturally rush in. But their season of flowering is reduced in the heat, they need more coddling, and more to the point, they just look more right in dappled shade. We are wise, therefore, from both cultivational and aesthetic points of view, to match our plants with an approximation of their original habitats.

BORDER SITING

My own main border is about 75 feet (23 m) long. As the plan shows, it faces north and is backed by the split-cedar fence of the vegetable garden. A gently serpentine front edge causes it to vary from 8 to 12 feet (2.4-3.7 m) wide and also adds bits of near easterly and westerly aspects. Aspect matters little, so long as there is no direct tree overhang and no more than a couple of hours of summer shade from buildings or distant trees. It is more important to site the border where it is best enjoyed.

One narrow Toronto Cabbagetown strip I know is all herbaceous border, with a serpentine path leading through it, almost like one of those idealized Surrey cottage gardens that Helen Allingham painted at the turn of the century. In other words, it has two borders that face each other, both backed by fences. In essence, these borders repeat the sort of scene that Gertrude Jekyll adapted from such cottage gardens. The genre is alive and well in Ontario. In most home gardens, some logical backing is desirable. A border will often be sited against a boundary fence or hedge. In the case of the latter, however, one must be concerned about the twice-per-summer clipping of the hedge and competition from its roots. A two- or three-foot (60-90 cm) service access is necessary between the face of the hedge and the back of the border. Though this sounds extravagant in small spaces, maintenance of hedge and border alike is difficult without it. In small gardens, there may be only one possible choice of position for a border, and one must make the best of it.

Perennials can also be grown in island beds without any backing. Here, of course, the taller plants will be grouped toward the centre of the bed rather than at the back, and the display will be viewed from all sides. This is highly effective on a large scale, as can be seen at the Royal Botanical Gardens, where different free-form beds concentrate upon different colour associations and visitors find themselves being led naturally from one to another. A pair of long, relatively narrow canal-like beds with a walk between is another good way to use perennials in a more formal fashion. These long beds may take the eye to an object, within or beyond the garden space,

82

....

My own main border includes liatris, day lilies, astilbe and sedum, fronted by annuals such as nicotiana, poppies and dusty miller.

that closes the vista. Such beds might sensibly concentrate upon soft, low plants with accent clumps of grasses, irises or yuccas.

Consideration of the border's front is also necessary. That wonderful tumbling exuberance of the admired English garden is impossible when a rigidly tidy front edge has the inevitable visible band of soil which must be kept cultivated. On the other hand, a front row of plants allowed to fall forward will either kill the grass or be chewed up by the mower. I regard those plastic or metal strips used to edge beds as abominations, and anyway, they do not help this situation at all. What is needed is a band, a "mowing strip" of paving slabs or bricks or interlocking stone about a foot (30 cm) wide onto which the tussocks of catmint or *Phlox subulata* or whatever can flop to soften the edge. The band is laid on a shallow layer of sand and is slightly lower than the level of the grass so that the mower can run on it: no edge to cut, no plants mistreated. With an island bed, the stone mowing strip needs to be on all sides, and with the canal beds, the inside strips may be widened so that they meet to form a central paved walk.

When land stays soggy despite your initial deep diggings with additions of compost or spent mushroom soil or any other well-rotted organic matter, the edge of the border can take the form of a low retaining wall of stone laid without mortar, six inches or a foot (15-30 cm) high, to give a raised bed. Wet roots are the death of many perennials. A sloping site is also best so treated, producing, in effect, a low terraced bed. The front-row plants then happily tumble over the edge.

So the position and aspect of one's perennial borders are chosen. What now of the plants? The choice is enormous. There are dozens of wild species from around the world, and almost all of them have special forms that keen gardeners have selected over the years. Others, such as day lilies and delphiniums, have vast numbers of named cultivars created by plant breeders over the last century. How to choose? Fortunately, many of us planning a new border will not be starting entirely from scratch. There are some Shasta daisies over there, a good clump of hostas in the front yard ready for division, and a friend down the road is lifting some overcrowded irises. All could be grist for the mill, and initially at least, nothing is to be despised.

But perhaps one has already reached the stage of that happy miscellany of inheritances and donations when some conscious rearranging is called for. One's perennials give reasonable summer colour but seem not to hold together. Glossy magazines show borders of incredible beauty. One wants something similar. We all have a tendency to expect too much of a given space – it's those magazines again. (Thank heavens for the camera. Even at home, it cleverly records moments of perfection and frames perfect pictures that eliminate next door's washing. Anyone can do it.) We have to accept that no one border can produce a blaze of colour from May through October, but it can give interest throughout that time and, indeed, beyond.

Planning to scale on a bit of squared paper is obviously a help in situating the plants in the right place for their height and spread and in managing the right associations for texture and effect, colour and season – shocking pink bergamot next to orange-scarlet Oriental poppy is fine for the most delicate sensibilities because a full month separates their flowering times. Thus, along a given border, one should try to plan a series of successional plant pictures: as one grouping goes over, another one takes our attention. With care (and a bit of luck), it is also possible to arrange

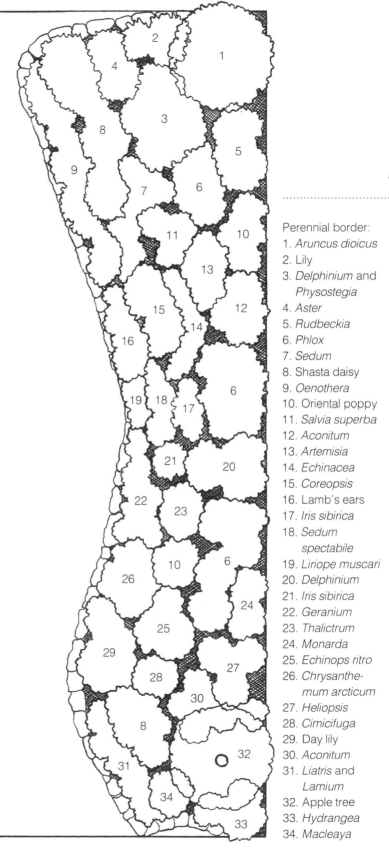

83

Perennial border:
1. *Aruncus dioicus*
2. Lily
3. *Delphinium* and *Physostegia*
4. *Aster*
5. *Rudbeckia*
6. *Phlox*
7. *Sedum*
8. Shasta daisy
9. *Oenothera*
10. Oriental poppy
11. *Salvia superba*
12. *Aconitum*
13. *Artemisia*
14. *Echinacea*
15. *Coreopsis*
16. Lamb's ears
17. *Iris sibirica*
18. *Sedum spectabile*
19. *Liriope muscari*
20. *Delphinium*
21. *Iris sibirica*
22. *Geranium*
23. *Thalictrum*
24. *Monarda*
25. *Echinops ritro*
26. *Chrysanthemum arcticum*
27. *Heliopsis*
28. *Cimicifuga*
29. Day lily
30. *Aconitum*
31. *Liatris* and *Lamium*
32. Apple tree
33. *Hydrangea*
34. *Macleaya*

for the demise of one plant to be masked by the later growth of another.

Because they are the first to flower, the shade-tolerant plants of North American woodlands and comparable habitats around the world are bound to begin this survey of perennials throughout the seasons. Europe and the Far East have also been sources of wonderful shady-border plants collected avidly for gardens in the past. It is apt to be forgotten that such an old favourite as bleeding heart is a Japanese native introduced first to English gardens only in 1816. The exotic and North American species, selections and hybrids complement each other to give garden interest under trees and shrubs or to the lee of buildings from March long into fall.

EARLY SPRING

In my garden, some of the first floral stirrings come in the cold northwest-facing border overhung by a big horse chestnut tree. Pushing through its own winter-torn leaves come the furry flower clusters of *Pulmonaria rubra*, whose coral-red bells open only an inch or two above ground. But with the warming days of April and early May, the stems become nine inches (23 cm) long, flowering the while and building up a clump of long, pale, velvety leaves that will remain green until next year. And as they bloom, they are joined by other species. All the pulmonarias, forget-me-not relations, are valuable plants at this time and for their long-term foliage. Several have typically blue flowers (P. *longifolia mollis*), while others have pink buds, open purplish and turn blue, with all colours occurring at the same time on the same plant, suggesting the old name soldiers and sailors (from a time before military uniforms became safer but boring camouflage). Another common name, lungwort, a translation from the Latin *pulmonaria*, refers to the lunglike appearance of the grey-spotted leaves. There are a number of especially well-marked forms that have been selected by observant gardeners with an eye for a good plant; one such (P. *longifolia* 'Roy Davidson'), given to me by Elizabeth Sheldon, makes a great wheel of silver and green that is spectacular until covered by snow. Once built up into a large stock by division, it will make a wonderful ground cover under forsythias.

Showing the earliest spring colour with *Pulmonaria rubra* is the first hellebore. By all reasonable expectation, this should be the Christmas rose, *Helleborus niger*, but even in gentler winter conditions than ours, it very seldom lives up to its name. Here, those exquisite bowls modelled, as it seems, in finest white porcelain are more likely to open for Easter, but even then, what a treat they are. More suitably in line with the festivals of the church are the Lenten roses (none of which, of course, are botanically roses; they are really upscale, upmarket buttercups). The first is H. *atrorubens*, which will make a clump of foot-high (30 cm) stems, each carrying half a dozen nodding flowers of deep plum-purple. They are good for a month at least and are followed by fine-fingered foliage. A little later comes H. *orientalis*, which shares the same pattern of growth, but the flowers can be white, dusky pink or sombre purple, all elegantly spotted in the cup. All the hellebores are expensive to buy, but once you have them, you can slowly increase your stock by careful division after flowering or by sowing seed as soon as it is ripe in pots or scattering it beneath the parent. It is impossible to have too many.

These pulmonarias and hellebores, partnered with bergenias, with their glossy purple overwintered leaves and their early pink flowers, help to alleviate the often overpowering yellowness of spring, when even unfolding foliage can be as gold as in fall. In bigger gardens, they are plants for woodland edges and around shrubs. Where space is limited, these are the perfect plants to go with carefully chosen bulbs in shaded or half-shaded borders against the house. (Out with the dreary junipers!) They will accept full southern exposure, but this is better kept for things that need it. In my garden, we also use them on the way to the front door so that in bad weather, their daily development can be noted and enjoyed and it will not be necessary to slop across a soggy lawn to find signs of spring.

By mid-April, a walk in the woods shows that spring really has sprung: exquisite bloodroot, hepaticas of blue, white and pink, trout lilies, mayapple and trilliums are in flower or showing buds. All these are worthwhile garden plants—indeed, these and many more of our common native woodlanders are specialist nursery stock in Britain. Shady borders therefore can hold these and their kissing cousins from around the world. While Ontario's provincial flower, the white *Trillium grandiflorum*, is the best of the genus, others such as T. *sessile* will always catch the eye. Stand-

The spring garden is bright with creeping phlox and just a glimpse of *Paeonia mlokosewitschii*, accompanied here by additional excellent edging plants: aubrieta, buttercups and dwarf irises.

ing upright on a triad of horizontal mottled leaves are three corn-yellow petals. The whole thing looks like an art nouveau candlestick.

From the Himalayan foothills, where I have collected it at 8,000 feet (2,400 m), comes a mayapple, *Podophyllum hexandrum* (P. *emodi*). While the native North American type (P. *peltatum*) has creamy nodding flowers and yellowish fruit, this has an upright pink flower like the most delicate rose and, in August, a bright red plum-sized fruit.

LATE SPRING

A month later, the diversity of wonderful plants for shaded situations is positively daunting (and dealt with more comprehensively in my *Plants for Shade and Woodland*, Fitzhenry & Whiteside, 1987). There are little lamiums with gold or silver leaves; wild gingers, soft and downy or glistening in the low light; tiny creeping phloxes, pink, blue or white; strangely sculpted green dragons (*Arisaema dracontium*); and Jacks-in-the-pulpit – or is it Jack-in-the-pulpits? Now, the bigger shade lovers begin to fill up their allotted spaces, covering the already yellowing foliage of snowdrops and scillas. The arching stems of bleeding heart are a couple of feet (60 cm) high; the typical form has clear pink locket-shaped flowers that sway in the wind,

and a pure white form is just as beautiful. This comes true from seed, and self-sown seedlings should be moved to positions of their own.

Like so many woodlanders, bleeding heart's period above ground is a gay but short one. By mid-July, it is gone again, so its companions should be chosen for foliage longevity. Sweet Cicely (*Myrrhis odorata*), for instance, is a sort of perennial Queen Anne's lace with an early fountain of feathery, aromatic leaves and flat heads of tiny white flowers. If the whole plant is cut down after flowering, it will shoot up from the base and look fresh for the rest of the year.

More statuesque are the Solomon's seals (*Polygonatum* spp). Whenever I have a big gap under trees, I fill it in with P. *multiflorum* – three-foot (1 m) arching stems lined with smooth, paired leaves and dangling white bells. It maintains its presence until the hard frosts of late fall. Our native false Solomon's seal (*Smilacina racemosa*) is just as beautiful, with heads of fluffy cream flowers followed, in September, by sprays of little red fruits. For such a berry display, not normally expected of herbaceous plants, smilacina can be joined by the actaeas, one with heads of brilliant scarlet and one, *Actaea alba* (A. *pachypoda*), with heads of white. Each berry is enhanced by a swollen red stalk and

In June, blue campanulas and delphiniums share the spotlight with orange lilies, yellow red-hot pokers and pink annual poppies.

a central black spot, hence the common name doll's eyes. This is a real showstopper, standing tall in August above an area devoted to spring bulbs (now out of sight) and joined by a few white or red auratum lilies.

In sunnier borders, tulips – perennials themselves – can give early colour to a border of otherwise summer-blooming perennials. (A separate chapter follows on hardy bulbous plants that are, by definition, perennials and cannot be entirely left out of the discussion, but in this chapter, they are rather taken for granted, planted under or around other things. They are apt to be either early-flowering, like daffodils and tulips, or late-flowering, like colchicums, and are entirely out of sight during most summer months.) A couple of clumps of crown imperials (*Fritillaria imperialis*), both the yellow and orange forms, will give not only flower colour in May but a sudden statuesque exclamation mark of shining green foliage when other things are still looking over their shoulders for fear that winter might return. Plant them toward the back so that their foliage, which declines as quickly as it came, is soon hidden.

Soon afterward come the Oriental poppies, with their luscious crimped petals of vermilion, pink or white, each carrying a near-black blotch at the

base. These, too, have disappeared by the end of June. Their sudden explosions of colour need little aesthetic concern, so long as they are framed by surrounding foliage that in turn hides their decline. Gertrude Jekyll was keen to use gypsophila for this and grew nasturtiums over it in turn. I find *Gypsophila paniculata* safer in a well-drained, open position above a stone retaining wall but use grey wormwood (*Artemisia absinthium*) to do the heavy work in the border. Lupins and peonies are flowers of early June, and they, too, can be something of an embarrassment for the rest of the season. Such long-lived plants as peonies, it seems to me, are best planted with old-fashioned roses or fronting shrubs, so that they are not upset by the necessary lifting and dividing of other things around them.

PLANNING FOR JUNE

It becomes clear, then, that though there are delicious herbaceous hors d'oeuvres to be enjoyed as early as late April, the main courses do not arrive until June. This is when a basic concern for colour association is vital. White, pink and the pale pastel shades are easier to deal with than strong yellows, orange-reds and flame colours, which initially one might avoid or experiment with in some separate spot. I do not intend to elaborate on colour theory in the garden – there are several recommendations in the reading list at the end of this book – but I will say that it is better by far to plant at once with every possible mistake than pussyfoot around for fear of breaking the rules. So often, the recommendations in books seem to be meant for an impossibly grand scale: a yellow border here, a white garden there. But on a smaller scale, one can plan the border to change its colour emphasis as the season progresses. June catmints, baptisia, hardy geraniums and delphiniums in shades of blue can give way in July and early August to the bright pinks of phlox, monarda and hybrid lilies. Then it is the turn of the yellow daisies – heleniums, heliopsis and helianthus – sunflowers all.

While it is certain that our native woodlanders are the pride and joy of shade gardeners around the temperate world, it is equally true that North America has also provided the lion's share of the base material for all the grand herbaceous full-sun borders that ever were. The difference is that until recently, American natives have had to go to Europe to be bred up and made, as it were, sufficiently socially acceptable for polite garden society back home. Over there, they were exotic, their humble roadside origins unknown. They were merely beautiful. Black-eyed Susans (*Rudbeckia hirta*) and several different asters that blow into this garden are local examples that I consider carefully before weeding out. Some of the small-flowered asters such as *Aster ericoides* are left around our few old-fashioned roses and enjoyed for serendipitous fall colour in a spot that would otherwise offer little interest at that time. These daisies are plants of open meadows and wide prairies. They are perfectly adapted to the herbaceous border; after all, that is how they grow in the wild. A gardener merely substitutes more desirable things for some of their natural neighbours and competitors and, to some extent, lets them fight it out.

This is, of course, a gross simplification; we each have personal likes and dislikes ("Goldenrod? Don't be ridiculous"), colour preferences ("Malignant magenta over there? Certainly not") and seasonal requirements. Obtaining the desired effect involves balancing a huge range of pros and cons, plant by plant. This is not to say that it is difficult. Certainly there is great art and technical know-how involved in producing one of those vast

If true geraniums are cut back after flowering, they will produce cushions of fresh green leaves. Here, they are accompanied by golden alyssum, a pink rose and a white one, blue veronica and the yellow daisies of goatsbeard.

Jekyllian borders. But with her, as with any of us today, such achievements must be the product of apprenticeship and trial and error, which in themselves give pleasure and satisfaction.

The sort of sequence outlined above does not mean that the early blue-purple area is without subsequent interest. It might be backed with the tall, creamy spikes of aruncus, which keep their form into winter. Delphiniums and catmint will flower again if cut down, fed and cosseted after the first display. Geraniums are also cut back and will produce cushions of fresh green leaves. And there is no reason why one should not add obedient plant (*Physostegia virginiana*), a New England aster, and the essential *Sedum spectabile* 'Autumn Joy,' with its wonderful grey-green fleshy leaves and flat heads of pink-turning-to-bronze flowers.

At two feet (60 cm) high, 'Autumn Joy' is a second-row forward (in rugby football terms), and since it is rather stiff, it needs a bit of front-row help. Bergenia's bronze-green elephant-ear leaves are admirable, and I add sundrops (*Oenothera fruticosa*) as well. The jolly yellow flowers in late June may upset the colour purist, but the rose-pink fall colour of the foliage is just what is needed then. The oversensitive could always pick the buds off or go away for a while.

Day lilies are most beautiful if one chooses a flower colour to suit the spot. These are growing beside complementary geraniums.

Despite the emphasis on flower colour and associations within a herbaceous border, it should not be forgotten that plants are individuals and that some have a particular ability to stand out from the crowd. Such plants may be particularly tall, such as the seven-foot (2 m) *Boltonia asteroides*, which makes a light and airy cloud of tiny daisies, or have especially fine foliage, such as *Cimicifuga racemosa* and *Macleaya cordata*, or some other architectural presence. There are examples of good foliage in every size of perennial, from the near-black tussocks of *Ophiopogon planiscapus* 'Nigrescens' (a name that once learned is unlikely to be forgotten) to the soft grey of felted lamb's ears (*Stachys byzantina*) to smooth sea kale (*Crambe maritima*), ferny *Myrrhis odorata* and statuesque *Rheum palmatum*. Some are natural front-row forwards, while others are plants to bring forward *because* of their height, to avoid too bland a profile to the border.

GRASSES AND LILIES

All the monocotyledonous plants, such as irises, day lilies, yuccas and, above all, grasses, have narrow, arching, almost vertical foliage that adds an important dimension of contrast to associations of mainly broad-leafed species. Their usual habit of holding their flowers high on leafless stems is also distinctive, and when the blooms are over, the foliage effect usually remains worthwhile for months. Grasses, rushes and sedges are apt to be thought of as weeds in our gardens. We pull them out and mow them within an inch, often literally, of their lives. I heard lawn described dismissively at a recent seminar in Berkeley, California, as topiary grass—flat topiary at that. If we suspend our prejudice and allow grasses to flower, we discover some of the most beautiful plants we can grow. Flower colour is obviously restrained—as wind-pollinated plants, why should grasses pander to the vagaries of bees?—but after pollination, the flower spikes remain to decorate the garden, often throughout the winter.

For most users of this book, I must accept that to recommend any of the woody grasses, such as bamboo, is a bit unfair. Canadians can manage one or two in the warmest areas, but even there, these tropical plants do not maintain the fresh green one sees in milder climates. But we can all grow the herbaceous perennials and should be grateful. Fortunately, the hot summers that most of us enjoy suit the best of the big grasses; Oriental species of miscanthus flower so much better here than in the grand gardens of Britain. It is comforting to think there is something one can do better than the late Vita Sackville-West at Sissinghurst Castle.

With *Miscanthus sinensis*, wonderful rustling wands shoot up to six feet (1.8 m) or so by August before breaking out into silky flower heads. Garden forms offer leaves with white longitudinal variegation or golden bands across the leaves. Even bigger is the Mediterranean reed grass, *Arundo donax*. This can reach 10 to 12 feet (3-3.7 m) in a summer, and a clump of just half a dozen stems waving in the breeze is a splendid sight. A brilliant striped form is less vigorous and possibly less hardy. Here, I dump a couple of buckets of leaves over the rootstock in November and hope for the best; all is well so far. A bit could be overwintered indoors for insurance in colder areas.

Very common and not to be despised in any way is ribbon grass, also called gardener's garters (*Phalaris arundinacea* 'Picta'). This makes wide clumps of white-striped leaves, all of which turn pale buff to see out the winter. Smaller yellow-striped grasses include *Hakonechloa macra* and the sedge *Carex morrowii*, which make a fine strong statement in a front-of-border position. The bigger ones, too, can come well forward because of their lightness of effect.

Day lilies are particularly valuable so long as one chooses, from the vast range available, those with good foliage and flowers of a colour to suit the spot. They vary from palest ivory cream through every shade of yellow to apricot, orange, bronze, dusky pink and mahogany red. New cultivars appear all the time, but older ones that have lasted have passed at least some of the tests of time and preferably have retained their scent. They will also be less expensive. A number of dwarf cultivars are now available. I am rather ambivalent about these. The day lily 'Stella d'Oro' is very popular, but apart from finding the colour harsh (like a yolk from a very free-range hen's egg), I feel it lacks the arching grace of even the small species such as *Hemerocallis middendorffi*. Nonetheless, complaining the while, I grow it.

Of course, *the* perennial for shady spots is hosta, another lily. No plant could be easier to grow, and the commoner forms are amazingly tolerant of dry shade under trees. But once hooked, one seldom wants to keep to the commoner forms, however useful, for the diversity of hostas is now extraordinary. To use a musical analogy, the theme of thick clumps of lustrous, heart-shaped leaves from which grow summer stems of white or lavender lily flowers develops into one of intricate foliage variations with gold and cream obbligato. There is every shade of green, from gunmetal grey to near blue with variegated edges or centres. Some clumps are no more than six inches (15 cm) across (*Hosta venusta*), while others, such as H. *glauca*, span more than a yard (1 m). Specialist nursery lists offer dozens, and not surprisingly, there is a hosta society in the United States.

Although hostas can be grown from seed, seedlings take three years to produce good ground-covering clumps and are unlikely to be better than existing named forms. Of these, precious individuals can be lifted in spring and the crowns gently teased apart to increase one's stock, while big clumps can have a slice or two chopped out with a spade in spring as if one were cutting a plum cake. The hole is filled in with good compost, and no harm is done.

Inevitably, because they are easy, hostas are prey to pseudosophisticates who profess to be bored with them. What nonsense. Like all plants, hostas need careful siting to do a specific job and make a planned effect. Under tall trees, a line of *Hosta lancifolia* edges the sidewalk in a downtown Hamilton garden. Nothing could be simpler, more effective or less trouble: fine foliage all summer and fine flowers all September. In another spot, the dramatic blue-leafed 'Krossa Regal' sends up five-foot-high (1.5 m) flower spikes like exclamation marks.

While plants happy in shade commonly give a spring and early-summer show, a few lovely things suited to shade save their visual treats for fall. Combinations of *Kirengeschoma palmata* and toad lily (*Tricyrtis hirta*) or hardy *Begonia grandis* with *Cyclamen hederifolium* just cannot be bettered. Then, at last, the hostas that have been such a stalwart support to the summer scene turn clear gold and bid the year a final farewell.

Using these shade-tolerant plants—and there are many other good ones—offers a peculiar satisfaction. There is no difficulty building up complementary associations, because flower colours are almost invariably soft and gentle. The ineffable "rightness" achieved comes from the fact that here are plants which share a common environmental need just as they would if they had met in a wild woodland glade. In the most favoured gardens, their surrounding may be just

that or a bit of a ravine. Equally, it may be the whole of a tiny, shaded town yard or the north-facing lee of a single shrub. Plenty of organic matter added to any soil will bring success for the plant and pleasure to the planter.

MOVING AND MULTIPLYING

So far, I have emphasized the diversity of perennials available for our gardens—although only mentioning the merest few by name. This emphasis is made to indicate the range from which to choose, not for one moment to suggest that even big gardens should try to cram them all in. A perennial border gives a much better effect when planted with relatively large numbers of relatively few types of plant. Big permanent plants with wide foliage such as aruncus, the miscanthuses or yuccas are often able to stand alone, or they may be planted in larger borders in groups of three. Most other things need to be in at least half-dozens. Numbers can be worked out by calculating from the area envisioned. To use my own border as an example, a front-row band of gayfeather (*Liatris* spp) six feet (1.8 m) by 18 inches (0.5 m) would require 15 plants or so; a midborder group of coneflowers (*Echinacea purpurea*) five or six feet (1.5-1.8 m) by four feet (1.2 m), 12 plants; a strong back-of-border display of macleaya, 8 plants for three square yards (2.5 m²). It will be noted that clumps are more like swaths, longer than deep. They overlap with others, and hence, as each passes its best, no huge gap is left.

Planning a new border *de novo* on this scale can be a formidable prospect from a financial point of view, and though the outlay is probably small in comparison with furnishing a room (and the analogy is worth repeating), it can be enough to inhibit development of proper balance and effectiveness of the garden space. Planning well in advance can help enormously, as it will be possible to bulk up the numbers necessary at home over one or two years. Most perennials can be grown from seed. A packet of delphinium seed sown indoors in early spring will probably produce more seedlings than ultimately needed. Lined out in the vegetable garden, many will flower—though with small spikes—in the fall. Those with the best colours can be marked and moved into their border positions the following April or May.

Many plants can be increased by division. A decent-sized clump of day lilies bought in spring can be washed clean of soil and gently teased apart so that each bud with its roots makes a single plant. Again, a well-fed year in a nursery row brings on sufficient stock to produce the effect planned on the scale that the border demands. Of course, this process is apt to be continuous. One is always reviewing the garden scene, noting infelicities, discovering an unusual plant and considering new plant associations for this spot or that. So always, when the addition or the change is made, it is satisfying to have the necessary plants just waiting to be used at a not inordinate cost.

Planting of new material is best done as spring growth starts, as the soil warms up and is still moist. This is also the best time to renovate existing plantings. As mentioned in the chapter "Year-Round in the Garden," it may be that no one year is redo-the-border-from-scratch year. It is too big a job with so many other tasks demanding their turn. But every spring, some plants are lifted and divided. Their space is forked deeply, and some compost is added before they or other things are put back.

It is in spring, too, that I enjoy the final bonus of not having cut down last year's herbaceous growth in October in the traditional frenzy of tucking up the garden for the winter. We have had the visual pleasure of the architectural shapes and textures of the growth for the last six months, wild birds have fed on many of the seed heads, other seed heads have been gathered for house

91

A hosta plant in bloom beneath Mediterranean reed grass reveals the flowers that identify it as a type of lily.

decoration, and the plants themselves have benefited from the winter protection of their own growth, which helps hold the protective snow in place. Now, the tops remind me by their size and their thickness that this clump of phlox or those heliopsis must be thinned or that the Japanese anemones must be brought forward in the border. Thus, one works from one end of the border to the other over a couple of weeks, cutting down last year's dead growth as one goes, only as the decision is made to leave or lift. A dressing of rotted compost scattered over the whole is a last benediction. Now, it's up to them.

It would be obscurantist not to mention that this leave-till-spring regime is apt to be considered by many people a disastrous invitation to small rodents to take up winter quarters in and play havoc with the resting plant organs. Here, over a number of years, only a couple of tussocks of Siberian iris seem to have been affected, and this is not enough to outweigh the manifest advantages. If the problem did develop and our invaluable cat were unable to cope, I would certainly attempt to deal with the rodents directly rather than live with a winter-bare border and not be able to remember what grew next to what when it came to border renovation time.

92

The best way to treat daffodils such as these 'King Alfreds,' foreground, is informally, inspired by a Wordsworthian ideal: ''Continuous as the stars that shine / And twinkle on the Milky Way.''

FLOWERING BULBS AND CORMS

pring is a time for enjoying every type of flowering bulb that is available—a sort of floral antipasto. In order to take advantage of the diversity of spring bulbs and to ensure as long a display as possible, it is important not to concentrate upon large quantities of just a few sorts. This is at variance with my recommendations for choosing herbaceous border plants. With bulbs, restraint is necessary only for formal plantings.

What are bulbs? They are places where the old year meets the new more dramatically than in any image of a scythe-carrying ancient with newborn child. This is not symbol but fact, a miracle of the turning years that we celebrate every time we plant spring bulbs. If you should be so extravagant, when hyacinth bulbs first go on sale in September, take a plump bulb, slice it in half, and you will see a meeting of seasons made manifest, a turn of the year that predates human calendars by untold millennia. In your hand is the product of warm spring and early summer in suspended animation. And if you look closely, you will see next spring in perfectly formed embryo: layers of leaf bases swollen with stored food enclose a cluster of flowers already faintly tinged with colour. All appear gift-wrapped in white, purple or pink tissue, and a rough, dry beard of old roots is still attached to the base. The same prepacked miracle occurs with tulips and daffodils and many smaller bulbs—scillas, chionodoxas, camassias, and so on.

That dissected hyacinth demonstrates clearly what a bulb is. Within a papery "tunic" is a series of overlapping leaves; these and a flower stalk are attached to a compressed basal stem from which roots grow on the lower side. On the normal elongated stem of a mature plant, there are invariably buds in the axils of the leaves. Similarly, on this compressed stem, there are buds,

The bulb season begins with snowdrops, which give pleasure out of all proportion to their diminutive size.

and each year, a couple of them develop more strongly and cause the bulb to divide. In this way, the clumps of many garden bulbs increase. Bulbs are not only storage organs, they are methods of vegetative propagation as well.

BULB HABITAT

Bulbs are biological responses to environment, to that combination of terrain and climate which, if it is to be "home," has to be adapted to in very specific ways. Virtually all true species of tulips, daffodils (*Narcissus* spp) and hyacinths grow wild in the lands around the Mediterranean Sea and eastward into Asia Minor. Do children in public school still chant on demand the description of a Mediterranean climate: hot dry summers and moist mild winters? I doubt it. But this climatic fact is worth recounting, because it expresses the essence of one type of bulb habitat that is repeated in several other areas of the world, in similar latitudes and in both hemispheres—in parts of California, Chile, southern Australia and southern Africa.

Other invaluable plants for the garden have developed different methods of dealing with that same climatic pattern. Crocuses and gladioli have another type of storage organ, corms, wherein the basal stem comprises almost all the food store and little growth buds enclose the embryonic flower on top. Further variations on the same storage-organ theme include rhizomes (bearded irises) and stem tubers (winter aconites and cyclamens). Together, they provide a vast range of perennial plants for spring and early-summer flowering in our gardens.

It is the pattern of the climate that is important, not the actual amounts of sun or rain or cold. And that pattern is very constant. Following an almost cloudless summer, the autumn rains provoke a sudden flurry of plant growth. Dormant seeds germinate, buds swell on shrubs, and resting underground storage organs—the bulbs and their kin—begin to stir. Some immediately thrust up their flowers from still unsoaked ground (which is why colchicums flower on garden-centre shelves in August, looking as pathetic as puppies in a pet-shop window), most put out roots at once, some start to shoot, and all soften and swell. As our calendar year goes into decline, their new year has begun.

There is no difficulty for species native to the mild maritime parts of the Mediterranean, where growth is gentle and continuous—which is why I have been able to pick bunches of *Narcissus tazetta* on Christmas Day in coastal Crete and have seen the tiny hoop-petticoat daffodil (N. *bulbocodium*) blowing in the sea breeze on the cliffs in Portugal in January. The former is a parent of 'Grand Soleil d'Or' that we grow as a pot plant and is not hardy enough to be a garden plant for us. However, all is not plain sailing elsewhere. Climb the hills, or go east into Turkey and beyond, and you will find those growth-stimulating autumn rains something of a snare. Winter there is for real, with the heavy frosts and deep snows with which many North Americans can readily identify. The whole point of this somewhat protracted introduction, then, is to show that there are many hardy bulbs that can easily grow in our climates.

Nevertheless, it is necessary to choose sites for spring bulbs as thoughtfully as for anything else. In the early part of the year, aspect and protection can make a difference of a month in the flowering time of the same plant in the same garden. As I write in the first week in February, one clump of snowdrops against the house is showing white buds. Thirty yards (27 m) away, where I know the main display will take place, there is not the slightest sign of even a green shoot. The sunny sheltered spots, then, are best for the earliest bulbs and for those that need sun to open: crocuses and species tulips. Those that flower later are best placed where they receive a little shade for some of the day; even the bare branches of deciduous trees and shrubs are a help. Sites with more shade but not full evergreen-tree shade can be used for bulbs such as later daffodils, summer snowflakes, Spanish bluebells and hyacinths, as all will unfold without direct sun.

The growth regime here repeats that for which bulbs are evolutionarily adapted. We plant dor-

Hardy spring bulbs such as chionodoxas flower for a short time, then build up their strength through the summer for the next year's flowering season.

mant spring-flowering bulbs in the fall in time for root development to occur – and this is vital for success. Just for interest, dig up an established clump of daffodils in August, and you can see them already at work, making the most of the weather while they may. Their roots will continue to grow as long as soil temperatures remain above freezing – long after fall frosts have disposed of the tender annuals. In many years, shoot growth will also begin, and the garden will enter winter with tulips and daffodils an inch or two (2.5-5 cm) above ground. This invariably provokes worries that the climate is changing, that there will be no spring display and other prognostications of doom. The only real worry, however, is that hungry squirrels may also notice the tulips; a light mulch of bark or woodchips once the ground is fully frozen may solve the problem. Putting the superannuated Christmas tree through a chipper gives the perfect material. The wonderful thing about bulbs is that success is virtually assured; so long as the most basic procedures are followed, spring is bound to be a joy.

WOODLAND BULBS

The season opens, predictably enough, with snowdrops (*Galanthus* spp). Soon after Christmas,

every time there is a thaw, I take a look at the base of an old clipped boxwood at the back of the garage where our first snowdrops can be expected to appear. By the end of January, the shoots are a couple of inches (5 cm) high. A few mild days, and they may be blooming (and a letter comes from Scotland, a thousand miles [1,600 km] to the north, to say that the woods below our house there are already white with snowdrops). But it becomes cold again, and these apparently frail creatures enter a state of suspended animation until conditions improve. It may be a week or a month. Then pairs of leaves part, a stem extends, the sheath at the top splits, and the bud falls out, held by a delicate pedicel. Three petals spread back like wings, while three form a bell to protect stamens and stigma. The first of the spring bulbs are out, the weather can now do as it will, and as far as I am concerned, spring has sprung.

Snowdrops give pleasure out of all proportion to their size and even to their show. You need lots to make any effect at a distance, but not only are they delightful in their own right – with a delicious scent if you can get your nose down there – but they are a promise of even better things to come.

All of which makes it strange that they do not exist in every garden. There are a couple of reasons. One is that many people just do not "think gardens" at this time of year, and the season passes them by. Another is the failure rate of autumn-planted snowdrops. It will already have been noted that there are spring bulbs that do not fall into that rigorous Mediterranean growth pattern. What about eastern North America's trout lilies (*Erythronium americanum*) and their western cousins? These are plants of woodland, so their reliance on their bulbs comes from different environmental requirements.

Here is what botanists call an ecological niche just waiting to be filled, and as nature abhors a vacuum—as someone else has proclaimed— some clever plants have been able to take advantage of that short but valuable season under high deciduous trees, where there is protection from wind and soil warms up quickly when the sun penetrates the still leafless canopy in spring. But by May, leaves have cut off the light from above, and tree roots have limited the water from below. Anything growing here has got to be quick to bloom and then must survive quietly in relative darkness for some months to come. These flowers have bulbs, but as they do not receive the sort of summer baking the others do, they are less able to endure drying on the garden-centre shelves. It is the same with snowdrops. If we are rewarded with a 50 percent success rate from those little late-planted packets of desiccated bulbs, we've done well.

There are two approaches, then, to planting snowdrops. One is to buy them as soon as they appear in the stores, shake them in a bag of moist peat and leave them for a week or so to plump up before planting. The same trick helps with the tiny tubers of snowdrops' obvious associates, winter aconites (*Eranthis hyemalis*). But it is better to beg a clump of snowdrops from a friend as soon as flowering is over in spring. This is what the aficionados call "planting in the green." The clump is teased apart and two or three bulbs— some no bigger than a pea—are dibbled into holes just a little deeper than they were before, the ground having been forked over and a handful of bonemeal added. All they need now is watering; all we need do is wait.

While this system is ideal for galanthus, it is worth considering for any clump of bulbs that is becoming too crowded—but not as long as it is performing well. Most are best dealt with rather later in the season, just as the foliage yellows but

before it disappears; it is extraordinary how poor one's memory is when searching for bulbs that have gone to rest. (For that same reason, if you are offered any plants you covet when visiting other gardens, you should take them there and then. The kindest of donors are apt to forget by fall, and you are too polite to remind them— another opportunity missed.)

The common snowdrop (*Galanthus nivalis*) is erratically native to most of Europe, producing variants in the wild such as the fall-flowering *G. n. reginae-olgae* and *G. corcyrensis* from Greece and Corfu, respectively. More fun are those selected in cultivation. 'Scharlockii' has a pair of long bracts that stand up behind the nodding bell like a rabbit's ears; 'Viridapicis' has green spots on both layers of petals; 'Lutescens' is a pale horn-yellow, and so on. The more snowdrops you grow— including the wonderful Asia Minor species such as *G. elwesii* that can be nine inches (23 cm) tall— the more variations you learn about. They are ideal plants for the "layered garden" I continually advocate. Grow them around shrubs or perhaps under English ivy, itself planted under hostas and combined with bigger, later bulbs.

Snowdrops seem to nudge spring into life, and before they are over, they are joined by other little bulbous plants. None has made itself more at home here than *Scilla sibirica*. In sugar maple woodland on the thin alkaline soils of the Niagara Escarpment, this bluebell can cover the ground like a quilt of the clearest blue through which native bloodroot shows brilliant white. A little later, glory-of-the-snow (*Chionodoxa luciliae*) produces starry blue flowers with a white eye. Before this— late March with us—the crocus season has begun.

EARLY SPRING

That crocuses emerge from corms and not bulbs is to us entirely by the way, but it is not to our little furry friends, those wretched squirrels that choose crocus corms for breakfast as we do cornflakes. Depredations are erratic. Some gardens cannot keep a single crocus, while others remain unscathed. Just as sparrows can get into the habit of tearing up yellow crocus flowers (black thread stretched into a sort of cobweb on a series of six-inch [15 cm] sticks is the answer here), so can squirrels acquire a taste for the corms. Rather deeper planting can help—three to four inches (8-10 cm) down—and clumps of expensive ones can be laid under a square of small-mesh wire net-

ting placed just below the soil surface so as not to be seen. The crocus flowers and leaves come through easily – just in time to be nibbled down, in this garden, by a cottontail that takes up winter quarters here. Rose and gooseberry prunings discourage him enough that we do enjoy a crocus display. It is worth the bother.

The first crocus to appear with the last of the snowdrops is the bright yellow *Crocus ancyrensis*. Soon after, the cloth-of-gold crocus (C. *susianus*) shows its deep yellow petals veined with bronze feathering on the outside, while the cloth-of-silver crocus from Italy and the Balkans (C. *chrysanthus*) is palest lilac painted on the outside with darker stripes. The reverse of the petals is as important as the inside face, because crocuses open and close with the sun, a habit that indicates their need for light. A position around high deciduous trees and shrubs is ideal.

There are many other species and named selections that together give a six-week display. Their spring season ends with the big Dutch crocuses derived from *Crocus vernus*. Some in the catalogues have been in cultivation since the 1600s, but other early cultivars, such as the lavender 'Little Dorrit' and purple-striped 'Pickwick,' hint of a Dickensian 19th-century origin. 'Jeanne d'Arc' is a superb pure

white. As with most spring "bulbs," the leaves extend greatly after flowering to build up next year's food store. The leaves of Dutch crocuses have a central silver band that is quite distinctive.

Crocuses naturalize wonderfully when happy, making great pools of bright and sombre tones as they open and close. Their relations, the little bulbous irises, however, keep to themselves, only gradually building up clumps with a few more flowers each year. For pockets in the rock garden or in raised beds in sheltered positions, nothing is more beautiful. Coming from the chilly uplands of Turkey and beyond, they are utterly hardy, but the delicate flowers are easily battered by wind, which destroys their perfect shape. I*ris danfordiae* is the first to appear in March, bright yellow and only four inches (10 cm) high. This needs really deep planting, nine inches (23 cm) down at least, to discourage the bulbs from breaking up into a lot of little flowerless bulbils.

Soon after comes I*ris histrioides*, only a little taller, with robust flowers of clear sky-blue, and then the range of cultivars of I. *reticulata*. The true species is purple with a flash of yellow on the falls – the petals that curve downward – and is exquisitely violet-scented, a good reason for a raised-bed position. 'J.S. Dijt' is darker still, 'Cantab' pale blue. All are lovely.

Soon following are the first fritillaries, a word that suggests marble-winged butterflies to a lepidopterist but bulbous plants, some with a similar marbling on the petals, to a botanist. Sadly, because these flowers are mainly fly- or bee-pollinated, we are unlikely ever to see a fritillary *on* a fritillary outside of those wonderful Dutch-painted still-life pieces that so happily deny both sense and season. Our fritillaries, which are related to lilies, belong to a genus comprising over 100 species spread around the northern hemisphere. Most are strangely attractive rather than pretty, but there are certainly three I would not want to be without.

Fritillaria imperialis is the well-named crown imperial, which often dominates those flower paintings with its ring of great orange bells crowned with a leafy pineapple topknot. It is just as dominating in the early-spring garden. A bullet-shaped shoot pushes through the soil as soon as the ground thaws and rushes up to three or even four feet (1-1.2 m) tall within a month, unfolding shining leaves as it goes. Then comes a nine-inch (23 cm) gap of bare stem, so the dangling bells

Dutch crocuses, which are distinguished by a silver band on the leaves, bloom a little later than many of the smaller species. They have relatively large flowers and can be purchased in a range of colours.

98

The well-named crown imperial, here grown in front of grape hyacinths and a flowering currant, is as showy as it is malodorous.

stand out all the more dramatically. Turn one up, and at the base of each petal is revealed a great teardrop of nectar miraculously held against gravity. The yellow form is just as fine, but both do have a drawback. In Britain, they say crown imperials smell of old coffee grounds. That is because they don't have skunks. We know better.

But the odour of this flower is no reason for not growing a clump or two. Combined with purple honesty (*Lunaria annua*) and *Helleborus atrorubens*, the orange form makes one of the strongest spring statements possible. The yellow form effectively shines through a pool of blue *Scilla sibirica* or glory-of-the-snow.

Another worthwhile fritillary is *Fritillaria persica*,

from Iran and Afghanistan. A leafy stem supports a two-foot-high (60 cm) carillon of bells of an extraordinary grape-black colour. This is a plant for May that, like the earlier crown imperials, soon goes to rest. Its place needs to be marked if a careless fork is not to spear its bulbs during a fall tidy-up.

Fritillaria meleagris is the snake's head, a classic bulb. Shoots indistinguishable from those of the grasses that surround it in its native English meadows suddenly produce strangely checkered bells, pinkish purple or creamy white. They need a bit of moist shade. We have a small clump growing through the shining leaves of the European wild ginger (*Asarum europaeum*) at the base of the big bottlebrush buckeye. Allowed to ripen seed, they are gradually increasing their gentle effect.

From similar moist meadows in Britain and continental Europe comes *Leucojum aestivum*, whose common name, summer snowflake – foolish, because the flower is over long before summer is in sight – was probably coined to distinguish it from the six-inch (15 cm) *L. vernum* that flowers with the snowdrops. The summer snowflake has big daffodil-like bulbs, and as the leaves emerge in late winter, extending a little every time there is a day or two of thaw, you begin to expect daffodil flowers. But no. In May, when the two-foot-high (60 cm) stems hang out a series of white, green-tipped bells that swing in the wind, nothing could be more charming. By the south entrance of the Royal Botanical Gardens, they grow against a splendid star magnolia, white on white, a serendipitous association well worth copying. Add *Lamium* 'Beacon Silver' for the snowflake to come through and to clothe the ground when it has gone to rest.

Adding shades of blue to the spring garden are grape hyacinths (*Muscari* spp), whose new leaves will be gone by October. Spanish bluebells (*Hyacinthoides hispanica*, *Scilla hispanica*), true hyacinths (*Hyacinthus orientalis*) and *Ipheion uniflorum* all deserve consideration, and all are beautiful.

But the main spring bulb displays consist of daffodils and tulips. Without them, no garden deserves the name. Because the range of tulips and daffodils is so great, there really is no justification for the oft-repeated statement that it is hardly worth growing these bulbs in the northeastern climate because they are over so quickly. (This goes with another cliché that we do not have any spring and rush straight from winter to summer without a pause.) Certainly, there are years when a hot spell in early May knocks out bulbs in flower within a week. One is understandably annoyed. This is most likely to happen if, as is so often seen, they are planted amongst the conventional foundation junipers against the south wall of the house. Of course, there they just cook.

So where to start? What to choose? Let us review briefly the riches of the genera *Tulipa* and *Narcissus*. There are, after all, about 100 wild *Tulipa* species strewn in a band from southern Europe as far as China and, derived from them, literally thousands of cultivars. The arid hillsides of Asia Minor and Iran are home to the most spectacular wild tulips. The wild distribution of 30 species or so of daffodils and narcissi, all members of the genus *Narcissus* (we generally call those that have long trumpets daffodils and those with short trumpets narcissi, but the use of the names is purely a matter of convenience), is more westerly and also extends south of the Mediterranean Sea into the Atlas Mountains of Morocco. Yet again, there are almost untold named garden forms.

The outdoor period of daffodils and tulips is almost exactly the same. In this garden, I expect to see the first pink and white water-lily tulip (*Tulipa kaufmanniana*) open and buzzing with bees during the last days of March. *Narcissus* 'February Gold' will be in hot pursuit. Eight weeks later, the wonderfully scented pheasant-eye narcissus 'Actaea' closes the season with the late double peony-flowered tulips, which are almost as big and lush as the true peonies with whose blooming time they just overlap.

TULIPS

Consider first the genus *Tulipa*. Deep planting, eight or nine inches (20-23 cm) down, is necessary so that the bulbs are not damaged during later cultivation if summer annuals are to share the space. This does, in fact, replicate what occurs in the wild, where a number of species of beautiful tulips actually become weeds in cultivated ground, keeping their bulbs below the depth that the primitive ploughs still used in some areas can penetrate. I have seen the pink *T. bakeriana* flowering in April in the little stony fields high on Crete's Omalós Plateau, where they are able to begin their summer rest by the time the farmers come up from the valleys to cultivate the land. With us, the other advantage of deep planting is that it outwits the digging squirrels, which enjoy nothing more than a tulip or two after crocuses for starters.

The diversity of tulips is so extraordinary that every garden can find suitable spots for at least a few. The smallest can go into pockets in the rock garden or along a woodland edge with other spring bulbs. All are suitable, along with other early things, for beds on the way to the front door. All they need is good drainage and good light conditions during their short March-through-June period above ground.

The season begins, as I have said, with the water-lily tulip, which opens flat on stems no taller than six inches (15 cm). Soon afterward comes *Tulipa fosteriana*, taller with gleaming scarlet flow-

One of the secrets
of creating a bed
of early-flowering
spring bulbs is to
interplant them
with foliage that
will obscure their
less appealing
later life.

ers as wide as eight inches (20 cm). Almost as dramatic is T. *greigii*, whose effect is enhanced by purplish stripes on the leaves, clearly a dominant gene, because these striped leaves appear on all its hybrid children.

These species have been combined by breeders into what are often listed as peacock tulips. They retain the short stems and relatively early flowering habit of their parents, so are ideal for informal situations where the big soldier-straight garden tulips can look out of place. Nonetheless, they are also splendid for early-to-midseason bedding. As has been described earlier, we have some of these succeeding year after year as perennials growing through a permanent ground

cover of lamb's ears (*Stachys byzantina*) and never give a thought to lifting them.

The species continue: low-growing T*ulipa tarda*, which produces multiflowered stems of yellow, white-edged flowers above shining foliage in April, cream-coloured T. *batalinii*, pink T. *pulchella* and scarlet T. *hageri*. One of the very last to flower is the lovely lady tulip (T. *clusiana*). Only a foot (30 cm) high, it is as slender as a classical nymph on a Greek vase, with narrow pink buds that open to pink and white candy-striped stars. It is named for Carolus Clusius, a professor of botany who in the 1570s grew tulips for the first time ever in northern Europe. Clusius' tulips had come from Constantinople and were already sophisticated garden plants, having been selected over several centuries at the courts of the caliphs.

Clusius' famed tulip collection was stolen and spread around the Netherlands. By the 1630s, gardeners' desire for these new plants had become such an obsession that prices for single bulbs reached ridiculous heights—one bulb of the red and white 'Semper Augustus' is recorded as selling for 5,000 florins. Tulipomania made fortunes for successful speculators. Although the bubble burst in 1637, the tulips remained and soon became one of Holland's staple horticultural crops.

Any good bulb catalogue lists scores of hybrid tulips that can trace their ancestry back over the 400 years since garden tulips burst upon the European gardening world like a display of exotic fireworks. They are listed under a number of categories reflecting their flowering period and habit. Thus the Single Early tulips and their long-lasting double forms begin the season in late April. These are only a foot (30 cm) or so high. Much taller and opening in succession are the Triumphs, Darwins, Single Late (Cottage) and Double Late tulips. Every imaginable flower colour, except true blue, in every combination is available. Petals can be flamed with contrasting shades or fringed like filigree. Most bizarre are the Parrot tulips, with huge flounced flowers in strange combinations of colours: red and gold, orange and green, purple and bronze. They bloom late enough to associate with the first bearded irises, with which they share a certain flamboyance.

Incredibly restrained by contrast are the Lily-Flowered tulips, with elegant carafe-shaped buds whose pointed petals eventually open to wide stars. 'China Pink' and 'White Triumphator' are among my favourites. They are wonderful standing proud above the developing foliage of the perennial border, which modestly conceals their declining postflower leaves.

DAFFODILS AND NARCISSI

The other main spring bulb genus is *Narcissus*. While daffodils are used in formal bedding schemes, this always seems to me a mistake, both cultivationally and conceptually. The cultivational aspect is the long growing season that daffodils need. They really should be in the ground by the beginning of October, when the previous summer's bedding plants still have a couple of weeks to run. And at the other end of their season, their foliage is still in full growth in late May, when the new summer's things are bulging out of their boxes and calling for the space. Obviously, the bulbs can be lifted and moved to a nursery bed, but it seems an unnecessary effort. Surely the better way to treat daffodils is informally, inspired by a Wordsworthian ideal: "Beside the lake, beneath the trees, / Fluttering and dancing in the breeze. / Continuous as the stars that shine / And twinkle on the Milky Way."

We may well have neither lake nor enough room for daffodils in stellar profusion, yet they have a freedom of form that calls for informal planting in the biggest quantities one can afford. And they must be considered permanent perennials. If they are happy—and they can accept heavier ground than tulips but not really bad drainage—clumps will increase over decades without any attention.

It must be emphasized that, as perennials, they deserve decent treatment at planting time: those lovely stainless-steel bulb planters look splendid, but the method confines the bulb and its roots to a narrow tube of loosened soil. Much better for naturalizing bulbs in established turf is to roll back a square foot or two (900-1,800 cm^2) and plant beneath it. Remove six inches (15 cm) of soil from the exposed spot, and for tidiness, pile it on a plastic sheet. Fork over the soil beneath, adding a handful of bonemeal, firm it and arrange six or eight bulbs four inches (10 cm) apart. Cover them with the sheetful of topsoil, then replace the turf. The slight hummock will soon settle down. In borders and under shrubs, the process is the same, but if planting large quantities, it is best to plant in furrows, as in the vegetable garden. Place the bulbs six or eight inches (15-20 cm) deep in each trench. Work backward, so that digging the next trench will cover the bulbs already in place. If they are situated carefully, they will not appear to be in rows.

Again, it is important to emphasize that daffodils and other bulbs used thus are part of a consciously contrived series of plant associations. They give early interest to a spot that also holds lilies and hostas among late-flowering shrubs, and they complement spring shrubs and follow the early bulbs. Their roles are legion, and it is almost impossible to have too many. They are completely trouble-free once established, although gardeners should pick dead flowers, for the effort of seed production is better avoided.

Foliage must never be removed until it is entirely yellow, and that fool habit of "tidying" by plaiting the declining foliage must be resisted. If this stage of daffodils' life cycle is so distressing, it should be disguised by other planting. In a lawn, similarly, the mower must not be used until the bulbs' leaves are really yellow.

Because of the huge choice of colour and form available, one must pore over the catalogues or the bulb displays with care. It will be seen that there is a horticultural classification of divisions that groups narcissi into trumpet, large cup, small cup, and so on. These have most significance for the show bench. For gardens, it makes sense to keep the more exotic types and vivid colours close to the house in cultivated beds. I have some reservations about the doubles in the open garden, where their heavy heads are knocked down by spring squalls then chewed by slugs. Use the traditional sorts for naturalizing in grass and on woodland edges, but not in dense woodland, where daffodils will survive but not flower, since they need sunlight after the time when the deciduous canopy closes in.

Which, then, of the dozens of big garden daffodils to choose? Only personal preference can decide, and it seems one's choice changes through the years. In addition to well-loved traditional yellow daffodils, I am now especially fond of white trumpets such as 'Mount Hood' and 'Beersheba' and white-cupped 'Ice Follies' and have always been devoted to the late pheasant-eye narcissus, 'Actaea.' Somehow, I find the pink-cupped 'Salmon Trout' and 'Salome' (exquisite with tulip 'Apricot Beauty') more attractive than I once did, but bunch-flowered 'Geranium' and 'Cheerfulness,' both wonderfully scented, have always been great favourites. Every daffodil grower—and that means everyone with a garden—will have their own. So if one adds a few dozen each year, the garden reflects one's developing taste. Incidentally, it is worth mentioning that high-priced bulbs are not necessarily better, just newer and slightly different; in a few years, they will be more affordable. Quality, however, remains vital.

Then, of course, there are all the wonderful little *Narcissus* species such as hoop-petticoat daffodils, jonquils and N. *cyclamineus*, whose intensely swept-back petals are inherited by its lovely progeny, Lent lilies and angels' tears. All are ideal for pockets in the rock garden, for raised beds or just for a small garden if you wish to possess a diversity of daffodils without being overwhelmed by their size. Among the dwarf hybrids, yellow and white 'Jack Snipe,' yellow 'February Gold' (which flowers in March for us) and pure white 'Thalia' are especially irresistible.

SUMMER BULBS

The end of the tulip and daffodil season does not presage the end of the bulb season. On the contrary, it continues in waves throughout the summer. In many books, there is a classic picture of Rosemary Verey's laburnum tunnel in her Gloucestershire garden, where myriad golden chains almost meet the crowds of drumstick heads of A*llium aflatunense*. Texture is superbly contrasted, the yellow and violet-purple perfectly complementary. Why don't we do it here? Do we find it too extravagant or just too much work? If so, perhaps it is best to simply settle for the alliums and leave the training of the laburnums to Mrs. Verey.

A*llium aflatunense* is one of the first of the ornamental onions. It comes on immediately when the daffodils and tulips leave off, so is perfect for that strange in-between season when spring declines but before summer leaps lusciously forward. Bigger still is A. *giganteum*, with heads like lilac grapefruits on four-foot (1.2 m) stems. We have four or five of these coming out of a clump of sedum 'Autumn Joy,' which is able to jostle with the onions' rather coarse leaves until they yellow and then fully fills the spot, leaving no sign of competition save the dead, dry allium heads still swaying above the border. These, of course, are invaluable for winter arrangements indoors.

Only half the height but with even bigger heads of starry flowers is A*llium christophii*. In our garden, it grows near the apothecary's rose, with whose bloom time it just overlaps, and it follows honesty in the same spot. Catalogues should be consulted for other onions, from tiny six-inchers (15 cm), such as the rosy red A. *oreophilum*, to the blue, two-foot (60 cm) A. *coeruleum*. All are plants for sunny borders and, once planted, should be left alone.

With the last of these ornamental onions in late June and July come the foxtail lilies, species of *Eremurus*. These do not have proper bulbs but adapt to the rather prairielike climate of their native Asian hillsides by dying back to a great wheel of fleshy storage roots immediately after flowering. And that flowering is dramatic in the extreme. E. *robustus* thrusts up as high as 10 feet (3 m), a vast

bottlebrush consisting of hundreds of starlike, palest pink-buff flowers that open gradually from the bottom. The show lasts a month, then suddenly, the spike and the ground-level spread of strap-shaped leaves have gone for the year. Golden yellow E. *stenophyllus* and the pink, white and orange Shelford hybrids are easier to use in the garden scene, but all need the same treatment. Drainage must be perfect. Spread the starfishlike rootstock over a heap of grit or coarse sand with the top of the central bud a couple of inches (5 cm) below the soil surface, and add a loose mulch for the winter.

The problem with eremurus is the huge gap left when the plants go to rest at a most inconvenient time of year. The same problem occurs earlier with crown imperials and later with *Crambe cordifolia*. Scillas and snowdrops help at the beginning, and big-leafed *Hosta glauca* clumped nearby will give later foliage that is not too competitive. The devising of suitable associations is particularly necessary for such plants, but the planning is half the fun—and what a triumph when it works!

LILIES

As summer really blooms, so do more bulbous plants, including the true lilies, species of *Lilium*.

This is a huge genus, with exquisite plants from all over the northern hemisphere. Indeed, we have our own fine wild species native to North America: in the wet river valley below our house, one of them grows to perfection, looking as exotic as any bulb imported from the Near East. The orange-spotted Turk's cap (*Lilium michiganense*) thrusts six-foot (2 m) stems above the lush grasses every July. Nothing could be finer, but it is very choosy about lifestyle, and there are many easier lilies to grow in the garden.

Although hybridization has mixed them up, wild species have flowers of three distinct types: the Turk's caps have downward-facing flowers and reflexed petals; another group has clusters of flowers that look up; and yet another group, the trumpet lilies, has outfacing flowers. These last include the classic Madonna lily (*Lilium candidum*) depicted in paintings of the Virgin Mary since the Middle Ages. Still a desirable plant, it has the strange habit of coming into leaf in August and, even in our climate, keeps this rosette over the winter to flower the following June. So there is a very short time of rest when it can be planted (and then only just below the soil surface, unlike all other lilies). The other trumpet lily that everyone knows is the Easter lily (L. *longiflorum*), sold by the millions as a pot plant to be thrown away in almost equal millions after flowering. Better to pick off the dead flowers, tip out the soil ball and plant the whole potful in a depression so that the original soil surface is three or four inches (8-10 cm) below the garden's soil level. Fill this in when the lilies take a short early-summer nap, and they will regrow the same season, often flowering again in fall, although you may need to cut them for indoors to prevent the frost from damaging the flowers. A mulch of leaves will help the bulbs overwinter and ensure the next year's display.

The easiest of the trumpet lilies is the white, gold-flushed Himalayan *Lilium regale*. We grow them amongst hostas, and they go on for years with no attention at all. These are also the easiest to increase from seed and, grown this way, may flower in a couple of years. L. *regale* has had genetic input into the Aurelian hybrids, huge trumpet lilies as tall as six feet (2 m). All are splendid but need to be carefully staked.

Two other hybrid groups precede and follow the Aurelians, so the garden can offer lilies throughout the summer. The Asiatic hybrids have

Alliums, ornamental versions of onions, have a blooming season which overlaps that of tulips and daffodils and extends into June and July.

sprays of outward- or upward-facing flowers in every colour but blue. (Like roses and tulips, blue lilies just do not exist.) Later come the Oriental hybrids based upon the amazing *Lilium auratum*, the golden-rayed lily of Japan, and L. *speciosum*, a superb Japanese Turk's cap. Flowers of the Oriental hybrids can be eight inches (20 cm) across, white, pink or rosy red and spotted and banded with gold.

Lilies are not difficult to grow. This is a statement that can be made without reservation. But their growth pattern must be understood. Unlike tulip and daffodil bulbs, lilies never go fully to rest. Some roots remain fleshy, and the bulb, which is made up of loosely layered scales not enclosed in protective skins, is less adapted to survive a completely arid period either in the ground or on the garden-centre shelf. It resents being long out of the soil. Yet because lilies are summer growers, they cannot be available till late fall, by which time it is rather late for planting – but one perseveres.

The Ontario bulb company Cruickshank's publishes a mouth-watering catalogue that makes the sensible suggestion that intended sites for lilies should be prepared in advance of the arrival of the bulbs. Try deep digging and add lots of well-rotted compost plus some grit if drainage is doubtful. For three bulbs, dig a hole a foot square (900 cm²) and eight or nine inches (20-23 cm) deep. Fill it with leaves to keep it from freezing. Then when the bulbs appear, take out the leaves, set the bulbs in place, fill the hole with unfrozen soil and pile the leaves on top as a mulch for the winter. Sometimes, in spite of good intentions, the lilies come just too late or you pick up an irresistible bargain (simply because it is so late). Still, all is not lost. Lilies will overwinter quite well in barely moist peat in the coolest place you can find – but do not let them freeze. Plant them when the ground can receive them in spring. (Any greenish mould found on the bulbs is likely to be harmless penicillin feeding upon the sugars on bruised outside scales.)

UNUSUAL CHOICES

With the blooming of the latest lilies, the season for hardy bulbs is virtually at an end. But the last lilies are joined by a trio that plays the strange game of flowering before their leaves appear. *Lycoris squamigera* looks for all the world like a pink amaryllis, and one never ceases to be surprised

that this tropical-looking Japanese native is hardy to zone 5. The same is the case with the little *Cyclamen hederifolium*. (Plant these tubers with the smooth, rounded side down, just below the soil surface.) Then there are the autumn crocuses, both real *Crocus* species, such as the lilac C. *zonatus*, and members of the genus *Colchicum*, with clusters of robust flowers like pink champagne flutes that push through the bare, dry ground after the first September shower. These are good naturalized in thin grass both for their fall flowering and for the lush shining spring foliage that contrasts with the daffodils. We grow some in front of day lilies, before and after which the colchicums make their mark.

The wonderful world of plants has yet further bulbous treats for our summer gardens. While the hardy bulbs use their underground organs to help them survive the winter, a number of subtropical genera that we are wise to use have developed such storage organs to deal with the dry season in their native lands. Although none of them are safely winter-hardy with us, they are so easily stored indoors over the winter that May planting and October lifting are not much of a chore. *Gladiolus* is the classic South African contribution; there are many elegant species not generally in cultivation and vast numbers of named hybrids. I find the big hybrids whose corms are sold in supermarkets in spring difficult to use in the garden scene, but the delicate butterfly gladiolus, derived mainly from G. *primulinus*, is fine in mixed plantings. Invaluable, too, is an Ethiopian relation, *Acidanthera* (*Gladiolus*) *murieliae*. This is four feet (1.2 m) tall with a delicate spike of fragrant white flowers, each with a purple throat. It flowers late, even into October, and looks lovely with pink and white cleomes. Keep the pea-sized "spawn" corms that are attached to the big ones when they are lifted. Sown like peas in a row in the vegetable plot, many will build up to flowering size in one season. If not, bring them in for the winter and give them another year.

Anyone wanting unusual flowers for the summer should leaf through the spring bulb catalogues for further treats: jewel-like tigridias from Mexico, pineapple flower (*Eucomis* spp) from South Africa and the fragrant chlidanthus lily from the Andes. All are easy and, given care, will go on from year to year. There is just no excuse for having a dull garden.

104

The most popular
of the summer
bulbs, types dug
up in fall and
overwintered
indoors, are
hybrid gladioli,
which are flam-
boyant but clearly
difficult to use in
the garden scene.

Annuals such as impatiens, coleus and alyssum are flowers of our short summer, and we celebrate the season with their brilliance and beauty.

ANNUALS FOR
SUMMER DELIGHT

nnuals that are to be used in dominant spots must be as carefully and consciously chosen with regard to their size, shape, texture and colour – especially colour – as are the perennials in any grand border. In my garden, there are a couple of small beds that contain permanently planted tulips. I add pelargoniums or petunias in June, and when fall frosts finally do away with them, I lightly fork over the ground with a little well-rotted compost and plant it with clumps of forget-me-nots culled from around the garden. They require only watering, and the tulips will flower next May through a haze of blue. I use impatiens in containers on the shady terrace and in clumps, again, above resting spring bulbs in the woodland beds, keeping to softest pink or white there; the brilliant scarlets are too fierce in such informal spots. In high summer, a display of morning glories on a trellis provides daily excitement as we go out of our garden door: how many flowers are out today? All of these flowering plants except the bulbs are considered annuals by gardeners because they occupy the garden for just a single season.

Indeed, annuals are not quite what their name suggests: in our climate, they do not last a year. They are mainly plants of our short summers, and while we celebrate the season with their brilliance and beauty, the garden does not disappear with the impatiens and wax begonias at the first frost. A wise gardener will not depend entirely upon annuals, then, but will use them and enjoy their brief contributions of colour and form.

TRUE ANNUALS

An annual, botanically speaking, is a plant that is able to encompass its whole life cycle within a single growing season. The seed is a sort of genetic time bomb all ready to explode into growth when the conditions are right again for the next generation. The seed germinates, and the seedling develops into an adult, mature plant that sometimes within only a few weeks is capable of flowering, setting seed and distributing it.

Some seeds germinate as soon as they are shed—no waiting for a period of further ripening and winter dormancy broken by spring thaw. Such plants, often termed "ephemerals," have several overlapping generations on the go at once and are invariably able to capitalize on every suitable spot of soil that becomes empty. Leave a bit of the vegetable garden alone after a crop has come out, and there they are at once—quick-germinating annuals, the weeds of cultivated land that humanity has taken around the world. Chickweed, bitter cress, purslane and a host of others make up a cosmopolitan flora of highly successful annuals that have hitched themselves onto our agricultural coattails. And however well one has weeded and weeded again, it is only necessary to dig the ground, and there they are once more, grown from seeds brought to the surface and released from their state of suspended animation by the triggers of warmth and light. The apparently miraculous ground cover of scarlet field poppies in Flanders at the end of World War I can be credited to this phenomenon.

Not surprisingly, this group of horticultural opportunists offers little to us as good garden plants —we are only too busy trying to get rid of them. Field poppies (*Papaver rhoeas*) are an exception. From them have come the lovely Shirley poppies in every shade of red, soft pink and cream. Though these annual poppies are native to northern Europe—during the 19th century, the Reverend Mr. Wilks bred Shirley poppies from a plant with white-edged petals he found in the corner of a field in southern England—they spread south to the shores of the Mediterranean Sea, where they are joined by a number of annual plants less ephemeral and more enthusiastically welcomed by gardeners, though no doubt their weedy origins are similar.

HARDY ANNUALS

The plants that gardeners term hardy annuals because of their ability to endure some frost include pot marigold (*Calendula officinalis*), night-scented and Virginia stocks (*Matthiola bicornis* and *Malcolmia* spp, respectively), love-in-a-mist (*Nigella damascena*) and scabious (*Scabiosa* spp). The Mediterranean climate seems perfectly attuned to these plants, but of course, the situation must be the other way round: this is another pattern of growth that has evolved in response to a climate where, after a hot, baking summer, autumn showers will almost immediately trigger germination. The relatively mild, moist winter that follows encourages gentle development of the seedlings into strong plants. With spring warmth, cultivated fields, olive groves and roadsides become ablaze with flowers that have a short but brilliant life. By June, all have produced and shed their seeds. As seeds, they survive the high summer temperatures and complete drought that soft green plants could not endure.

Even with our cold North American winters, these hardy annuals will often self-sow in the garden and overwinter as small seedlings, just as they do on the Côte d'Azur. Although we cannot really depend upon autumn sowing outdoors, such self-sown seedlings certainly produce the easiest plants for next year, so it is always worth scattering spare seeds where, if all does go well, there will be a bonus early-summer display, perhaps following the spring bulbs.

There are two plants in my garden that play this game to perfection without any effort of mine. Strictly speaking, both, I suppose, are biennials— that is, their self-sown seeds germinate in summer and the plants flower the following year— but in a sense, they could be considered annuals because this certainly happens within a 12-month period. One is forget-me-not (*Myosotis sylvatica*); the other is honesty, or silver dollar (*Lunaria annua*).

In milder climates than this, it is usual to plan spring bedding schemes with, for example, tulips or hyacinths coming out of a ground cover of white arabis, wallflowers, polyanthuses, and so on. Such a ground cover provides a furnished appearance much greater than the bulbs do alone because of the cover's leafy growth as well as its flowering period, which usually starts before the bulbs and continues later. In much of the north, as we well know, a sudden hot spell means that a bed of tulips can pass in a week.

So it makes sense to look for other plants that will do this spring furnishing job. Forget-me-nots seed themselves everywhere, so there are always spare plants to move to considered positions. The same process is repeated elsewhere with honesty. There are forms that come true from seed—so long as different types are not grown

Many popular annuals such as petunias and alyssum can be purchased at garden stores in spring to fill the bays at the edge of a border.

close enough to cross-pollinate—with two-foot-high (60 cm) spikes of purple or white flowers or with variegated foliage. With rather more effort, one can have spring colour from the so-called winter-flowering pansies sown the previous June. It seems to me that gardeners willing to spend some time and thought on a spring display could add a number of plants to the list, all of which would help to avoid the common complaint that northerners "don't have any spring; we go straight from winter to summer." It really isn't true.

But back to those hardy Mediterranean annuals. Because the seedlings can accept quite a lot of frost, they are plants that those of us without seriously heated greenhouses or banks of basement propagating lights can nevertheless grow to perfection. The pattern is exactly as described for sweet peas (see page 31), which are indeed members of this group—Sicily is probably their original home. It will also be realized that this is the way to start the earliest vegetables—lettuce, carrots and radishes, for instance—and to furnish the herb bed. Almost all the common culinary herbs, with the exception of the truly tropical basil, are also wild wayside plants native to what the ancients called the Middle Sea. A six-plug pack of each of marjoram, savory, fennel, chervil, et cetera, sown in a cool place, will provide all that most families require.

That "hardy" attribute is as valid at the end of

Tender perennials, commonly used as annuals in northern climates, should be as carefully and consciously planned with regard to size, shape and colour —especially colour—as the hardy perennials in any grand border. Here, the colours of these pelargoniums, heliotrope and fuchsia are complemented by the grey tones of *Helichrysum petiolatum.*

the season as at the beginning. There is, to my mind, nothing more maddening than waking up after a sudden cold night in mid-September to black dahlias and soggy impatiens, only to have the next month entirely frost-free. Such a sudden snap has no effect upon the group under review. They can still provide a bit of colour into November. Cold, however, is not the only limitation to floral abundance. In general, although we will enjoy three months of flowers from hardy annuals, it is unreasonable to expect the plants that were started early in the season to carry on into fall. If a late show is wanted for a special spot, it will be necessary to make a further sowing, either in pots or outdoors, in July or even early August.

When we look for more fine hardy annuals, we are not disappointed, because other countries share the Mediterranean climate, with its hot, dry summer and moist, mild winter. California offers clarkia, godetia, baby blue eyes (*Nemophila maculata*), poached-egg flower (*Limnanthes douglasii*) and, of course, the wonderful California poppy (*Eschscholzia californica*). Anyone doubting the value of these simple sown-*in-situ* flowers should visit Santa Barbara Botanic Garden in March to see blazing fields of orange eschscholzia as a foreground to views of the mountains beyond.

Southern Australia provides most of our everlastings, immortelles and strawflowers (species of *Helipterum, Xeranthemum* and *Helichrysum*), which give both good summer garden displays and material for winter arrangements indoors. In addition to the ubiquitous blue lobelia (essential with sweet alyssum and *Salvia splendens* for patriotic red, white and blue displays), southern Africa has given North American gardeners a splendid range of brilliant daisies, generically known as South African daisies. These include species of *Dimorphotheca, Ursinia, Venidium* and more. Neighbours of our country house in Scotland always grow a bed of eye-stopping Livingstone daisies (*Dorotheanthus bellidiformis*) that flower wonderfully even there, 500 feet (150 m) up in the hills, where summers are cool and can be cloudy. But because most of the African daisies close their flowers when the sun is not out—a not uncommon habit among hot-climate species—they are an even better bet in Ontario and other places where summers are mostly sunny.

The Californians and their friends from the southern hemisphere are not quite so cold-tolerant as the true Mediterraneans, but since they can take near-freezing temperatures at the seedling stage, they are perfect for home sowing in

March and planting out six or eight weeks later. On light, well-drained soils, seeds can also be sown directly outdoors from late April onward, and they may self-sow.

These annuals are useful in the bays that naturally appear along the front of a shrub border, where they will give colour as long as the soil stays moist. The ground is loosened and a thin scattering of seeds raked in. Alternatively, the idea of a border composed entirely of hardy annuals has much to commend it. It is also wonderfully inexpensive in comparison with the cost of buying the usual pregrown tender annuals. The system is simple. A bed or strip of border is chosen with at least three-quarters sun exposure, because most annuals are sun lovers. Make a simple plan on paper, more or less to scale, showing an elongated clump of each type of plant. Colour combinations, ultimate size and shape will determine position exactly, as for a perennial border. Fork the bed over and rake it smooth, just as if you were preparing for vegetable seeds. Transfer the plan to the prepared site, either scratching the outlines of the clumps into the soil with a pointed stick or marking them with a trickle of sand. Then scatter seeds within each clump and lightly rake them in; they need to be just barely covered. The soil should be damp at planting time, and frequent watering is necessary until the sprouts appear.

This method is perfectly acceptable, but it does have one problem: as has already been mentioned, many seeds of annuals other than the ones you have sown are just waiting to come up in your carefully prepared bed. Without some subterfuge, the weeds will win every time. Not only will they germinate first, but you may well find yourself cherishing these usurpers, not having recognized them at the seedling stage for what they are. If the chosen seeds are sown in short rows six or nine inches (15-23 cm) apart across or along the allotted space, it will quickly become clear which are the botanical sheep and which the goats. As they grow, the pattern of the rows becomes unnoticeable.

Germination of freshly packeted hardy-annual seeds is usually extremely good, so sowing thinly is essential. Even so, further thinning is usually necessary. At first, leave the seedlings three inches (8 cm) apart, and later thin them to stand as far apart as the space between the rows. Plants with room to develop make better individuals – though they soon meet their neighbours – and

they flower for much longer than those competing for space and sun.

INSTANT GARDEN

Although this sort of direct seeding is sensible, it does require some patience. The usual expectation of summer annual displays is a rigidly-adhered-to pattern of late-May planting of plants already in flower. Both breeders and growers work hard to develop these early bloomers, finding, not surprisingly, that the prospect of immediate effect is what sells. This is something of a snare if a season-long display is really the aim. Often, plants put out when they are blooming have already reached maturity because of root systems that have been too long restricted by their containers. They never bulk up and fill their positions in the garden. From an annual's point of view, after all, to have succeeded in flowering is the culmination of life expectation: set a few seeds, and life is done.

As gardeners, we need to keep this in mind by ensuring that the plants we put out are healthy, pest-free and growing strongly. They will come into flower in their own good time. Fortunately, summer annuals are not very particular as to soil type, but they fare best if the soil has been well dug with some compost or other organic matter in order to encourage strong root growth. The deeper the roots go, the more resistant the plants will be to summer drought and the longer will be their effective season. It would be an unusual year if further irrigation, after the obviously essential watering in, were not necessary at all, but it is good to do what one can to reduce the need in advance. There is little doubt, too, that excessive overhead irrigation, especially in times of high temperatures and atmospheric humidity, encourages the spread of moulds, which shorten the plants' lives and make them look foul as they die.

I have already made it very clear that, to my mind, depending too heavily upon tender annual plants for garden interest is a great mistake, not only because one misses some of the best flowering plants but also because it is labour-demanding and expensive. Nonetheless, not to use the best from the wonderful range available would be self-defeating. For an important bed leading to the front door, perhaps, or edging a terrace or deck in continual view, different schemes with tender annuals can be planned each year.

As with perennial borders, it is best not to use

too many different plants but to concentrate the effect upon just two or three types. Thus, bordering a path, a narrow bed on each side 4 feet (1.2 m) wide by 20 feet (6 m) long might have a blue and white theme. Planted nine inches (23 cm) in from the edge is a single row of blue ageratum; 'Madison' would be a suitable cultivar, compact and uniform in size. If the plants are set at regular intervals, about 60 will be needed for a band to frame each bed. The centre of the bed is filled with white multiflora petunias a foot (30 cm) apart in three staggered rows. About 50 plants will be needed. Then, in place of three or five petunias in the centre of the bed, single dot plants of *Salvia farinacea* could give a vertical emphasis and repeat the blue of the ageratum. The blue and white bands can be reversed using sweet alyssum to enclose verbena or taller China asters (*Callistephus* spp). Marguerites, so-called Paris daisies (*Chrysanthemum frutescens*), might be dot plants. Every colour combination is possible in such formal beds: pink and blue from geraniums (*Pelargonium* spp) and petunias, scarlet and grey from *Salvia splendens* and dusty miller, orange and purple from marigolds and *Verbena rigida*. Again, one keeps in mind the colours of existing features—house, paving, deck, and so on.

Obviously, gardeners with time and suitable facilities for raising their own tender annuals from seed can plan the most original combinations; the catalogue lists are the limit. There are pages and pages of petunias, marigolds and pelargoniums alone, all ostensibly different and described in the most enthusiastic tones, this year's 'Orange Delight' utterly outshining last year's 'Tangerine Beauty.' I wonder. But many of these, or something very close, are available from the garden centre or the local nursery, and personally, I am happy to take advantage of their expertise. Better to use my limited space and time to grow from seed those things that are otherwise less easy to find. I would hate to be without, for example, spider flower (*Cleome hasslerana*) or those lovely mallows, *Lavatera trimestris* 'Loveliness' and the forms of *Malope trifida*, all possible to seed outdoors in late spring (though better sown under glass and planted out), as is the clear, glowing orange-scarlet tithonia from Mexico. And there are so many additional annuals capable of giving a more lush, luxuriant effect than that of the formal beds discussed above, which inevitably use the rather tight, regular plants needed for "carpet bedding."

Unfortunately, breeders' activities seem to have concentrated upon producing ever more dwarf, compact forms, as if this were the only need, not always to the benefit of the exuberant garden effect we would like.

PLANT CONDITIONING

Presuming one has the heated greenhouse space to raise such plants, starting them around March, moving them on into plugs or single pots and then planning a final hardening off outdoors in late May, there is, if all goes well, the ability to have the young plants in really good condition for planting out, which they will accept without any shock. Plants bought off the garden-centre shelves are not always so prepared. Packed closely together and forced to have open flowers at the time of purchase, they are often in a state from which they take some time to recover. A worthwhile exercise is to buy one's requirements as soon as they appear for sale, which is often well before safe postfrost planting time, and immediately move the young plants from their trays or six-packs into larger individual containers that can be kept on sunny windowsills or in a bright porch where temperatures do not drop below freezing. Well spaced out, fed, watered and gradually hardened off, these plants will give much more generously.

The geographical origins of the hardy annuals discussed previously make it very clear that they are plants for sunny sites. Give them overhanging trees or more than a third of the day in the shade of a building, and they lose their virtues. Thin, etiolated growth and poor flowering is the result. The same applies to the tender annuals so far mentioned: pelargoniums are from southern Africa, where, in fact, they grow as subshrubs that last for years. Marigolds (*Tagetes* spp, the so-called French and African types) and *Salvia splendens* are Mexicans, while the original wild *Petunia* species originated farther south in subtropical South America. All are sun lovers that become progressively less effective as shade increases.

SHADY CHOICES

Shade, however, is a fact of gardening life and indeed one to be cherished, because it offers the potential for growing a wonderful range of plants evolutionarily adapted to it. But very few of these shade plants are true annuals; woodland just does not offer a habitat in which the annual lifestyle has naturally developed. Fortunately, however, there are a couple of tropical plants—both strictly subshrubby perennials in their home environment—that have been transformed into superb shade-tolerant "annuals" for our summer gardens. These are impatiens and wax begonias.

Impatiens walleriana, from tropical East Africa, was introduced to Britain as a plant for warm greenhouses in the 1890s. Its ease of cultivation—cuttings root like weeds in a glass of water—soon took it from specialist collections of botanical curiosities to kitchen windowsills across the temperate world. It gathered names as it went: water plant, busy Lizzie, patience, patient Lucy, and so on. The last two are obviously derived from the scientific name but entirely miss the point: *Impatiens*, from the Latin for impatient or touchy, refers to the explosive seedpods that shoot ripe seeds several feet away from the parent. (Another species is called, redundantly, *Impatiens noli-tangere*.)

In the north, during just the last couple of decades, impatiens has progressed from a houseplant—sometimes propagated vegetatively and put out in the summer—to one of our most valuable seed-grown annuals, able to accept any position so long as summer moisture is constant. Colours now vary from white through every shade of pink to lilac, salmon, scarlet and orange. Striped or double forms with flowers like tiny, exquisite roses can also be raised from seed. Selections vary from six inches (15 cm) high to twice that, and all grow a bit taller in shade. It should be remembered that as with all annuals, impatiens cultivars bred for dwarfness in height are also compact in habit, and more are needed to fill a given space.

Raising impatiens from seed requires a nighttime minimum of 70 degrees F (21°C) and high humidity in late February, if plants are to be at flowering stage for the end of May. Thus, most home gardeners, sensibly, will buy their busy Lizzies. Doing so early and potting them on, as mentioned above for other annuals, has a bonus here, because the tips of the plants can be pinched off—which is recommended anyway in early May to encourage the plants to bush out—and quickly rooted in water. These cuttings make usable plants within six weeks. It is also possible to do this at the end of the season and to overwinter a few selected forms. A variegated form whose leaves have brilliant white edges that contrast with its pink flowers is particularly desirable and

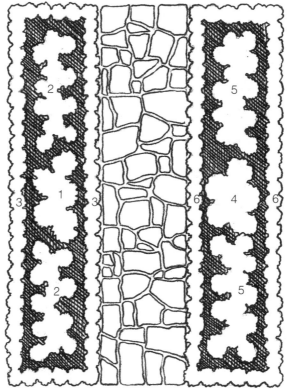

....

Both of the formal
annual beds lining
this pathway
should be planted
the same way.
One might choose
the blue border,
left, or the white,
right.

1. *Salvia farinacea*
   (blue)

2. Petunia (white)

3. *Ageratum* (blue)

4. Paris daisies
   (white)

5. *Verbena* (blue)

6. Sweet alyssum
   (white)

has to be propagated vegetatively. This is a wonderful container plant for a shady terrace.

Although impatiens can be used in the garden in any position that requires bright summer colour, its wonderful shade tolerance is bound to affect one's planning (but beware the New Guinea hybrids, bred from different species, which need sun to flower well). At the Royal Botanical Gardens' spectacular rock garden, mixed impatiens planted on slopes under big pines seem to flow like a Technicolor cascade. In the formal circles at the base of flowering crab apples, when complementary spring bulbs have gone out of sight, impatiens in single colours give the effect of a bright basket from which each tree seems to grow. In dry periods, they can go rather limp, but they perk up immediately after a shower, natural or contrived, and are well worth their keep.

The other most important shade-tolerant summer annual is the fibrous-rooted, or wax, begonia. Here is a plant that, either because of popularity or ease of pronunciation, seems never to have needed a common name. Begonia it is. There are more than 1,000 wild species strewn around the tropics and subtropics of the world and some 10,000 recorded hybrids. The wax begonias are derived mainly from the Brazilian *Be-*

gonia semperflorens, whose species name indicates what it does for our summer garden: it flowers all the time – until first frost, that is.

As a true tropical plant and a perennial, it needs both early sowing – January is usual – and temperatures as high as for impatiens. The seed is like dust – with more than two million seeds in an ounce (28 g), begonias would make a much better model for the biblical parable of the mustard seed – and the seedlings are the size of pinheads. For most of us, then, it is better to let the professionals get on with raising begonias. But again, the game of buying early and then rooting cuttings makes sense. Wax begonias seem less happy in the informal parts of the garden than are impatiens. The upright plants, the glossy foliage, green or bronze, and the flowers – from white to all shades of pink and red and, recently, yellow and orange – have a certain formality that is best respected.

Other South American species of begonia from areas that have a marked dry season have evolved resting tubers, and these tuberous begonias, too, have been brought into cultivation and hybridized again and again, resulting in the most exotic individual flowers of any plants we can grow as a part of summer bedding schemes. Some have frilled petals, and others are like enormous formal double camellias held above the typical off-centre leaves of the genus.

Tuberous begonias are not for mass planting but for concentrating in small beds or containers where they can receive individual grooming and some shade, because full sun causes delicate petals to burn and bleach. They are best kept over the winter or bought as resting tubers in March or April. Pot them shallowly in a moist, peaty compost, and keep them warm until the dormant tubers slowly come to life and produce new shoots. As with all the family, early June is soon enough for them to take the outdoor air.

Mimulus and torenia, both foot-high (30 cm) foxglove relations, can also take as much as three-quarters of the day in shade. The first blooms in a range of yellows and reds, often amusingly spotted. The second has pale blue, purple-cheeked flowers rather like snapdragons of an unlikely colour. But though pleasant, neither makes much of a show, and they do not flower long. Better, though not for really shady spots, is Madagascar periwinkle (*Vinca rosea, Catharanthus roseus*), whose flat flowers, pink or

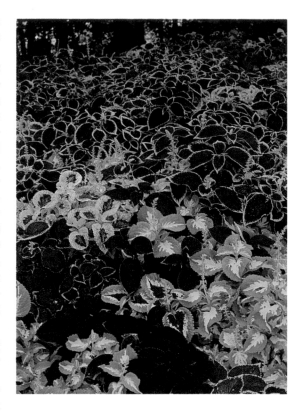

white – often with a contrasting eye of the other colour – stud low bushes of shining leaves.

FOLIAGE PLANTS

For deeper shade, one must turn to those annuals whose foliage makes the dramatic impact, their flowers being unimportant to us and hence not demanding of sun for their development. All of these are truly perennial. Coleus, or painted nettle (*Coleus x hybridus*), is indeed virtually a shrub in its tropical East Indies home, but again, careful selection has made it possible for home gardeners to produce good plants from seed in a short time. Although the brilliant, colour-splashed forms are effective in shade, the golden- and lime-green-leafed forms make the best impact, lighting up dark corners wonderfully if fed and watered liberally throughout the season. Accent plants for shady spots can also be found amongst our common houseplants. Few are as ornamental as the variegated spider plant (*Chlorophytum comosum*), which will build up fine tussocks of green-and-white-striped leaves from spring-potted offsets. Or one can set out the big plants that have been indoors all winter and then pot up the plantlets that appear naturally at the ends of long stems for the house. No plant is easier.

114

Coleus is a typical annual for shade and is grown for its dramatic foliage. Its range of brilliant colours is unusually wide and varied.

Finally, there is caladium (*Caladium x hortulanum*), an elegant aroid—a Jack-in-the-pulpit relative from tropical South America whose fleshy rhizomes are treated like tuberous begonias—started in warm, peaty compost in March. The big, shield-shaped leaves can be red with green veins or the reverse or, perhaps the most spectacular of all, pure white with green veins. Caladiums need moisture and shelter from both wind and full sun to give the tropical effect of which they are marvellously capable.

Further annual foliage plants from seed take us back into the sunnier spots, where they offer the sort of size and presence that are so often lacking in the normal run of summer annuals. *Canna* species and cultivars are the easiest of all. From fleshy rhizomes, strong shoots rise as high as five feet (1.5 m) and produce broad, paddle-shaped leaves rather like those of bananas, bright green or deep purple. Spikes of flowers, which bloom in shades of orange, red and pink, are splendidly statuesque at a distance but disappointing in detail. Cannas are superb as dot plants in bedding schemes and also for filling the gaps in perennial borders that even careful planning seems not always to avoid. They are usually treated like caladiums, started indoors in warmth in March and April to ensure immediate effect when planted out. But indoor starting is not essential: rhizomes—especially good clumps of one's own kept from last year—planted three inches (8 cm) deep in late May will soon start to earn their keep. The richer the soil, the lusher the growth.

Dahlia cultivars can be treated in exactly the same way. Tender perennials normally considered summer annuals, they have an extraordinary diversity of floral form, from tiny formal rosettes to shaggy flowers the size of cabbages. While the coarse foliage of the bigger types and their need for individual staking make them difficult to use in the mixed-garden scene, dwarf varieties and seed-grown bedding forms are, of course, exceptions. We grow just one dahlia, a very old four-foot (1.2 m) cultivar called 'Bishop of Llandaff,' which superbly combines delicate purple foliage and clear red, single daisy flowers. It is the perfect red border plant, and each year, we combine it with purple-leafed cannas—a marvellous textural contrast—with an identical red impatiens at their feet, growing out of the black-leafed grassy *Ophiopogon planiscapus* 'Nigrescens.' Purple-leafed *Perilla frutescens* and another edible

plant, the related 'Dark Opal' form of basil (that most aromatic of herbs), are also added toward the front. If I needed more instant height in this association, I would add half a dozen castor oil plants (*Ricinus communis*) at the back. This plant attains small-tree status in the tropics, and in the north, even from spring-sown seeds, it will produce huge, eight-foot (2.4 m) plants with great fingered leaves, purple, metallic or green. Nothing is better for quick furnishing in a new garden.

Although castor oil is a member of the spurge family, it does not have the typical white latex that immediately distinguishes some other spurges, the true euphorbias. One of these, *Euphorbia marginata*, has a valuable summer role with its two-foot (60 cm) mounds of striking green and white foliage. Often called snow-on-the-mountain, this is an annual that will grow anywhere after being sown under glass or even *in situ*, and it will take the poorest soils with impunity.

On one hand, the floral brilliance of summer bedding schemes is just what we hope for, but on the other, their real effectiveness lies not just in unrestrained colour but in the careful combinations of flower and foliage. With so much brilliance easily attained, it is very important to be able to cool it, in both senses of the phrase. For this, grey foliage is invaluable. It gently combines with the misty blues and pinks and purples, softens reds and is an obvious part of white gardens. The various dusty millers supply it splendidly. They include the cultivars 'Silverdust,' 'White Diamond' and 'Cirrus' of *Senecio cineraria*, a Mediterranean seaside perennial subshrub that will sometimes overwinter even with us, and *Pyrethrum* 'Silver Feather.' Except for tight carpet bedding, one will want to avoid the dwarfest forms that catalogues seem more and more to rejoice in: it is lightness and delicacy of form that is needed here, not blobs—even grey blobs.

Several annual grasses—untouched by human hands, one could say, for they have not been the object of plant breeding—can help provide lightness and delicacy. Hare's foot (*Lagurus ovatus*) and quaking grass (*Briza maxima*) are foot-high (30 cm) Mediterraneans for long-lasting border-front effect and for later drying indoors. Once established, self-sown autumn seedlings will overwinter to flower the next June so long as they are recognized as the desirable plants they are. Unfortunately, when it is a couple of inches (5 cm) high, one grass looks much like another and can be eas-

Dahlias, such as this small orange collarette type in a container with lobelia, verbena, dianthus and alyssum, are tender perennials normally treated as annuals.

ily weeded out by mistake. Vastly bigger and again invaluable in new gardens are the striped-leafed forms of sweet corn (Zea mays). While these are splendidly striking, so, too, is perfectly conventional culinary corn. Perhaps one might grow half a dozen plants of 'Peaches and Cream' amongst the flowers in the hope that, so disguised, they will be missed by the local squirrels and raccoons, and (provided there are enough plants to allow for pollination) we might at last enjoy fresh-picked corn of our own growing. No doubt surrounding them with the most highly scented of annuals, such as tobacco plants (Nicotiana spp), stocks (Matthiola bicornis), heliotrope (Heliotropium arborescens) and mignonette (Reseda odorata), would help keep the predators away. All of these fragrant annuals are also wonderful grown close to where the family sits on the patio in the evening, when the scents are at their most delicious.

VINES AND CLIMBERS

Several references have already been made in this book to the need for quick height, especially in new gardens. Fences, trellises, panels of netting or wigwams of poles all offer support for annual climbers, those quickest-growing of all plants. Ten or even twenty feet (3-6 m) of growth in a June-to-October season is entirely possible, but of course, the effect is apt to be thin for the first half of the season. Thus these plants are often best planned to add late colour to spots that already support early-flowering clematises or roses or to scramble over early-flowering shrubs. For this role, one must choose climbers with delicate foliage that will not compete too much with the host's leaves, which are working to build up next year's flower buds. Thus the Chilean glory vine (Eccremocarpus scaber), a tendril climber with sprays of orange, yellow or red flowers, and the

yellow canary creeper (Tropaeolum peregrinum) are ideal. So are the cypress vine (Ipomoea quamoclit) and other elegant morning-glory relations.

The true 'Heavenly Blue' form of morning glory (Ipomoea spp) is possibly the most dramatic of all annual climbers. The way in which its clear blue trumpets shade to white in the tube is exactly mirrored by a summer sky paling to the horizon. When it is hot, their display is over soon after midday, but as the weather cools, the trumpets can stay open until dusk, gradually taking on a purplish tinge. The flowers of the cup-and-saucer vine (Cobaea scandens) are longer-lasting, and although the general effect is less striking, both the purple and greenish white forms are well worth growing and last well when cut. Like morning glories, the seeds can be germinated indoors in early April.

Sweet peas (discussed on page 31) are the best-loved of all annual climbers. Their effect is generally over by August. A worthwhile relation, the hyacinth bean, which rejoices in the Latin name of Dolichos lablab, is a sort of symphony in purple: leaves, flowers and pods are all variations on the theme. It looks especially fine sharing a support with flame-flowered climbing nasturtiums (Tropaeolum majus) or the black-eyed Susan vine (Thunbergia alata), whose clear orange trumpets have a jet-black eye.

For a really dense late-summer screen, there is nothing better than the whole family of gourds and squashes, though for this job, you must stay away from the bush types. The huge round leaves are as effective as that traditional perennial front porch cover, the old Dutchman's pipe (Aristolochia durior). Conventionally, gourds and squashes are allowed to roam horizontally, but their tendrils indicate clearly that they have vertical pretensions, though as the fruit develops and becomes heavy, some extra help in the form of loose nets may be needed to hold them up. Bottle gourds (Lagenaria spp) with soft, downy foliage, bristly loofahs (Luffa cylindrica) and ornamental gourds in every shape and size (Cucurbita spp) can be supplemented by edible acorn and butternut squashes. Rich soil is essential, with plenty of moisture in the early stages as well as full sun for effective ripening of the fruit.

CONTAINERS

It will be agreed that there is hardly a spare corner of summer garden that cannot be home to

suitably chosen annuals, yet there are further opportunities still. Annuals can take to the air in hanging baskets, and in a sort of intermediate position, they are the best of plants for containers. In this garden, that is their major role. A big Chinese pickled-egg jar 18 inches (45 cm) across and 24 inches (60 cm) deep or something similar can hold a surprising cornucopia of growth. A single central marguerite surrounded by eight or nine double-flowered petunias tumbling over the sides or a cabbage palm (Cordyline australis) with three spider plants and six impatiens are the sort of combinations one can create. These examples are for sun and shade, respectively. Once the containers are obtained (and they have a furnishing value of their own), this is an economical way to use annuals, because the small numbers of plants needed give an effect that is out of all proportion to their cost. Watering and feeding can never be neglected, of course, because of the necessarily restricted root run.

The same must be emphasized of hanging baskets. Because they have air circulating all around, they dry out incredibly quickly on hot, windy days. It is wise not to get carried away at the beginning of the season with more hanging baskets than can be looked after, because a daily visit to the baskets is essential unless one is able to arrange a semiautomatic irrigation system with capillary drip lines. One big, luxuriant basket by an often used door and another in view of the kitchen window may be quite enough.

By July, it will be hoped that the container itself is virtually invisible, hidden by a curtain of growth of plants especially chosen for the job. Cascade petunias, pendulous begonias and fuchsias, ivy-leafed pelargoniums and trailing lobelias are just a few of the possibles. To be avoided at all costs are things like stiff little marigolds and cockscomb celosias, both beastly things at the best of times. Again, gardeners can plan for colour combinations or just keep to one lush plant and some complementary foliage used extravagantly.

This rapid review of the wonderful world of annual plants has only scratched the surface of the possible, which any survey of seed catalogues will quickly expand. It may seem ungrateful and ungracious, then, to conclude the chapter by repeating the warning that throughout has been implicit (and, at the risk of redundancy, explicit as well). Annuals have no claim to be the permanent "bones" of the garden. We, as garden makers, are ostensibly in control, and we must use them wisely and sensitively.

Vegetables can be
ornamental as well
as useful. Grown
in plots or patches,
salad ingredients
of various hues
present a picture
that adds to
the landscape
as a whole.

DESIGNER VEGETABLES

A t the grand château of Villandry in the Loire area of France, one of the vast, formal parterres below the house is laid out entirely in vegetables. There are square, rectangular and circular beds, arabesques and scrolls, each reflecting the next in wonderful rococo exuberance. Their brilliant colours come from the foliage of lettuce, leeks, beets, beans, chard, cabbages and fennel in a multiplicity of forms, just one type of vegetable to a bed. As the crop in a bed matures, it is harvested en masse, usually to be replaced at once by fresh transplants. The effect is visually dazzling.

Villandry takes to the absolute limit the French concept of the *potager*. The French presumption is that vegetables, herbs and often trained fruit trees have as important a part to play in the design of the garden as a whole as have perennial borders and other flowerbeds. This concept reflects the traditional French attitude toward food, which raises the culinary arts beyond what Anglo-Saxons consider morally acceptable. It is another manifestation of what in sociological terms might be called a sophisticated peasantry, a reverence for the basics.

It is unlikely that any of today's home gardeners will take up the Villandry idea wholeheartedly unless they have an entire village to feed or are uncommonly devoted to lettuce soup—which is indeed a wonderful way to deal with the not infrequent double row that matures all at once and threatens imminent bolting—but the potager principle has great potential for us all. It takes design into the vegetable plot and brings the food plants close to home.

I have always had a sneaking suspicion that many authors of gardening books do not practise what they preach. Some, I fear, do not even have a garden to practise on. So it would be wise to confess at this point that I do not have a proper

Planks in my
kitchen garden
provide peripatetic
paths so that one
need not walk on
the ground and
working is easy
even when the
ground is wet.

potager; but my kitchen garden increasingly resembles one.

Years ago, when we moved to Ontario from England, I inherited a conventional rectangular plot surrounded by wire fencing that was intended to reduce the depredations of rabbits and groundhogs. (It did a fairly poor job. In our first year, never having met a groundhog, socially or otherwise, I was utterly mystified by a row of peas that obstinately stayed two inches [5 cm] high. Daily crack-of-dawn pruning by this wretched rodent eventually proved to be the problem. The subsequent addition of a dog to the family scene has remedied the situation, but I keep the wire netting just in case. There are hungry rabbits that get up earlier than the dog.)

The plot has grown. It is now about 75 feet by 20 feet (23 by 6 m). Divided into a number of sections, bounded by split-cedar fencing and incorporating other permanent features, it begins to suggest the potager ethos of separately identified areas linked by appealing eye-catchers. The eastern two-thirds is cut in half lengthwise by a single sunken line of railway ties, so the vegetable rows on each side are only 10 feet (3 m) long. Three or four rows placed closer together than is usual create a space-saving block of vegetables divided from the next by a wider gap. Planks provide peripatetic paths so that one need not walk on the ground—a necessary consideration on my heavy clay—and cultivation and harvesting are made easy even when the ground is wet.

As the plans in this chapter indicate, the whole kitchen garden has eight distinct areas. At one end is what I call rather grandiloquently the bean arbour, a 10-foot-high (3 m) netting tunnel the width of the plot, upon which climbing snap beans and acorn and butternut squashes fight for predominance with a couple of morning glories

that contribute floral brilliance. The effect works only during the three months of high summer, but then, when one walks under beans and squashes hanging down like some extravagant harvest festival at a country church, the tunnel does seem worthwhile. A classical sculpture at each end would give it the architectural emphasis of my pretensions. I must work on this. Actually, I have started. Beyond the far arch is an enormous Chinese pot that is a good eye-catcher. It is also useful: topped up by the garden hose, it provides acclimatized water for my watering cans.

On the arbour's other side is a simple cold frame. Its railway-tie sides were once glazed with old storm windows; they worked well enough, but I have replaced them with pieces of double acrylic, which seem even better. To the west is a permanent asparagus bed bounded by red currants and gooseberries. This end, undefended by wire netting, gets more shade than I would like from a huge Amur cork tree that is unthinkable to remove. Separated from this area by a band of raspberries are four quadrants of the pseudo-potager, with the split-cedar fence on three sides. These divisions and permanent features, whether woody plant growth (the fruit bushes) or artifacts, combine to give the kitchen garden the potager feeling of a separate room. The analogy, I suppose, is to a house with a cathedral ceiling.

POTAGER POSITION

As in a house, so in a garden one must decide which room will go where. The decision about location for a vegetable plot is most important. Some plants will grow in unpromising situations, but vegetables demand the best: a simple recipe of full sun and good, well-drained soil. Consider something of the background of these plants. Many come from the tropics. Beets, asparagus and cabbages and all of their tribe are natives of the European seashore—sandy soil with perfect drainage, no trees, no shade. Of course, our vegetables could no longer survive in the wild, for, bred to be highly productive, they require what their ancestors had and more—plenty of water and plenty of food to produce lush crops.

The designed garden will include some shade because of its fences and fruit trees, and thus it will demand more thought than a traditional flat plot. In recompense, the potager-inspired garden can be productive from early spring until late fall.

A well-planned plot need not and often should

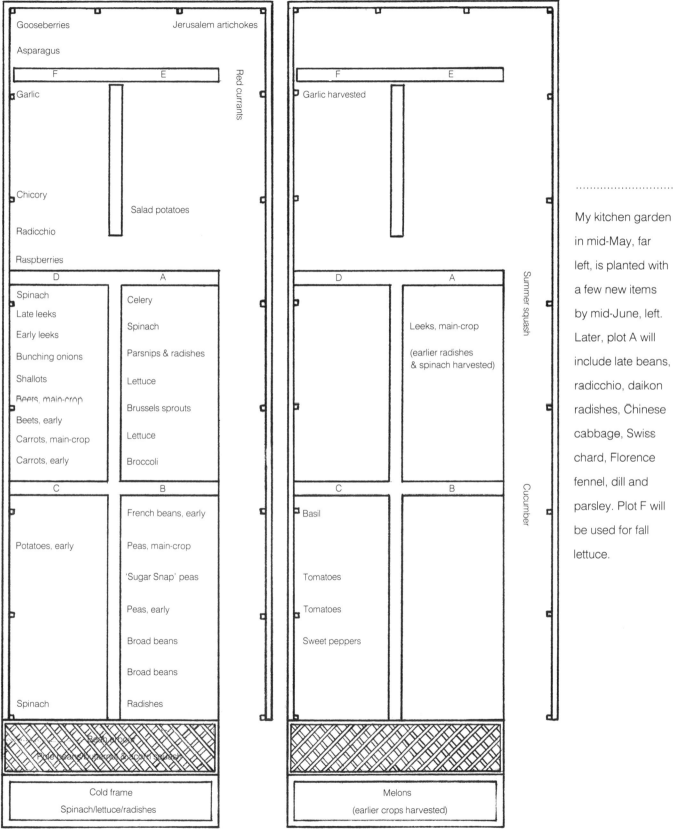

Gooseberries   Jerusalem artichokes

Asparagus

Red currants

| F | E |

Garlic

Chicory

Salad potatoes

Radicchio

Raspberries

D	A
Spinach	Celery
Late leeks	Spinach
Early leeks	Parsnips & radishes
Bunching onions	Lettuce
Shallots	Brussels sprouts
Beets, main-crop	Lettuce
Beets, early	Broccoli
Carrots, main-crop	
Carrots, early	

C	B
Potatoes, early	French beans, early
	Peas, main-crop
	'Sugar Snap' peas
	Peas, early
	Broad beans
	Broad beans
Spinach	Radishes

Bean sprout
Pole beans/butternut & acorn squash

Cold frame
Spinach/lettuce/radishes

Garlic harvested

Summer squash

Cucumber

| F | E |

D	A
	Leeks, main-crop
	(earlier radishes & spinach harvested)

C	B
Basil	
Tomatoes	
Tomatoes	
Sweet peppers	

Melons
(earlier crops harvested)

My kitchen garden in mid-May, far left, is planted with a few new items by mid-June, left. Later, plot A will include late beans, radicchio, daikon radishes, Chinese cabbage, Swiss chard, Florence fennel, dill and parsley. Plot F will be used for fall lettuce.

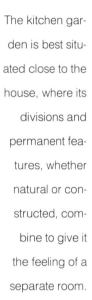

The kitchen garden is best situated close to the house, where its divisions and permanent features, whether natural or constructed, combine to give it the feeling of a separate room.

not be at the end of the garden. A wide lot may provide space at the side. The vegetable plot may even make sense in front of the house, sacrificing some of that endless, pointless, featureless grass between front door and street. The Gallic idea, in which the aesthetic is combined with the utilitarian, is that the kitchen garden should be close to the house and the associated herb plot right against the kitchen door.

Fortunately, winter provides some time to plan. My kitchen gardening year begins just after Christmas, when the seed catalogues come. (At least they do if I have remembered to order catalogues or if I ordered seeds last year. There is a catalogue source list at the end of this book.) The catalogues come when the outdoor temperature is still far below freezing and the wind is whirling the snow into a crescendo that only the weather forecasters enjoy describing. But by the living room fire, I easily cultivate the most wonderful kitchen garden ever. All the old faithfuls are there in the catalogues: early peas with fingerling carrots for June; for later, melons fit for a king and a root cellar stacked with overwintering potatoes and squashes and beets sleeping in sand. And because my January dreams are nothing if not original, this year will see a progression

of exotics from arugula and finocchio to radicchio and wong bok.

Some of my choices – most, I like to think – are rational, although I do grow rather too many perfectly ordinary potatoes because I enjoy the look in early July of impeccably earthed-up rows and, later, the rich harvest of smooth pink or yellow tubers, the separation of the little ones from the big, the immediate use of those I was foolish enough to spear with a digging fork and the full baskets in the cellar. All a little silly and certainly atavistic, but wonderfully satisfying in an ever more impersonal age. (I do, however, plan to search out unusual varieties, such as the waxy, sausage-shaped 'Pink Fir-Apple.')

More sensible and the *raison d'être* for most of my choices is the possibility of utterly fresh produce, grown without unknown fertilizers and pesticides or with none. My family wants fresh things as early as possible and as late as possible, and we want types bred for flavour, not for their ability to travel happily from Florida and sit on a supermarket shelf for two weeks. Specialist catalogues offer a good selection while affording the gardener time to sit and peruse the pages.

Seed firms vary greatly. Some are all glitz and glitter, aglow with glossy photographs of gorgeous goodies, while others quietly describe their heritage seeds on recycled paper. There is a catalogue for everyone. I like to patronize companies from a climate comparable to mine, especially if they grow their own seeds; if they can do it, I like to think, so can I. Their cultural directions in the catalogue or on the seed packets are often engagingly personal.

Ordered early—there may be a small discount for doing so—your seeds will be with you by late January or early February. For those of us without a heated greenhouse, that is plenty soon enough. Store the seeds in a dry, cool place; high temperatures and humidity can lower their germination rates.

FEBRUARY

On Valentine's Day or thereabouts, I start my vegetable seeds. Two small pots of lettuce are sown in a purchased peat-based planting mix, then watered and put in a plastic bag. My dressing room becomes the propagation house, and because it has to double as a spare bedroom, I hope no one comes to stay. In four or five days, when the seedlings emerge, I immediately move them to a sunny windowsill so they will not grow lanky and pale; forget them for just a day, and they are ruined and one has to start again. Before a pair of true leaves develops, the youngsters are moved singly into six-pack containers of the same soil mix. I do one boxful of 'Little Gem' and another of 'Winter Density' for succession crops, both of them romaine types. These should provide us with a fresh supply of lettuce from May through June, when my conventional late-May garden planting has not yet produced a thing.

The sequence is this: a couple of weeks on the warm windowsill, then to a high, lighted shelf up against the windowpane in our barely heated garden room described in the next chapter (where camellias, spring bulbs and *Jasminum polyanthum* flowering below give the seedlings some idea of the standard expected). On the coldest nights, the dog's water bowl has a skin of ice, but nothing comes to harm, not even the dog. By the end of March, the seedlings are sufficiently developed for transplanting—leaves touching, roots circling the inside of each plug in the six-pack. Outdoor exposure now would be too unkind, so they go into the cold frame east of the bean arbour, where the sheet of double acrylic, though in no way fully sealing out the weather, shelters a crum-

bly soil that is just right. I leave about six inches (15 cm) of space all around each plant so that the earliest harvests, in late April, will act as a necessary thinning and give us our first salad at a time worth boasting about.

Every year is different. One year, thick late snow made planting in the cold frame impossible, so we ate our first two salads straight from the boxes—a box lunch. More seeds were sown at once. Another year, a mild mid-February permitted sowing radishes straight into the frame for the lettuces to meet later. All this activity is apt to sound somewhat laborious, but it is almost as quick to do as to describe. Besides, at that time of year, there is no other gardening activity demanding my attention, and sowing does help to foster thoughts of spring.

Also in February, I prop some old windows over a few feet of ground to encourage early thawing where the first of the outdoor vegetable seeds will go, those whose packets say, "Sow as soon as the ground can be worked." This does not refer merely to the soil temperature but to its physical state: moist without forming soggy lumps. A light forking leaves it in a state easily broken down with a rake.

MARCH

March brings brighter days and the prospect of milder weather. Amazingly, it is still almost three months before most people believe they should plant their gardens. This is a ridiculous length of time to wait, especially if one is willing to make use of a few windowsills indoors. Indeed, I believe it essential to get ahead of the game.

So this coming weekend—today, as I write, is the last day of February—I shall sow one small pot of Brussels sprouts and one of broccoli, a dozen plants of each. In the garden, there will be two rows of each, three feet (1 m) apart, with plants 18 inches (45 cm) apart in the rows. The sequence is the same as with last month's lettuce: the seeds germinate in a week and move to the windowsill. In another few days, they are big enough to transfer to the six-packs. I do three of these of each vegetable to ensure that the 12 plants do not include any runts. A week or so later, out they go to the high, sunny shelf in the garden room. Grown in this simple, amateur way, the newly germinated seedlings are always rather leggy with weak stems, so when moved to single plugs, the individual cells of the six-packs, they need to be set more deeply, with the pair of seedling leaves at soil level.

At six inches (15 cm) tall in mid-April, the plants are ready to go outside, having already been taken out for a few days to acclimatize, like babies in their strollers, and brought in at night. In a mild year, no protection is necessary, and they can be planted directly in the open garden, but they will be slow to move forward. In most years, this is where some of those old windows, propped a few inches above the garden soil, continue to earn their keep. Under them, the soil is warming, the wind is kept off, and the growth of young plants is dramatic by comparison with their open-ground counterparts. It is important that the plants be watered thoroughly, with the help of a little fertilizer. Once more a couple of weeks later should be enough, by which time the weather may have improved sufficiently for the protection to be removed.

The broccoli cultivars 'Saga' and 'Paragon,' both of which do well here, represent a relatively recent trend concerning this delicious vegetable. Within two months of planting out, a central green flower head develops and is soon ready for cutting. Unlike cutting a cauliflower, which marks the end of the harvest, the removal of the broccoli head spurs further growth of side shoots well into fall. One word of warning: holes in the leaves probably indicate feeding by cabbage butterfly caterpillars, which sometimes hide in the heads you have cut. To avoid that most unappetizing sight—a cooked caterpillar crouching on one's plate—cover broccoli heads with salted water for an hour or two before plunging them into a saucepan of boiling water. Cooking only briefly is essential to enhance the brilliant, fresh colour.

The Brussels sprouts will not be ready until late October, which is fine, because I want to ensure that we have them to go with the Christmas turkey. Those from the supermarket deep freeze may look just the same, but that wonderful nutty flavour is utterly lost.

APRIL

April is described by the poet T.S. Eliot as "the cruellest month." For gardeners, however, it is the month of potential, when one works up to the sowing crescendo of May. April here still brings some night frosts and even late snow flurries, but these are the exception to the rule of progressively warmer, longer days. I do my best to take advantage of the good weather. The more one can do now, the less likely there is to be a frantic rush later and the more time will be available to enjoy both gardening and its results.

Soil preparation is not an exciting thing to write about, nor indeed to do, but it is critically important in the production of good vegetables. If the plot is divided up in the potager pattern, it is less possible to rush in with a tiller, so one has to dig more by hand. But each area is so small (and hopefully so productive) that an hour of applying compost or turning in the rye that overwintered and is now green manure is enough preparation for the next sequence of sowing. None of this need degenerate into the category of chore.

My garden plan on page 121 shows area B full of peas and beans. These leguminous crops, all members of the pea family, have a symbiotic relationship with bacteria living in nodules on the roots (which you can easily see if you gently pull up a plant). The bacteria convert atmospheric nitrogen into usable plant food. Hence the crops actually add to the soil's fertility—one good reason to remember crop rotation when planning.

Broad, or fava, beans go in first. They are not as popular in North America as they are in Europe, but my family considers them one of the treats of the vegetable year. The big seeds are sown six inches (15 cm) apart, two inches (5 cm) deep, in two pairs of rows as soon as the soil is fit to be worked—they can easily take our April frosts. Some varieties grow four feet (1.2 m) high, but the dwarf sorts, such as 'The Sultan' or 'Toto,' are much more suitable for my short rows and are almost as productive. Each chubby pod holds half a dozen flat beans reclining in soft green fur.

My earliest peas go in at the same time. 'Kelvedon Wonder,' or 'Little Marvel,' an old but excellent variety that my grandfather grew almost a century ago in Suffolk, reaches only 18 inches (45 cm) high. Again, a double row with seeds two inches (5 cm) apart gives an early picking a couple of months from sowing, like the broad beans.

The main-crop 'Green Arrow' and 'Sugar Snap' peas are climbers that have tendrils. Traditional support is twiggy brushwood pushed in alongside the rows in a near-vertical tent pattern. I would do this if twigs were easily available and I had plenty of time, because the twigs add attractive height and structure to the garden (and we have agreed that a vegetable plot should look good), but I have degenerated to the simplicity

The more the plot is divided up, the less possible is the use of a tiller, but each area is so small and productive that the hand labour required need not be a great chore.

of a strip of wire netting three feet (1 m) high with reinforcing rod supports every three feet (1 m). As soon as good germination is apparent, I install this fence down the centre of each double row, and the young plants quickly clothe it as they climb.

Full circle brings us around to area C. Here, at the very end of April, I plant two rows of early potatoes. Although potatoes can be grown from true seeds — seeds from the fruit, which is in fact like a small green tomato — it is seldom done in the home garden. The "seed potatoes" gardeners buy are virus-free tubers specially grown in areas away from commercial crop production for the best chance of disease-free growth. I buy the tubers as soon as they appear — just 20, ideally

the size of a kiwi fruit. I put them in a box in a warm, bright place, with the end having the most eyes upright. Sprayed lightly with water, the eyes soon produce little purplish shoots, which in the dark would grow long, white and wormlike, as we have all seen on potatoes stored too long. In mid-April, the potatoes are moved to a cooler place to be acclimatized for their move to the garden a week later, one foot (30 cm) apart each way and four inches (10 cm) deep, buds up. If the weather is warm, growth can be evident in two weeks. A subsequent frost will blacken the tender shoots overnight, so for a week or two, the gardener should be prepared to add straw, newspapers or some other suitable "pyjamas" to cover the

Peppers, backed here by a morning glory, are often purchased as seedlings in a garden centre, a small investment that pays delicious dividends.

sprouts on frosty nights. Like our pyjamas, these covers are taken off in the morning.

MAY

By mid-May, area B is full. 'Green Arrow' peas and 'Sugar Snaps,' eaten pods and all, have been sown in early May and a little later. I take a risk on the last frost by soon following with a double row of dwarf French beans. They are very sensitive to cool soil, and the first batch is bought pretreated with a fungicide such as Captan; brilliant blue or pink powdered seeds show this has been applied. Keen organic gardeners will avoid fungicides, sowing untreated seeds somewhat later, around the end of May.

In May, the other plots fill up as well. The broccoli and sprouts are joined first by parsnips, sown as soon as the soil can be easily worked; these long white roots are very slow to develop. Six or eight seeds are sown in groups every eight inches (20 cm). When at last the seedlings appear—and they can take about a month—they are thinned to two and then to one at each spot. It is a good idea to sow radishes with the parsnips; they emerge quickly, break up the crust of soil that forms over the nonappearers and are harvested as the parsnips begin to show. Parsnips are won-

derfully winter-hardy. They are harvested as long as one can get a fork into the ground in fall, and any that are not lifted and brought in before the soil freezes are still there when a thaw sets in. The later the harvest, the sweeter the roots.

A botanically related crop, also slow to mature, is celery. It needs to be sown indoors in March— the usual windowsill and cool-garden-room treatment. Forty-eight little plants in six-packs provide me with two rows planted out in late May. I choose a green type or the so-called golden self-blanching celery, neither of which needs the laboursome and space-hungry earthing up of the conventional white-hearted sort. Because of the work involved and because the stores sell a good product that stays crisp on their shelves, celery is a rather unpopular home garden crop. But it happily takes to the shade and overly moist soil in my A and D plots close to the raspberries.

Most of area D is a typical sow-when-you-like-so-long-as-it's-in-May sort of plot. More spinach —it is almost impossible to have too much, and it freezes well—is joined by carrots and beets. There are varieties of each that mature in 50 days or so; little fingerling carrots or bite-sized beets are among the joys of early summer and are soon harvested. Others take another month but produce higher yields. Then again, there are varieties bred for winter storage. But as with celery, such good carrots can be bought throughout the winter that it is really wiser to concentrate on summer crops if the plot is small.

Light, compost-rich soil soon warms up, and growth is rapid. By mid-June, one can start to scratch at the base of a potato plant or two to see how things are progressing. Soon after, the very first potatoes of the year are ready, the size of walnuts. It is nonsense, economically, to harvest perhaps only four or five meals from two rows, but new potatoes are among the culinary highlights of the year and they use the space for such a short time. A row of basil, that most marvellous of garden herbs, takes the potatoes' place as soon as they are out of the way.

TOMATOES

Meanwhile, the other summer tropicals can be started indoors. These are all potato relatives: sweet peppers, eggplants and, most important of all, tomatoes. No summer garden is complete without tomatoes, even if they are the only vegetable grown. In my bit of southern Ontario, it is warm enough for self-sown tomatoes to produce a crop in September or early October. These are the plants that often appear in the garden in June or July where a fruit dropped last year. Obviously, then, I could sow tomatoes outdoors, but I want them as early as possible.

Without bright light and a warm indoor place, the earliest crops cannot be started from scratch, so for these, I head down to the garden centre. Half a dozen plants bought in little pots in early May can be moved into bigger containers and cherished on a warm windowsill until the weather is fit and the soil is warm. These can well be in flower by the time they go out and will yield the first ripe tomatoes of the year. Unfortunately, it is seldom possible to buy as plants the particular varieties I choose from the seed catalogues. Given the dressing-room and sunny-windowsill treatment, these become later main crops, productive from early August until frost.

I usually grow four varieties. My choices vary from year to year, but 'Marmande,' a traditional French beefsteak variety of wonderful flavour, is always included. Some of the fruits weigh a pound (500 g). There are also yellow- and pink-fruited variations of this. Quite different are the cherry tomatoes with long sprays of small fruits. 'Sweet

100' is my favourite and a prodigious grower. 'Gardener's Delight' is another fine one.

Ideally, these varieties should be sown in early April at a temperature of about 80 degrees F (27°C), lowered to about 60 degrees (15°C) a week or so after germination. In the absence of a real greenhouse, one must resort again to sunny windowsills and garden rooms, helped, perhaps, by a fluorescent light setup in the basement. Tomato-seed germination is quick, and the robust seedlings can soon be moved singly to six-pack plugs. Daytime temperatures indoors are high in spring, but nights are still too cool for the tomatoes to go out, so when the leaves meet, the young plants must be moved into three- or four-inch (8-10 cm) pots. It is vital to prevent their getting leggy at this stage. Equally, the gardener must watch out for whiteflies, which can build up to an infestation of alarming proportions and spread havoc through the tomatoes and hence to the beans, squash, cucumbers, and so on. Nowhere is the "stitch in time" proverb more true. Insecticidal soap is a remedy if used in time.

If there is plenty of space available, tomatoes in the garden can be allowed to grow unchecked or can be half-confined in cages. I don't have that much space, so I tie each plant's main stem to a four-foot-high (1.2 m) length of steel reinforcing rod and reduce side shoots to avoid a tangle.

PEPPERS

Whether on the bedroom windowsill or in a temperature-controlled greenhouse, tomatoes are robust and easy. They seem to want to grow. Sweet peppers are much less keen in the early stages. They should be sown in March. After two weeks at 70 degrees F (21°C), they do best with subsequent night temperatures around 65 degrees (18°C), a regime difficult to sustain without professional greenhouse help. Peppers often require another visit to the garden centre.

Still, there is a technique or two that will improve crops subsequently. Plants are usually available by mid-May, a full month before I want to set them out in the open. But if they are set into larger pots and fed and cared for at this stage, I am well ahead of the game, and they take their place in the garden—just a dozen plants—as June really warms up. If the first good-sized fruits are harvested in August, before they have ripened to red, orange or yellow (depending on variety), production should continue well into fall.

I have stopped growing eggplants as a regular part of my vegetable garden. In the seedling stage, they demand higher temperatures than even peppers or tomatoes. Otherwise, the seedlings are apt to sit and sulk in a most depressing way. And although it is fun to see the variations in the high-summer garden—deepest purple, pink-striped ivory, white, big and small—I must confess to finding no difference in the flavour of fresh market eggplants.

BEANS

One of the few difficult aspects of vegetable gardening is figuring out the harvesttime. It may not be a problem if you plan to be at home all summer, but failure to be on hand when the vegetables are mature wastes that particular crop and slows production for weeks ahead. My family is often away in early August, just when the pole beans usually come into full production.

Thus for us, the usual early-June sowing time is too soon; we return from vacation to find the arbour dripping with tough, inedible beans. So it's a late-June sowing for me, a single line of beans on each side of the arbour. I sow three beans every six inches (15 cm) and reduce the seedlings to the best one at each station. It takes little more than a month for the vines to meet overhead, and the first beans are ready a couple of weeks later. From this point, it is essential that the arbour be picked every other day. Because it is extraordinarily easy to miss green beans among the foliage, only to find them when they are past their prime, I often grow yellow 'Kentucky Wonder Wax' and purple 'Climbing Purple Podded,' two coloured forms that stand out splendidly. Sometimes we grow a few scarlet runners, whose sprays of red pea flowers show why this variety was originally grown as an ornamental.

At one end of the arbour, just enough seeds of acorn and butternut squash are pushed in to produce two plants of each. The lush tropical leaves soon make a fine pattern, and the great hanging fruits, about two dozen in all, mature in early fall. These are for winter storage.

MELONS

At the other end of the arbour, one morning glory is planted on each side. In wet years, the vines make a terrible tangle that hardly helps the bean harvest, but the effect is memorable, creating a sort of processional entrance into the area. East of the bean arbour, it will be recalled, is the raised cold frame where those early radishes, beets and lettuces matured and were harvested by mid-June. Immediately, the soil is forked over, more crumbly compost is added, and it is watered well. This is the spot for melons. Longtime residents tell me that a place just along the road, where light sandy soils slope gently southward to the waters of Burlington Bay at the northwestern tip of Lake Ontario, used to be the best melon land in Canada. A couple of small fields still produce great ribbed muskmelons that are sold from roadside stands, but most of the land has gone to housing and yet more—generally unnecessary—shopping malls.

Unfortunately, that sort of soil stops a quarter of a mile (0.4 km) away, and mine, which is heavy clay a foot (30 cm) down, slopes equally gently but to the north. Not ideal melon land. Hence the need for the little extra help from the frame and the choice—instead of the big muskmelons or cantaloupes that need a lot of space—of 'Charentais,' a small, smooth-skinned French melon which I have seen grown by the acre in the south of France (surprisingly, at just the same latitude as my garden, with a not dissimilar summer, though winters are another story). With me, they are seldom much bigger than a croquet ball but have a lovely, rich flavour. Half a 'Charentais' with late raspberries is a dessert fit for a king or queen.

Here, a late mid-June outdoor sowing should allow enough time for a crop to ripen, but if this doesn't sprout, a couple of vital weeks have been lost. Melons need at least three months from germination, and with unripe fruit on the vines in mid-September, time is running out. So it is best to sow a few small pots of seeds indoors (three seeds to a pot, and thin to one seedling) at the end of May, or a little earlier if summers are notoriously short or if you just want an early crop—and who doesn't? Then, if for any reason disaster strikes, it is not too late to start again outside. There, with the soil warm and ready, one sows groups of seven or eight seeds every two feet (60 cm) or so. When these sprout, they are gradually reduced to the three best. This will result in a tangle of vines three or four feet (1-1.2 m) wide that in the open garden can engulf other things planted too close. That is another reason why I find the cold frame so satisfactory: not only can early and late protection be given if necessary, but the sides contain the growth.

The midsummer garden is highlighted by a pole of scarlet runner beans whose sprays of red flowers show why they were originally grown as ornamentals.

Considerations of space loom equally large with the other cucurbits (melons, squashes, cucumbers, pumpkins, ornamental gourds). The bigger winter squashes with their rambling vines can only be grown well if allowed their own plot in full sun. They do not make good neighbours. So although I hanker after those vast pumpkins and squashes – up to 200 pounds (90 kg), "great for fall fairs," the seed catalogues proclaim – I resist them. This shows great strength of character, for I have had a packet of the former in my desk for several years. On it is a picture of the gardener dwarfed by a barrel-sized monster he has nurtured like some vegetable sorcerer's apprentice. But perhaps he is a very small man.

SQUASHES AND CUCUMBERS

Which is why my winter squash fix is restricted to those acorns and butternuts fighting it out overhead with the pole beans and morning glories. One year, I shall add a cup-and-saucer vine (*Cobaea scandens*) for good measure. Summer squashes – zucchini, courgettes, marrows or whatever you wish to call them – are another matter, and they are irresistible. Although a single plant can easily cover a square yard (1 m²) of ground, they do not run about.

In England, not long ago, the idea of cutting vegetable marrows, or zucchini, before they were the size of the Goodyear blimp was likened to infanticide. Now the fashionable thing is to harvest them so young that the flower has barely opened. It is sensible in the home garden with space at a premium to have three or four plants at any one time and pick the zucchini as soon as the flower drops off the end. If the plants are well and robust, the fruit will be about six inches (15 cm) long; if they are poorly fed, only half that. So size is not the only criterion for readiness. The important thing is to harvest regularly. Leave the plants for a week in high summer, and one returns to clusters of monster incubi that the neighbours have to be bribed to remove. And the plants take ages to recover and resume their normal activities.

Thus on the outside of the split-rail fence go the zucchini. A few started early indoors give us some quick picking in early July. While they all taste the same – delicious – I like to vary colour of fruit and foliage, growing 'Greyzini' and 'Goldrush' in addition to the usual green 'Milano.' The bigger catalogues will tempt with other forms: pattypan-shaped 'Sunburst,' spherical 'Ronde de Nice,' and so on. It is easy to end up with a glut.

Gardener-cooks have always known that zuc-

Swiss chard is one of various cold-tolerant greens that help keep the garden productive until the weather really gives up in late fall.

chini flowers are delicious if picked fresh, dipped in batter and deep-fried. This is best as a luncheon dish, because they are apt to go limp in the evening. Now, the smart, fashion-driven restaurants are onto the idea, and a zucchini variety that is especially productive of male flowers, 'Butter-blossom,' is available. Of course, male and female flowers are equally edible, but the female ones are often left to produce zucchini.

My cucumbers share the same beyond-the-fence spot. I prefer the long, thin, seedless so-called English cucumbers, but these need greenhouse treatment. Nearest to them in quality but suitable for outdoors are the Japanese types and their recent hybrids, such as 'Sweet Success' or 'Burpless.' Like summer squash, cucumbers are apt to exhibit feast-or-famine tendencies. For a month, we dine on cucumbers at breakfast, lunch, tea and supper. Then there are none. Dealing with this is an annual game that is difficult to win.

At the other end of the garden, beyond the raspberries, are the potatoes I have already described. Plots E and F in alternate years give me eight short rows two feet (60 cm) apart with the potatoes planted 18 inches (45 cm) apart in mid-May. When they are six inches (15 cm) high, I scatter some general fertilizer and draw the soil up, almost covering them, so the rows look like long tents with furrows between them. This helps to ensure that the developing tubers (which come from shoots growing just below ground level, not from the roots) do not get to the light and become green and useless. And it also looks wonderfully professional.

CHICORY

Opposite, across the central railway-tie path, go some vital vegetables that we would be particularly loath to be without: forms of chicory. Many people in North America are not familiar with these elegant salad ingredients—red radicchio, tight ivory-coloured heads of Belgian endive, green, pale-centred escarole with flat or frizzled leaves. All have become almost inevitable as parts of mixed salads or garnishes in the smarter restaurants. Fortunately, fashion does not detract from flavour.

Chicory itself is the single fresh, homegrown winter salad of which one can be assured in our climate, where overwintering crops outside is not possible. Chicory cultivation is rather a labour, but one that is eminently worthwhile. A couple of short double rows are sown in late May. Germination is apt to be erratic, and if especially poor, it may be necessary to repeat the process. Growth is slow at first, but eventually, one has a bed of what appear to be very fine dandelions. In late October, after the first frosts but before real freeze-up, the tops are cut off just above the soil. The outside leaves are extremely bitter, but there is a small amount of pale edible heart that is worth keeping.

Trim the parsniplike roots to about eight inches (20 cm) long, pack tightly together and stand them upright in deep pots of peat or sand. Water them and keep them somewhere frost-free but cool. They must be kept in the dark; a black plastic bag can be put over top. During fall and winter, one at a time, our pots are taken to sit by the furnace and kept moist. Soon, they begin to produce those marvellous crisp chicons, which are cut off just above the root when about six inches (15 cm) tall. As long as the pot is watered and looked after, a second or even third cutting is possible, the shoots becoming a bit wispy by the third. With chicory, practice is the only way to time one's production, but as few as four 8-inch (20 cm) pots, each holding 10 or a dozen roots, can give a surprising supply from November through February and beyond. A chicory and orange salad is almost delicious enough to make winter welcome.

I sow radicchio at about the same time, finding 'Guilio,' which is like a fat, dark red cos lettuce, the easiest of the new varieties. It is productive from September until hard frost. The Cook's Garden in Vermont (see Sources at the end of this book) offers a number of different types.

While all this activity is going on at one end of the plot, I must keep in mind that broad beans and early peas will be finished by mid-June and the main-crop peas and early dwarf beans not much later. The concept of succession crops is essential to pursue if a diversity of vegetables is to be maintained. Obviously, wherever a gap appears—between the tomatoes before they join up, after the early beets—it makes sense to sprinkle in a few radishes or spinach or plant summer lettuce. When plot B becomes suddenly empty, I turn to a group of rapidly maturing Chinese and Japanese vegetables ideal for July sowing.

ORIENTALS

Some catalogues specialize in these. Stokes is very encouraging and offers a couple of dozen Orientals, from loofahs (which you can eat when immature or use to scrub your back in the bath when they are ripe and dry) to two-foot-long (60 cm) asparagus beans and chop suey greens. I am content to stick with one of the Chinese cabbages, such as 'Wintertime' or 'Jade Pagoda,' which give fine solid heads by late September and will store happily in the earth cellar until Christmas. I also like the long white daikon radish, which is equally accommodating.

This high-summer sowing usually includes other rather unusual vegetables. The delicious Florence fennel, or finocchio, has a bonus of lovely, fernlike foliage. Swiss chard is useful, as is a late sowing of parsley. The important thing is to keep the production going, little by little, until the weather really gives up. There is never a date that can be definitely predicted in advance, and that, of course, is half the fun.

It will certainly have been noticed that my plot has some glaring omissions: no corn, no cabbages, no true onions. I must explain. Lack of onions grieves me, because I so enjoy the visual pleasure of rows of blond bulbs ripening under the September sun, later to be lifted and plaited into ropes just like those the Breton onion boys used to bring around on their bicycles in southern England. But onions don't like my heavy soil. The family is represented only by leeks, shallots and some garlic. Corn does well, but it needs a lot of space, and my plot is only a few yards from the edge of a ravine with a wild population. I see no reason to cultivate corn to satisfy an early-morning lineup of squirrels and raccoons. Cabbages and cauliflowers do not fully earn their considerable space requirements and, like corn, are grown to perfection by a farmer not far away. Roadside stands provide all we need in season. Certain other vegetables are not in great demand in our kitchen. Celeriac, lima beans, turnips, okra, salsify and kohlrabi may well be other gardeners' favourites. Unless one has a great deal of space—and time—for a vegetable garden, it is almost impossible to grow all the vegetables a family needs.

It should not be thought, then, that this rather personal account is the only way to go about things. Vegetable choices will differ, and some readers will lack the space or the inclination to proceed with what might appear an overextensive and labour-intensive scale. One just has to make decisions and answer the questions posed in the first chapter: What do I want? What do I enjoy growing? What is my garden best suited to?

The fall and spring gardening seasons meet in the garden room, a place bright enough to keep plants blooming and at the right temperature to overwinter certain temperate outdoor plants.

THE GARDEN ROOM

y now, it must be obvious that the thread running through all of the chapters in this book is my concern that your garden be usable and enjoyable throughout the year. There are, as I have said, strange myths which take it as axiomatic that gardening in the north is an occupation for only the frost-free months and that the garden virtually ceases to exist for half the year. At this point, if you are still with me, these myths have been pretty well exploded, but the year-round status of the garden can be encouraged even more if you have a little covered garden. "Encouraged" is the right word. Protection from wind and cold encourages plants to start a bit earlier and last a bit longer; gardeners are similarly encouraged to think about plant care and cultivation over a longer period, which ultimately benefits the garden. Eventually, the growing seasons meet.

What one needs, then, is a relatively cool, bright room well suited to plant growth in winter: a garden room. The concept of growing plants under cover is hardly a new one. Two thousand years ago, before the age of window glass, the Romans were protecting plants with naturally translucent materials such as selenite and mica. And having done this, they sought to heat the enclosed spaces with hypocausts and hot-water runnels. Roses and lilies bloomed earlier, and tender fruit trees thrived. As the centuries passed, this almost symbiotic plant-person relationship continued whenever and wherever wealth and leisure became available to at least a few.

GREENHOUSES PAST

In the late 17th century, the famous British diarist John Evelyn first used the word greenhouse in the context in which we use it today. He meant literally a house for greens; that is, evergreens which needed winter protection. One is apt to forget that England of the 1600s was not the place of verdantly furnished gardens it is today. Britain has only three native conifers and the same number of broadleaf evergreens. The plant riches of the temperate parts of the Orient and the New World were yet to be discovered. There was not a single rhododendron until the diminutive Swiss alpenrose (*Rhododendron ferrugineum*) was introduced in 1652, and it had little visual effect. There were other known evergreens, as Mediterranean travellers continually reported, but sweet bay and olives and Italian cypresses were on the border of hardiness north of the Alps. So, too, were oranges, lemons and citrons, which had arrived over the centuries from subtropical Asia. Even the Italians had to take special care of these. For northern gardeners, they were the ultimate greenhouse "greens"—to the extent that a house to protect them in winter, an orangery, became an essential part of all great gardens. Louis XIV's Versailles orangery, built in 1685, was more than 500 feet (150 m) long, 42 feet (13 m) wide and 45 feet (14 m) high. It held around 2,000 tubbed and potted plants, all of which were taken out to the terraces in the summer and brought back indoors, with immense labour, in late fall.

Although the plants usually survived, they most probably did not do very well. Seventeenth-century heating methods were primitive, and often the orangeries had solid roofs, so light conditions were poor. But gardening has always benefited from current technology, and the greenhouse is no exception. Victorian buildings, such as Decimus Burton's famous curvilinear Palm House at Kew, are the prototypes of all great greenhouses around the world today, making possible under glass what could never happen outside. During the 19th century, too, architects took advantage of the domestic possibilities of attaching such buildings to houses. Whether these attached glasshouses were "winter gardens" on a large scale or "conservatories" on a smaller one, pictures of them remind us of crinolined women framed in palm foliage and ferns. What we do not see in these pictures are the rows of utilitarian backup houses and the staff that made their luxuriance possible.

The wheel of fashion continually turns, and it is interesting to note that only during the last decade or so has there been a real resurgence of interest in garden buildings attached to the house. That ideal of the early 20th century—a Lutyens house with a Jekyll garden, described in the chapter on perennials—hardly ever suggests any covered garden space except in association with the kitchen garden. Now, suddenly, it seems, in both cool temperate Europe and North America, the greenhouse is back. Here, however, it may have a different name, suggesting—often with an excess of pretensions—a rather different role. It is not a greenhouse but a sun room, a Florida room or a solarium. The trouble with these concepts, from my point of view, is that this glazed room is perceived and used as an addition to the house rather than a link with the garden. It is elegantly furnished with upholstery that resents water (which plants like) and is often heated to Floridan temperatures, so only hibiscuses, poinsettias and conventional houseplants thrive. It is so lovely that the owners live there happily all year and hardly use the original living rooms of the house at all. Worse, it does not help the year-round garden scene the way a cooler room can.

The slightly bitter tone of the preceding paragraph may, of course, arise from sour grapes and jealousy on my part because I don't own such a facility. Yet this is a gardening book and not an encomium to the House Beautiful, so in these pages, the solarium appears to be an opportunity wasted. If I can begin by calling it a conservatory or garden room, its wider role starts to evolve. Now it can develop as much as the gardener wishes, has time for or is able to afford. A keen gardener, retired from a full-time job—the sort of fortunate being who invariably tells you he or she cannot imagine ever having had enough time to work—can do more than those of us still gainfully employed, as the phrase laughingly has it.

Even members of the latter group, who for four months, from November to February, leave home when it is barely light and return when it is dark, so gardening either indoors or out seems irrelevant, have time on the weekend to relate again to the sane world of plants and to the extended season that the garden room permits. The room need not be large or elaborately equipped nor its workload too heavy to be included in a weekend devoted to relaxation.

MY GARDEN ROOM

Let me describe my own scene as it is now, as I write this bit in mid-January. My garden room extends out from our home's original single-glazed breezeway—never was a word more descriptive:

While snow settles outdoors, my garden room blooms with houseplants and summer outdoor container plants like azaleas, camellias and pelargoniums.

bottles of tonic water used to burst in winter on their way to the gin. Its floor plan consists of two joined rectangles, 16 by 14 feet (4.9 by 4.3 m) and 8 by 9 feet (2.4 by 2.7 m), respectively. The latter rectangle, a route to the garage, is predominantly a mudroom with shelves for small plants higher up. The larger rectangle holds in winter a round table where, if they wear sweaters and breathe in, four or five people can take a simple lunch on a sunny midwinter day.

Such an occasion is a great pleasure. The rich lemony perfume of *Daphne odora* drifts over one shoulder, 'Paper White' narcissi lean forward, an old pink double azalea is in full bloom, and a couple of big pots of *Jasminum polyanthum* are show-

ing buds, as are shoots from freesia corms which, years ago, somehow ended up in a pot holding a rosemary bush that has been in flower since well before Christmas. And the first great red camellia is just showing colour. At this time of year, we would find these things outdoors, in much the same state of bloom, if we visited gardens on the French or Italian rivieras or in Los Angeles, places with an enviable winter climate but where temperatures frequently fall to, or close to, the freezing mark.

Comparison with the Mediterranean winter is not entirely fanciful if one remembers that southern Ontario is at the same latitude as the south of France. A recent plant-study tour for Royal

Botanical Gardens (RBG) members—we do a couple most years—left a chilly Toronto in mid-March and arrived the next morning in Nice, which was ablaze with mimosas and bedded-out cyclamens and cinerarias. And—this is the point—every garden visited along the Côte d'Azur was *north* of our own garden at Hamilton. Of course, the Côte d'Azur climate is much milder than ours, but our day length is the same, and with just marginal protection from actual frost, we can grow all the same wonderful things. Space is the only restriction. At the RBG, we have developed an extensive Mediterranean garden under glass to capitalize on just these facts. With its high roof, it can display not only plants of the classical world but also cascades of mimosas and bottlebrushes from southern Australia and native plants from California and southern Africa, all of which have a comparable latitude and climate. All these plants are grist to this particular mill. All give colour and scent and indeed hope of spring renewed during the depths of our winters.

Of those things now in flower in our garden room, John Evelyn could have met only rosemary and perhaps narcissi. He would have recognized a four-foot-high (1.2 m), narrowly trimmed sweet bay (*Laurus nobilis*), a much bigger oleander (*Nerium oleander*) and pots of small-leafed ivies (*Hedera* spp), but neither southern African spider plants (*Chlorophytum comosum*) nor a couple of clivias (*Clivia miniata*) with strap-shaped leaves. They should flower in March. There is even a bird of paradise (*Strelitzia reginae*) with one spike of flowers just opening. This was a gift last fall, when, I suspect, it was already pregnant. Again, these are plants that would thrive in Mediterranean gardens, yet they are able to be interesting and beautiful now during a northern winter with very little added cost to the heating bill. In our garden room, there is one small baseboard heater, a wall fan that comes on only infrequently and, not least in importance, warmth provided by Guy, our large springer spaniel, who is commissioned to sleep under the mudroom's end bench.

Such garden-room plants, then, need only slight additional heat so long as effective double glazing is used. In fact, they should not be overly hot; a variation from about 35 degrees F (2°C) at night to as high as 65 or 70 (18-21°C) on a sunny day suits them fine. Flowers last for an amazing length of time: spring bulbs that flower for a week in the house last a month in the garden room.

There are other advantages these plants gain from so cool a regime: soil does not dry out quickly, so watering is seldom necessary other than on the weekend.

The emphasis, then, for this type of garden room is to reduce the need for heating in winter both by its design and by the choice of plants used to furnish it. Inevitably, the design of such a garden room has much to do with its heating needs. It must be given an aspect so that sun collection is possible, but it also has to be sited to fit the demands of the house for which it is the vital garden link. Sealed-pane, double-glazed windows are essential, top and sides. Even better are more sophisticated glazing systems whereby heat from the low winter sun moves up the vertical front panes and, instead of being lost in part through the roof, is, in fact, trapped and used. In summer, such panels act as heat reducers, when the higher sun enters through the roof. However, even with conventional panes, winter temperatures can be helped by a suitable floor. Ours is made of uncemented bricks tightly laid on edge, from which water drains at once. These bricks rest on a couple of feet (60 cm) of gravel that acts as a thermal reservoir. Double glazing on the roof has one disadvantage: because heat loss is reduced, snow can stay for ages, and on occasion, it becomes necessary to take a ladder out to clear it so that we can enjoy the sun.

SEASONAL LINKING

The garden room is not only an architectural link or just an intermediary between the indoor and outdoor living spaces, though it is both of these. It is also a link between the seasons. This role is absolutely essential from the point of view of a fully furnished year-round garden. It enables autumn to slide gently into winter and winter into spring, insulating gardeners—and, more important, their more tender plants—from those sudden seizures of the winter climate that can upset one's garden plans for months in the future. That unprecedented fall frost (unprecedented, that is, since last year) in late September or early October might give the kitchen-window hanging basket of tender annuals its comeuppance sooner than they or we would wish. Instead, the basket comes in to swing from the ceiling for a night or two. Most probably, it can return outdoors again for a couple of weeks of Indian summer, offering a visual extension of real summer that otherwise

would not have been enjoyed. There will doubtless be pots of other tender plants that can receive this response to a climatic emergency.

But there comes the time when the irrevocable can be delayed no longer. The season of (to misquote) frosts and mellow fruitfulness is upon us, and the tender annuals must go the way of all flesh. Or must they? Baskets and pots of unhurt things can come into the garden room, where one realizes how many of our summer "annuals" are in fact fully perennial in a suitable climate. Obviously, one cannot keep everything—there is just not the space—but it is comforting not to have to cart off healthy plants to the compost heap. So this year in my garden room, there are a few geraniums (*Pelargonium* spp) brought in from the terrace last fall. A pink one is flowering merrily now, in mid-January. In other years, salvias, petunias and others have had their turn. Unlike pelargoniums, these seem not to continue blooming for a second summer, though they will flower happily throughout winter and indeed until April.

One particular word of warning: if your plants can live from year to year, so, too, can their pests and diseases, so it is vital to bring indoors only clean stock. Whitefly is an especial problem. Every plant must be examined carefully

to ensure that it is whitefly-free—the little monsters are just looking for protected food and winter lodging as a base from which to launch their next year's depredations.

While some of the garden-room regulars, such as Christmas cactus (*Schlumbergera bridgesii*), spider plants and amaryllis bulbs (*Hippeastrum* cultivars), are as sensitive to frost as tender annuals, most are able to take a couple of degrees of it without coming to harm. These are, in fact, best left outdoors until the last moment. For instance, the flower buds of camellias (*Camellia japonica*) and jasmine (*Jasminum* spp), which are still maturing in late fall, are then able to benefit from the brighter outdoor light. But one keeps an ear on the weather forecasts and watches for a cloudless, chilly evening with quickly dropping temperatures. These are the conditions that lead to heavy frost. With us, the last weekend in October or the first in November seems to be the deadline. Again, as each plant is brought in, it is examined for pests. Dead leaves are removed, and all of the plants are arranged on big trays on the one long temporary bench—actually the summer dining table—and on the floor according to their needs for light. From now on, watering is reduced to keep pots just moist, and feeding is stopped until the turn of the year, when flower buds on the camellias, daphne and jasmines begin to show colour.

Until now, therefore, the garden room has excelled as a home for winter-flowering plants, and this role continues—as do the plants—into March and even beyond. The broadleaf evergreens are soon supported by a few pots of hyacinths, daffodils, *Iris reticulata*, and so on, that spent a few quiet months developing in the earth cellar below. Once they show a couple of inches (5 cm) of tip growth, they are brought upstairs. They spend two or three weeks on the floor of the garden room under the bench or wherever there is space, and then as flower buds appear, the pots are moved to positions where we can best enjoy them. Naturally, some will be brought into other rooms in the house, even though in those warmer places their time of beauty will be more than halved. After flowering, these plants continue to need light and full frost protection so that their leaves can build up their bulbs for next year. In spring, most can be planted in garden beds. It seems a pity to neglect them when their future contribution can be added to the open garden. Narcissi 'Paper White' and 'Grand Soleil d'Or,'

The garden room is an excellent place for forcing hardy bulbs, which are stored in the cool cellar and brought upstairs as soon as they show a few inches of tip growth.

In late winter, as the days lengthen, the garden room assumes its second role as propagation house for cuttings and seeds of vegetables, herbs and flowers. With a minimum nighttime temperature of 50 degrees F (10°C), tropicals like bougainvillea come into bloom.

however, are not worth keeping, since they will not take outside cultivation in our climate.

But as the days become longer – a wonderful fact that we convince ourselves is discernible by about January 3, however unlikely – the garden room starts to assume its other role, as propagation house. On a sunny Saturday or Sunday morning toward the end of the month, when the warmth of the sun is really apparent – although the outdoors is all white and the outside thermometer is hovering around 15 degrees F (−9°C) – it is wonderfully encouraging to sow the first seeds of the season. The round table is covered with newspaper, a bucket of purchased potting compost is moistened, a few pots are cleaned, and one is ready to celebrate the New Year in a more constructive way than one could at all those jolly parties a few weeks ago.

SPRING SEEDING

Earlier chapters have referred to what should or should not be started at this stage. Although the pots of newly sown seeds will go upstairs under a table in my dressing room for germination – there is no better place for ensuring a twice-daily glance, thus nothing is allowed to dry out or become thin and drawn – they will, after germination occurs, need to return to the garden room with its low night temperatures. It is still too cold there for tender annuals, so they are not started this early. But one square four-inch (10 cm) pot – more space-saving than round ones – apiece of near-hardy vegetables and herbs such as lettuce, thyme and parsley can be tried now. This early start makes a lot of sense for parsley, which can take more than three weeks to germinate and is very slow in the seedling stage. If it is sown outside in April or May, it is midsummer before one has any usable leaves. Sweet peas are sown now also, as are a few perennials, especially the seeds of things one has collected – a pod or two here, a capsule there – when visiting gardens the previous year. This is the ideal moment to plan to bulk up the perennial border at virtually no cost: delphiniums, columbines, echinacea, and so on started in early spring will flower a bit toward the end of this season in their nursery bed. Then, good colours can be noted and poor ones rogued out. The best plants will go into their permanent places the following spring.

The danger of a sunny Sunday morning in January or February is the euphoria that leads one to sow seeds of tender annuals which will germinate quickly. The resultant plants will suffer in the chilly garden room and, even if initially cosseted, cannot be kept healthy until after the last spring frost. This is three to four months away at the most optimistic, by which time the plants will be crowding their boxes, prey to fungal diseases. There are many hardy annuals, however, and a host of hardy perennials that do not mind cool weather in the seedling stage. The plants suggested above are examples of a wide range that will allow the gardener to get ahead of the season. Growing space in the garden room is limited, so one must be very strong-minded, keeping only as many plants as can be handled indoors and are really wanted outside.

The lettuce will probably come up first. When the first true leaf develops, good seedlings are transferred to individual plugs. A boxful of these will give me three dozen for March planting in the cold frame and cutting during May. I also want a whole box of parsley, not only because we use a lot of this herb but because I like to edge a kitchen garden path with its ornamental moss-curled leaves. But half a box of thyme and a dozen plugs of sweet peas will be enough. After pricking out, they have a week to recover from transplanting shock on a warm windowsill, then they must go to the high, bright shelves of the garden room and be very carefully watered – *not* overwatered. These shelves, out of sight from the "winter-garden" end of the garden room, do not affect the ornamental aspect of the room. I do not really want these early experiments to show, for this dead-of-winter activity is essentially a bit of horticultural therapy for me. Everything is done, within reason, to ensure success, but it is not the end of the world if it doesn't work, and there is plenty of time to resow if things go wrong.

The purposefully low but frost-free temperatures in the garden room have been emphasized: economy and the needs of the permanent, mainly temperate-climate inhabitants are the chief reasons. Sufficient light is just as important. While commercial growers supplement with artificial lighting either to extend day length or to increase light concentrations and many people raise their plants under fluorescent fixtures in the basement, I find it possible to manage remarkably well with very few technological aids beyond those provided by a normal, comfortable house – of which, of course, the garden room is a significant part.

In other chapters, it has been seen how, as January moves into February—a blessedly short month even in a leap year—and February into March, this bit of greenhouse space becomes more and more important and starts to creak at the seams. The dingy light from a half-window in the earth cellar combined with marginally warmer temperatures down there seems to be sufficient to trigger growth in the tender perennials that were stored there in fall. Fortunately, corms of gladioli, acidantheras and tigridias are willing to snooze until the outdoor soil temperatures are ready to receive them in May. But any piece of variegated giant reed (*Arundo donax*) that had been brought in as insurance against the winter, as well as cannas, pelargoniums and fuchsias, will all be stirring like back-row members of the corps de ballet when, centre stage, the Sleeping Beauty is awakened. In the earth cellar, all these potential beauties need to be repotted, watered and found places upstairs under the bench at the end of the farthest shelf around the side of the dog's bed. (Thank goodness, the cat can now scratch outdoors, and the precious 18 by 12 inches [45 by 30 cm] for her litter box can be devoted to more aesthetic ends.) Space, suddenly, is at a premium.

The next two months, from mid-March, are the busiest time in the garden room. The sun climbs in the sky. No longer, except in the evening, does it shine through the vertical front windows. It's now shining mainly through the roof, and with lengthening days, temperatures increase. My concern now is not whether the room is too cold, as it seems it was only a couple of weeks ago, but whether it is or will be too hot. Midday ventilation is probably necessary, but of course, we all leave the house early in the morning to go to work. To open a crack now or not is the daily question. Will one's botanical children chill or fry? Fortunately, plants are pretty resilient creatures. Sufficient moisture in the compost (but not too much) helps, because damp compost acts as an insulator, buffering extremes of heat and cold. Always, it is better to err slightly on the side of dryness. From this, pot plants—even if wilting pitiably—will usually soon recover, especially if stood in a bath of tepid water until all bubbles have ceased to rise. That same sign of distress, limp leaves, reveals overwatering. But recovery from this is slow at best.

As soon as possible, the really hardy plants—the perennials, herbs and vegetables—are moved out either to a cold frame, which is the wisest next step, if only for a few days, or to a spot in the lee of the wall just outside. This gives more space to the less resilient plants remaining indoors. Still there is not enough room, because in early May, as suggested in the chapter on annuals, one has bought a few early flats of tender tropicals to be potted up and strengthened before they are set out after frosts are really over.

All of this sounds frenetic, exhausting and, if one is honest, just a little bit silly. So it is. But no sillier than, for example, hitting—and losing—a little white ball out in the countryside. Both golf and gardening offer rewards not immediately apparent to an uncommitted observer. The garden obsession in spring involves working with the season and, whenever possible, getting a little bit ahead of it to increase the productivity of summer's lease, which we do not need a Shakespearean sonnet to remind us "hath all too short a date."

THE SUMMER ROOM

Fortunately, the end of this frantic garden-room activity is in sight. Depending upon where one lives, some date in May can usually be assumed to be the time beyond which no significant frost is likely. Virtually everything now goes outdoors, so the garden room can take on its other linking role. Throughout the summer, it is used more by people than by plants. Now, it is not sun that one wants, but shade, and as has been mentioned before, a good-sized deciduous tree just outside—which I am lucky enough to have—is the perfect answer. For a couple of weeks in late May, my family wishes the leaves on the yellowwood would unfurl a little faster, and in mid-October, we wish they would fall a bit quicker, but in between, it provides the ideal shade, keeping the place blessedly cool. Internal shading by blinds, which allow the heat of the sun to reach the glass, can never be half as effective and is only a fraction as beautiful. Just one addition is needed: anti-bug screens on the windows to permit full enjoyment of warm, fragrant summer breezes. Our small round winter table goes out on the terrace. The winter-plant trestle bench is turned at right angles and sports a smart cloth and, in the evening, candles in hurricane glasses.

This place is no longer for flowering plants but for traditional houseplants. Anthuriums, philodendrons and spider plants, jungle-floor natives, can flourish in this now shady spot as late-May temperatures rise through the 80s F (27-32°C). In fact, from the end of June until early September, even these plants are better outside, where there is more light, less heat and better air circulation. They make splendid outdoor furnishing in fully shaded parts of the deck or terrace, where they enjoy the air and the occasional wash from summer showers. It goes without saying that in dry periods, they must be well watered and also that even short periods of full sun will cause leaves to burn and bleach, injuries that will be visible for many months until those leaves are naturally replaced.

In our garden room, only the narrower, half-screened mudroom end maintains its year-round role. It is always important to have a place where a mess is acceptable—if only to show the other end more tidy by contrast. But we also maintain a big arrangement of cut foliage and simple flowers to screen it further at this time.

Thus for five months, almost every meal is taken in the garden room. From it, each changing day through the progressing season offers different aspects of the garden and its plants beyond. From morning mists to sunset, the views change with the light. On our small domestic scale, it is possible to relate to that extraordinary series of paintings Monet made of the west front of Rouen Cathedral, which seem even more dramatic than the famous water-lily series from his garden at Giverny. As the sun went round, Monet saw that great Gothic façade in tones of grey on a misty morning, blindingly white with blue shadows at midday and gamboge in the evening light.

Even without the eyes of an Impressionist—though they say it helps to be shortsighted: bully for myopia!—sitting in the same spot at a table at different hours of the day and consciously evaluating what one sees has real potential for the improvement of one's garden. Colours, and the effects those colours have, change amazingly during the day. In the morning, from our west-facing garden room, we see the light playing directly upon the long border to the left and ahead down the slope to the woodland edge. The colours now appear as true as they come yet are modified by long shadows from the low sun. As the sun rises and moves round, the shadows are dispelled, many of the colours become rather washed out and the border loses any sense of mystery. All is revealed—but not to its benefit.

Tropical house-plants, natives of the jungle floor, are the only green residents of the garden room in summer. Everything else has gone outside to furnish the terrace and beds beyond.

Now one realizes how important is the effect of chiaroscuro provided by deep shadows under the trees. Brilliant light and shade juxtaposed—perhaps this is more Mannerist than Impressionist. In any case, it is far more satisfying than no shadows at all.

But as the sun comes round to the west and starts to decline, it shines into one's eyes and everything sparkles. Colours no longer belong to individual plants but dance between them; shapes loom against the light. The sun drops behind the trees, colours briefly return and then are progressively lost in the dusk. The soft blues and purples disappear first, then the hot reds and oranges, and suddenly, pale yellow and white gather a strength they had not shown before, lingering lambently until dark finally falls.

All this can be watched from the garden-room windows, but the room is, of course, only the link. One is enticed out of it to other vantage points where a seat or some steps encourage one to stop. The sun and the light are now in different places in relation to the plants, and their appearance changes once more. With all this contemplation, valuable and pleasurable though it is, the most amazing thing is that one gets any work done at all.

SOURCES

Importing plants and plant materials such as tubers and bulbs into Canada requires a permit from the Plant Protection Division, Agriculture Canada, Ottawa, Ontario K1A 0C7. Most seeds can be imported without any such paperwork.

AIMERS
81 Temperance Street
Aurora, Ontario L4G 1R1
Flower seeds, bulbs, perennials. Catalogue free to Canada, $1 foreign.

ALBERTA NURSERIES & SEEDS LTD.
Box 20
Bowden, Alberta T0M 0K0
Flower and vegetable seeds, plants. Catalogue free to Canada, $2 foreign.

BAYPORT PLANT FARM
RR1
Rose Bay, Nova Scotia B0J 2X0
Rhododendrons, heathers, seeds. Send an SASE for price list.

BLUESTONE PERENNIALS INC.
7223 Middle Ridge Road
Madison, Ohio 44057
Catalogue free, to U.S. only.

BOUGHEN NURSERIES VALLEY RIVER LTD.
Box 12
Valley River, Manitoba R0L 2B0
Perennials, trees. Catalogue free, to Canada only.

BRICKMAN'S BOTANICAL GARDENS
RR1
Sebringville, Ontario N0K 1X0
Catalogue $2 refundable.

W. ATLEE BURPEE & CO.
300 Park Avenue
Warminster, Pennsylvania 18974
Seeds for vegetables, flowers. Catalogue free.

CHILTERN SEEDS
Bortree Stile, Ulverston
Cumbria LA12 7PB, England
Seeds of flowers, shrubs, trees, vegetables. Catalogue $4.

THE COOK'S GARDEN
Box 535
Londonderry, Vermont 05148
Seeds for gourmet vegetables. Catalogue $1 (U.S.).

CORN HILL NURSERY
RR5
Petitcodiac, New Brunswick E0A 2H0
Trees, berries, roses. Catalogue $2, to Canada only.

CRUICKSHANK'S LTD.
1015 Mount Pleasant Road
Toronto, Ontario M4P 2M1
Perennials, bulbs, seeds. Catalogue $3.

THE DAFFODIL MART
Route 3, Box 794
Gloucester, Virginia 23061
Daffodils and narcissi. Catalogue free.

DELAIR GARDENS
35120 Delair Road, RR4
Abbotsford, British Columbia V2S 4N4
Perennials, heathers. Catalogue $2 refundable.

FERNCLIFF GARDENS
8394 McTaggart Street
Mission, British Columbia V2V 6S6
Gladioli, dahlias, irises, peonies. Catalogue free.

FOUR SEASONS NURSERY
1706 Morrissey Drive
Bloomington, Illinois 61701
Perennials, seeds. Catalogue free.

FROSTY HOLLOW NURSERY
Box 53

Langley, Washington 98260
Seeds of shrubs, trees. SASE for price list, to U.S. only.

GARDENIMPORT
Box 760
Thornhill, Ontario L3T 4A5
Perennials, bulbs, seeds. Catalogue $4 for two years.

GARDENS NORTH
34 Helena Street
Ottawa, Ontario K1Y 3M8
Perennial seeds. Catalogue $3 to Canada, $4 to U.S.

GREER GARDENS
1280 Goodpasture Island Road
Eugene, Oregon 97401
Azaleas, rhododendrons, conifers. Catalogue $3 to U.S., $5 (U.S.) to Canada.

HAZELGROVE GARDENS
14219 Middle Bench Road, RR1
Oyama, British Columbia V0H 1W0
Perennials. Catalogue $1, to Canada only.

HERITAGE ROSE GARDEN
16831 Mitchell Creek Drive
Fort Bragg, California 95437
Catalogue $1.50 (U.S.).

HOLBROOK FARM AND NURSERY
115 Lance Road, Box 368
Fletcher, North Carolina 28732
Perennials, grasses, ferns, et cetera. Catalogue free, to U.S. only.

HONEYWOOD LILIES
Box 63
Parkside, Saskatchewan S0J 2A0
Lilies and day lilies. Catalogue $2.

HORTICO, INC.
RR1
Waterdown, Ontario L0R 2H0
Perennials, trees, grasses, roses. Catalogue $2.

J.L. HUDSON, SEEDSMAN
Box 1058
Redwood City, California 94064

Seeds of flowers, shrubs, vegetables. Catalogue $1 (U.S.).

JACKSON & PERKINS
Box 1020
Medford, Oregon 97501
Ornamentals, roses. Catalogue $2 (U.S.) to Canada, free to U.S.

KLEHM NURSERY
Route 5, Box 197
South Barrington, Illinois 60010
Peonies, day lilies, hostas, irises. Catalogue $2 (U.S.).

V. KRAUS NURSERIES
Box 180
Carlisle, Ontario L0R 1H0
Ornamentals, shrubs, trees, roses. Catalogue $2, to Canada or the U.S.

LINDEL LILIES
5510 239 Street
Langley, British Columbia V3A 7N6
Catalogue $1.

LOWE'S OWN ROOT ROSES
6 Sheffield Road
Nashua, New Hampshire 03062
Catalogue $2, to U.S. only.

MASON HOGUE GARDENS
3520 Durham Road #1, RR4
Uxbridge, Ontario L9P 1R4
Perennials for dry gardens. Send SASE for list, Canada only.

McMILLEN'S IRIS GARDENS
RR1
Norwich, Ontario N0J 1P0
Irises, day lilies. Catalogue $1, to Canada only.

MELLINGER'S NURSERY
2310 W. South Range Road
North Lima, Ohio 44452-9731
Seeds, plants. Catalogue free to U.S., $2 (U.S.) to Canada.

MILAEGER'S GARDENS
4838 Douglas Avenue
Racine, Wisconsin 53402-2498

Perennials, roses. Catalogue $1 refundable, to U.S. only.

MILLAR MOUNTAIN NURSERY
RR3, McLay Road
Duncan, British Columbia V9L 2X1
Irises, hostas. Catalogue $2.

MILLER BAY FARMS
248 Wilson Drive
Milton, Ontario L9T 3K2
Perennials, shrubs. Catalogue free, to Canada.

MONASHEE PERENNIALS
Site 6, Comp. 9, RR7
Vernon, British Columbia V1T 7Z3
Lilies, day lilies, Siberian irises. Catalogue $2.

MUSSER FORESTS
Box 340 588M
Indiana, Pennsylvania 15701-0340
Trees, shrubs. Catalogue free.

OIKOS TREE CROPS
Box 19425
Kalamazoo, Michigan 49019
Oak, nut, native fruit trees. Catalogue free.

OSLACH NURSERIES, INC.
RR1
Simcoe, Ontario N3Y 4J9
Dwarf conifers, trees, shrubs. Catalogue free.

CARL PALLEK & SON NURSERIES
Box 137
Virgil, Ontario L0S 1T0
Roses. Catalogue free, to Canada only.

PARK SEED CO., INC.
Cokesbury Road
Greenwood, South Carolina 29647-0001
Seeds of flowers, vegetables. Catalogue free.

PICKERING NURSERIES INC.
670 Kingston Road
Pickering, Ontario L1V 1A6
Roses. Catalogue $3.

PRISM PERENNIALS
Site 5, Comp. 45, RR1
Castlegar, British Columbia V1N 3H7
Perennials, irises, day lilies. Catalogue $2.

RAINFOREST GARDENS
13139 224 Street, RR2
Maple Ridge, British Columbia V2X 7E7
Perennials, hostas, ferns. Catalogue $2
refundable, to Canada only.

RED'S RHODIES ALPINE GARDENS
15920H S.W. Oberst Lane
Sherwood, Oregon 97140
Rhododendrons, azaleas, sedums. Send two U.S.
stamps for catalogue.

ROSEBERRY GARDENS
Box 933
Thunder Bay, Ontario P7C 4X8
Roses, azaleas, lilies. Catalogue $2.

ROSES OF YESTERDAY & TODAY
802 Brown's Valley Road
Watsonville, California 95076
Catalogue $3 to U.S., $5 (U.S.) to Canada.

SHADY OAKS NURSERY
700 19th Avenue NE
Waseca, Minnesota 56093
Perennials for shade. Catalogue free, to U.S.
only. No California orders.

KEITH SOMERS TREES LTD.
10 Tillson Avenue
Tillsonburg, Ontario N4G 2Z6
Trees, shrubs. Catalogue $2, to Canada only.

STIRLING PERENNIALS
RR1
Morpeth, Ontario N0P 1X0
Catalogue $2.

STOKES SEEDS LTD.
Box 10
St. Catharines, Ontario L2R 6R6
or
Box 548
Buffalo, New York 14240
Seeds of vegetables, annual flowers.
Catalogue free.

STRATA NURSERY
RR1, Site 2, Box 22
Port Moody, British Columbia V3H 3C8
Geraniums, hostas, ferns. Catalogue $2, to
Canada only.

THOMPSON & MORGAN, INC.
Box 1308
Jackson, New Jersey 08527
Seeds of annual and perennial flowers,
shrubs, vegetables. Catalogue free.

VAN BOURGONDIEN BROS.
Box A
Babylon, New York 11702
Perennials, hostas, lilies, day lilies. Catalogue
free.

WASHINGTON EVERGREEN NURSERY
Box 388
Leicester, North Carolina 28748
Dwarf evergreens. Catalogue $2 refundable,
to U.S. only.

THE WAYSIDE GARDENS
1 Garden Lane
Hodges, South Carolina 29695
Bulbs, roses, shrubs, perennials. Catalogue
free, to U.S. only.

WHITE FLOWER FARM
Route 63
Litchfield, Connecticut 06759
Perennials, shrubs. Catalogue $5 (U.S.).

GILBERT H. WILD & SON, INC.
1112 Joplin Street, Box 338
Sarcoxie, Michigan 64862-0338
Peonies, day lilies. Catalogue $3 (U.S.)
refundable.

WOODLANDERS, INC.
1128 Colleton Avenue
Aiken, South Carolina 29801
Trees, shrubs, vines, perennials. Catalogue $1
to U.S. and Canada; $3 foreign.

WYCHAVON NURSERY GARDENS
22 Winchester Avenue
Halifax, Nova Scotia B3P 2C8
Perennials, irises. Price list free, to
Canada only.

GLOSSARY

ANNUAL: A plant that completes its life cycle, seed to seed, in one growing season. Examples of true annuals are cosmos, dill, beans and marigolds. The term is also used to describe some plants, such as pelargoniums, bell peppers and impatiens, that are grown as annuals even though they are truly tender perennials and would survive winter if not killed by frost.

BIENNIAL: A plant that needs two years to complete its life cycle. In the spring of year one, seeds germinate and the plant builds up some type of storage organ that overwinters. The plant flowers, seeds and dies in year two.

COLD FRAME: A low surround of wood or brick with a glazed top, designed to gather sufficient solar heat to grow early flowers and vegetables.

COMPOST: A compost heap is an accumulation of organic garden and kitchen waste that breaks down into humus and is used to improve garden soils. In this book, I have used the term compost in the British sense, meaning homemade or purchased soil used for potting: a mixture of leaf mould, sand and soil.

CULTIVAR: A named *vari*ety of plant that appears in *culti*vation and is maintained by some form of propagation. Cultivar names are capitalized and enclosed in single quotation marks—for example, *Hedera helix* 'Baltica.'

CUTTING: Part of a shoot that can be encouraged to form roots; a means of plant propagation.

DIBBLE: A small pencil-like stick (or indeed a pencil) used for inserting cuttings into compost. The verb is "to dibble in."

DOUBLE: A flower whose normal number of petals has increased, often at the expense of stamens. A rosette pattern is usually formed. Some doubles have so many petals that they are virtual pompoms.

FLOWERS OF SULPHUR: A fine sulphur dust used to increase the acidity of soil in which one hopes to grow rhododendrons and other lime-hating plants.

FOUNDATION PLANTING: The conventional, frequently boring assemblage of small evergreen shrubs planted close to the base of a new building and subsequently neglected.

HARDEN OFF: To gradually accustom plants grown under glass to accept the cooler temperatures they will meet when planted outdoors.

HARDY: Plants that are able to flourish in all conditions of the site in which they are grown. It especially refers to frost-hardy: plants able to withstand the local winter temperatures.

HYBRID: A plant, occurring in the wild or in cultivation, that is a cross between two distinct species or cultivars.

OFFSET: Bulbs, corms and other storage organs frequently multiply by producing offsets, or bulbils. These smaller versions reach flowering size in two or three years.

PEAT MOSS: An important organic material used for mulching, for soil improvement and as a constituent of potting composts. Peat is now considered less environmentally acceptable than formerly because bulk extraction of it from the bogs where it forms harms the habitat. Well-rotted leaf mould should be used as an alternative whenever possible.

PEDICEL: The stem on which a flower is carried.

PH: A scale of 1 to 14 that denotes the acid-alkali continuum; used by gardeners in regard to soil conditions. A pH of 7 is neutral, lower numbers are increasingly acidic, and higher numbers are increasingly alkaline. A pH of 4 to 6.5 suits rhododendrons, while pH 5 to 8.5 is accepted by most flowers and vegetables.

PRICK OUT: To transfer seedlings from the containers in which they have germinated to pots or trays that provide more growing room. Hold seedlings only by the seedling leaf, which is described below.

SEEDLING LEAF: The first leaf or leaves appearing from a germinated seed, also called cotyledons. Lilies, grasses, et cetera, have one spearlike seedling leaf and are called monocotyledons (monocots). Most other plants have a pair of seedling leaves. These are the dicotyledons (dicots).

SINGLE: Flower with the normal number of petals for the wild species.

SIX-PACK: Apt to refer to a party contribution of beer; equally valid for a set of plastic cells, each holding a single plant, in a tray of annuals.

SPORT: A noticeable variation on a growing plant that is caused by cell mutation. Most dwarf conifers have arisen thus and have been subsequently propagated by cuttings to ensure that the form of the sport is maintained.

VEGETATIVE: Referring to propagation methods in which sexual seed production is not involved. Division, layering, cuttings and grafting are typical methods of vegetative reproduction.

FURTHER READING

Clausen, Ruth Rogers and Nicolas H. Ekstrom, *Perennials for American Gardens*. Random House, New York, 1989.

Druse, Kenneth, *The Natural Shade Garden*. Clarkson Potter, New York, 1992.

Fawcett, Brian, *The Compact Garden*. Camden House, Camden East, Ont., 1992.

Forsyth, Turid and Merilyn Simonds Mohr, *The Harrowsmith Salad Garden*. Camden House, Camden East, Ont., 1992.

Foster, H. Lincoln and Laura Louise Foster, *Cuttings from a Rock Garden: Plant Portraits and Other Essays*. Atlantic Monthly Press, New York, 1990.

The Harrowsmith Gardener's Guide series, published by Camden House, including *Ground Covers* (ed. Jennifer Bennett, Camden East, Ont., 1987), *Spring Flowers* (ed. Katharine Ferguson, Camden East, Ont., 1989) and *Vines* (ed. Karan Davis Cutler, Charlotte, Vt., 1992).

Heriteau, Jacqueline and Andre Viette, *The American Horticultural Society Flower Finder*. Simon & Schuster, New York, 1992.

Lima, Patrick, *The Kitchen Garden: Growing Vegetables and Fruits Naturally*. Key Porter, Toronto, 1992.

Lunardi, Costanza, *Simon & Schuster's Guide to Shrubs and Vines and Other Small Ornamentals*. Simon & Schuster, New York, 1989.

Osborne, Robert, *Roses for Canadian Gardens: A Practical Guide to Varieties and Techniques*. Key Porter, Toronto, 1991.

Paterson, Allen, *Herbs in the Garden*. Dent, London, 1985.

– – , *History of the Rose*. Wm. Collins & Son, London, 1983.

– – , *Plants for Shade and Woodland*. Fitzhenry & Whiteside, Markham, Ont., 1987.

Plants and Gardens, The Brooklyn Botanic Garden series of guides, such as *Small Gardens for Small Spaces* (#84), *100 Finest Trees and Shrubs* (#25) and *The Environment and the Home Gardener* (#82), available from BBG, 1000 Washington Avenue, Brooklyn, New York 11225.

Rix, Martyn, *Growing Bulbs*. Croom Helm, Kent, UK, 1983.

Sheldon, Elizabeth, *A Proper Garden*. Stackpole, Harrisburg, Pa., 1989.

Thomas, Graham Stuart, *The Art of Planting*. Dent, in association with the National Trust, London, 1984.

CLIMATIC-ZONE MAP

This simplified version of the U.S. Department of Agriculture's latest climatic-zone map indicates general temperature trends throughout Canada and the United States. The temperature ranges indicate average minimum winter temperatures. Colder zones have lower numbers. Nursery catalogues usually indicate the coldest zone in which a plant will thrive. Plants that are successful in your zone and in zones with numbers lower than yours should survive winters in your garden. Plants that prefer zones with higher numbers than yours may not be winter-hardy for you.

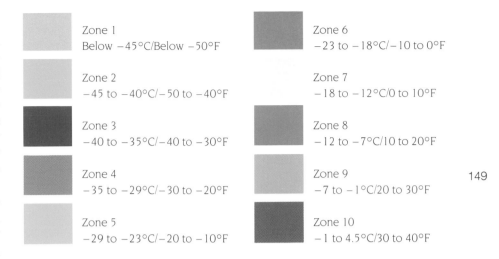

Zone 1
Below −45°C/Below −50°F

Zone 2
−45 to −40°C/−50 to −40°F

Zone 3
−40 to −35°C/−40 to −30°F

Zone 4
−35 to −29°C/−30 to −20°F

Zone 5
−29 to −23°C/−20 to −10°F

Zone 6
−23 to −18°C/−10 to 0°F

Zone 7
−18 to −12°C/0 to 10°F

Zone 8
−12 to −7°C/10 to 20°F

Zone 9
−7 to −1°C/20 to 30°F

Zone 10
−1 to 4.5°C/30 to 40°F

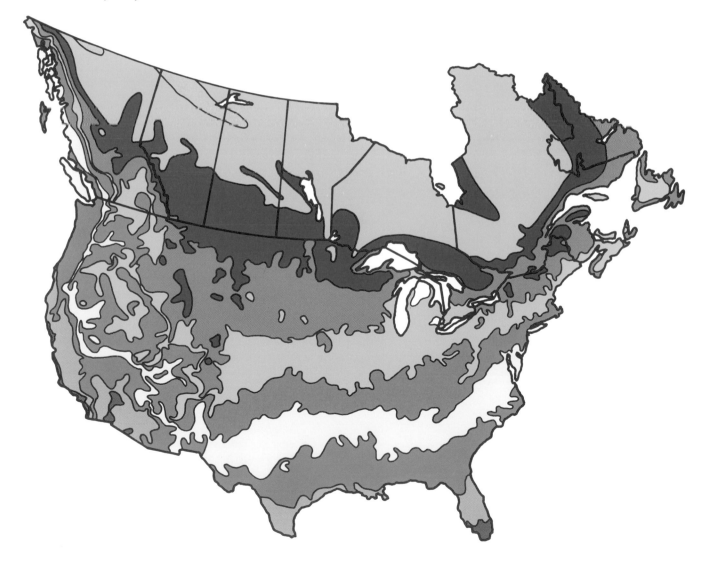

INDEX

CREDITS